TITANIC VICTIMS

IN HALIFAX GRAVEYARDS

BLAIR BEED

NIMBUS
PUBLISHING LTD

IN MEMORY OF MY MATERNAL GRANDMOTHER
GLADYS M. LEE, DECEMBER 1, 1901 - DECEMBER 24, 2000

Nimbus Publishing Limited
3731 Mackintosh St, Halifax, NS B3K 5A5
(902) 455-4286 nimbus.ca
Printed and bound in Canada

Design: Jenn Embree
Cover illustration: Marine artist, Yves Bérubé, Lunenburg, N.S. www.marineartgallery.com
    Original painting: 20"x 40" oil on canvas, 1993
    Title: Leaving Belfast, April 2, 1912

Library and Archives Canada Cataloguing in Publication

    Beed, Blair, 1955-
    Titanic victims in Halifax graveyards / Blair Beed. -- Rev. ed.
    Includes bibliographical references.
    ISBN 978-1-55109-897-5

1. Disaster victims—North Atlantic Ocean. 2. Titanic (Steamship). 3. Shipwrecks—North Atlantic Ocean.
4. Cemeteries—Nova Scotia—Halifax. 5. Halifax (N.S.)—History. I. Title.

FC2346.61.B44 2012   971.6'225   C2011-907644-6

NOVA SCOTIA
Communities, Culture and Heritage

Nimbus Publishing acknowledges the financial support for its publishing activities from the Government of Canada through the Canada Book Fund (CBF) and the Canada Council for the Arts, and from the Province of Nova Scotia through the Department of Communities, Culture and Heritage.

CONTENTS

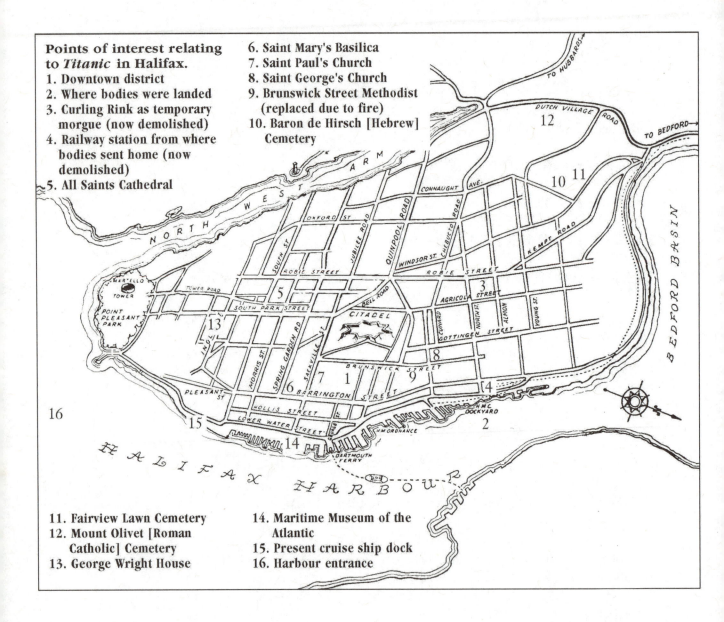

Points of interest relating to *Titanic* in Halifax.
1. Downtown district
2. Where bodies were landed
3. Curling Rink as temporary morgue (now demolished)
4. Railway station from where bodies sent home (now demolished)
5. All Saints Cathedral
6. Saint Mary's Basilica
7. Saint Paul's Church
8. Saint George's Church
9. Brunswick Street Methodist (replaced due to fire)
10. Baron de Hirsch [Hebrew] Cemetery
11. Fairview Lawn Cemetery
12. Mount Olivet [Roman Catholic] Cemetery
13. George Wright House
14. Maritime Museum of the Atlantic
15. Present cruise ship dock
16. Harbour entrance

Points of interest relating to Titanic in Halifax

ACKNOWLEDGEMENTS

Primary sources on the subject of the *Titanic* sinking and subsequent recovery of bodies and their disposition were checked through the records at the Nova Scotia Archives in Halifax. The resources of various archives and libraries were also drawn on: Harold Washington Library, Chicago, Illinois; Boston Public Library, Copley Square, Boston, Massachusetts; Archives of Ontario, Toronto, Ontario; Librairie Bibliotheque, Montreal, Quebec; New Brunswick Archives, Fredericton, New Brunswick; Southampton Public Library and Southampton Maritime Museum, Southampton, England.

Special thanks to: Donna Rae, Chicago, Illinois; Virginia Cooke, Woonsocket, Rhode Island; Charlie (the Whale) Lake, Boston, Massachusetts; Lesley Nelms Mroz, Connecticut, formerly of Southampton, England; Brian Ticehurst, Southampton, England; Senan Moloney, Dublin, Ireland; Anna and Alfred Clarke, Summit Acres Farm, Margaretsville, Nova Scotia; and in Halifax, Nova Scotia: Marilyn Gurney, director, Maritime Command Museum; Richard MacMicheal, Dan Conlin, and Jerry Lunn, Maritime Museum of the Atlantic; Gary Shutlack, archivist, Nova Scotia Archives; Alan Ruffman; Sara Yablon; Patrick Murphy; Stephanie Coyle; Sean Coyle; Shirley Ellis; Betty Browne; Carol Goodwin Goroff, Whitewater, Wisconsin; and the invaluable staff of the Spring Garden Road branch, Halifax Regional Library, for their contributions to this work.

HOW QUEEN MARY IS "REFORMING" LONDON'S FAST SET.

IT'S wash day in good old London town, with a queen at the "tub" and a "fast set" in the blueing.

There's no joy in the city on the Thames for those who now see that their time of favoritism has gone forever. Every day is Blue Monday.

Queen Mary, supported in her theories by the king, is determined that the old time set that found favor in the eyes of King Edward shall not rule the fashionable world of which London is the center any longer. And so those persons who have come under the royal disfavor are no longer requested to be in attendance at presentations, nor have any of the invitations which they sent the king and queen been answered with anything except "regrets."

And, of course, there is revolution.

Those who were in favor in another régime are disgusted with things in general. Things are too quiet. There is no royal favor for the fast little parties that once were supposed to be just the proper thing. To them Queen Mary's court is a sort of dowdy affair. It is dull and full of ennui. In common ordinary United States language, "there's nothing stirring."

The beginning of things came when Queen Mary decided that she should be the one to dictate what costumes should be worn at presentation. It was at just the time when hobble skirts were in favor and the queen didn't like them. She gave forth orders that no woman wearing a hobble skirt could be received in the royal presence.

Lady Paget Joins "Outsiders."

Of course, London gasped. But there was more to come! After the coronation, and especially after the royal trip to India, the invitations poured in to the king and queen to be present at various affairs given by old favorites of King Edward. Immense preparations were made for the reception of the

extraordinary birth or not just so long as they were interesting. And some of the things that came of that way of looking at things were interesting.

He was ready to pick up any one who offered promise of amusement. His life was one of merriment. One season in London he took about with him a young Austrian named Van Hoffman who had been introduced to him by Leopold of Belgium.

For a long time the companionship was the most interesting thing that London could find to talk about. "They went everywhere together. They were inseparable. Finally the blow came.

HOW QUEEN MARY PUTS 'EM THROUGH THE WRINGER!

She has refused to accept invitations to dinners given by friends of the late King Edward:

She has snubbed those who drink.

She has decreed that the hobble skirt must not enter her presence.

She doesn't like paint and face powder.

She is against picture hats.

She must know all about the person who is to be presented to her and if the examination isn't passed with a grade of 100 she "doesn't care to meet them."

The "fast set" must either be wiped out or reformed.

must observe a code of rules that are strict and from which there is no deviation. There must be no drinking and carousing such as there were in the other days of royal régime, there must be no gambling; there must be no painting and powdering; there must be no extremes of dress.

Reform Costly to Fashion Houses.

The fashion houses of London right now are being heavy, they say, simply because they cannot demand the prices for the goods they have to sell. Of course, in the dresses they make for those who would go before the queen they procure their usual profit, but

PREFACE

Titanic: the name conjures up many images. After its sinking, the pages of newspapers were filled with "thrilling" accounts of survivors and the parting words of the doomed. Jewels, evening gowns, and the net worth of the "thirty-three millionaires" lost at sea grabbed the attention of a world hungry for these stories. Among the souvenir books produced was *Story of the Wreck of the Titanic*. The cover drawing depicts the *Titanic* striking the iceberg and beginning to sink. Lifeboats riding huge waves are shown filled with passengers and manned

COVER DRAWING BY A. SCHMEDTGEN FROM *STORY OF THE WRECK OF THE TITANIC*.

by full crews of sailors. The truth is the night of April 14 was a beautiful, starlit evening with calm seas. The ship and iceberg quickly parted company. The lifeboats were not all full and were poorly crewed.

However, the band did play and history was made in the early morning hours of April 15, 1912. Historians will say that the year 1912 was one of the last calm years before the storm. The sun never set on the British Empire, so vast were its dominions, territories, and colonies. British gold was funding many new ventures in North America. The British Parliament was debating home rule for Ireland. In North America great waves of newcomers and many of the "newly rich" were joining the well-established "old stock." The United States was just discovering its economic muscle to the resentment of other countries and cultures.

The great highways of the world were on the water and the rail lines. Ocean liners were being

April 18, 1912: six flats in Montreal on offer for $15,500. A private suite on *Titanic* cost $4,350. A Los Angeles police officer made $83 to $102 per month.

built to standards of luxury never seen before. The wealthy travelled in style, maintaining houses, servants, and in some cases, mistresses, in different countries. New World rich girls often married Old World titles. Society maintained strict class lines and the upper classes were interconnected through family or investments. There was also a growing middle class, whose members had disposable income, allowing them to travel for pleasure. The poorest traveller would still be rich when compared to the poor who could never travel.

Under the surface of this golden age there was unrest. Unions were protecting the working class by striking services for better conditions and wages. Servants were leaving ancestral boundaries looking for new opportunities for themselves and their children. There were many types of political tension and the race between Britain and Germany to have the largest ships and most influence over commercial sectors was a sign of developments to take place just two years into the future. The year 1912, however, was far enough from war, taxes, and the stock market crash to be considered a frivolous time. New inventions, medical advancements, and larger buildings and ships made people in the western world feel that everything on earth could be controlled or conquered.

The newspapers were a major source of how the general public kept in touch with this changing world. Crime and scandal filled many a page. The activities and travels of the wealthy also provided reading material for the working people. The *Titanic* sinking would provide the newspapers with a lift in circulation. Though the newspapers profited from scandals, they also took a moral editorial position. Even while the sad stories of the sinking of the *Titanic* were still news, the *Chicago Sunday Tribune* ran a feature on "How Queen Mary is reforming London's Fast Set!" The accompanying cartoon showed the Queen laundering the upper class of its vices of drinking and gambling. Listed are those things that would disqualify people from entering Her Majesty's presence. There were those in first-class cabins on the *Titanic* who would have fallen short of the new Queen's standards. Redemption in the eyes of many came with the loss of life, as brave heroes were heralded in the press.

Reviewing press files one discovers the news of the sinking took three days to filter to the world. While waiting for the rescue ship *Carpathia* to arrive in New York with survivors, American newspapers filled their pages with speculation. They needed a villain for the piece and eventually chose the stiff Englishman, J. Bruce Ismay, the president of the White Star Line. There was little mention of the major owner, J. P. Morgan, who missed the voyage and was in France with "a friend." Many columns were filled with lists of names of those who were on board the ship. Many names were given identities that would prove false. For instance, first-class passenger Mr. H. Allison was thought to be an American senator when in fact he turned out to be a capitalist from Montreal. The lists often included people who had not sailed. These people are noted as receiving congratulations for having missed taking passage on the ship. Other families had to issue notices, days after the sinking, to correct reports of people saved who had actually perished.

Once the *Carpathia* arrived in New York, with its survivors, the news media had more to work with. While there were more losses in the third-class cabins and among the crew, the press wanted the stories of the rich. First-class survivors' recollections of April 15th were the most sought-after stories. Regardless of the newspaper, a few names made the headlines over and over because of their prominence in the financial world: Astor, Straus, Guggenheim, Hays, Widener, and Thayer among them. The newspapers led campaigns to raise funds for widows and orphans and gave coverage to the many benefit lectures and concerts held. *Titanic* was used for many a divine lesson. The words of the clergy on the error of putting confidence in material things and not spiritual needs were generously quoted in the press. Seeking comfort and wanting to be part of the great story, people crowded the churches; it was said "people are praying this Sunday who did not pray last Sunday." Reporters followed the official inquiries in the United States and England. Months after the sinking there were the stories of the settling of estates, the birth of children to the newly widowed and unveiling of monuments to the heroes. It all made excellent copy.

From the very beginning Halifax, Nova Scotia, was part of the *Titanic* story. The city was built to protect the interests of Great Britain. The large, natural, ice-free harbour is the closest mainland port to Europe. The harbour town welcomed soldiers and sailors, settlers, and the occasional wayward aristocrat. The cemeteries of the city contain townsfolk, pirates, and privateers. It was at Halifax that native son Samuel Cunard founded

HALIFAX, A PORT CITY THAT WAS SOMETIMES FORGOTTEN BETWEEN WARS, KNEW MANY STORIES OF SOULS LOST AT SEA.

the first transatlantic steamship company in 1839. It was here that the Cunard ship *Britannia* arrived with the mails from Liverpool in 1840. In 1849, the Associated Press was formed to ensure the fast delivery of the news of Europe from the Cunard ships in Halifax Harbour to the telegraph lines to New York. There is also a long history in Halifax of dealing with shipwrecks.

On April 15, 1912, the first news reports had *Titanic* being towed to Halifax. Other messages said passengers were being taken to Halifax. It was three days before the newspapers agreed that no living passenger or crew member from *Titanic* was going to Halifax from the wreck site. But Halifax would continue to feature in the newspaper pages for two months. Front-page curiosity of the arrival of the "death ship" carrying *Titanic* victims to Halifax Harbour would give way to page 12 notices of shipment of remains to Boston, New York, and other final resting places.

HEARSES CARRIED THE *TITANIC* DEAD PAST GOTTINGEN STREET, A WEALTHY RESIDENTIAL STREET.

Volunteer crews on the Canadian ships recovered 328 bodies. Of those found, 119 were buried at sea and 59 were sent elsewhere for burial. Halifax, with 150 graves in three different graveyards, is the largest land burial site for *Titanic* victims. The White Star Line purchased large plots and paid for gravestones. The inscription on the gravestone includes the person's name if known, the date of the sinking, and the number that was assigned to the body as it was recovered from the sea. Larger stones or extra wording was provided if the victim's family paid the additional cost.

Each generation discovers the story of *Titanic*'s sinking through poems, books, or movies. The passage of time varies the interest in *Titanic*, but it has never disappeared.

In learning any history, we have to know the language of the time. For instance the word "class" was much more restrictive than it is now. On airlines we still travel by executive class or economy class, but these terms do not have the same connotations they did a century ago. In 1912, first "cabin" (or "class"; the terms were interchangeable) did not guarantee that the cabin was any bigger than one located in second cabin. First cabin meant access to better arrangements such as food service. *Titanic* did have dormitory style cabins in third cabin but it did not resemble the crowded conditions of steerage in the 1800s.

HALIFAX STORES PROVIDED CLOTHING FOR THE *TITANIC* DEAD, PAID FOR BY THE WHITE STAR LINE.

Just as there were divisions between levels of passengers, the same was found among the crew. The men and the few women who served the passengers face-to-face had separate quarters according to the cabins they were assigned to work. The crew that kept the ship running was divided by trade and had separate cabins and messes. Ships had men who kept the coal fires burning; they were called firemen. Today we use that term almost exclusively for men who fight fires. For the purpose of this book I will refer to the steamship as the SS *Titanic*, the name found on the Halifax gravestones. The initials 'RMS' before the name *Titanic* were used to identify it as a Royal Mail Ship. This is also a correct title and is now used more widely in printed material. It is not always possible to identify the nationality of passengers on the *Titanic*. "British subject" included people from around the Empire. Many of the people on *Titanic*, even in third class, were well travelled. They were searching the world for opportunities to better their lives, and it is therefore difficult to tell where their citizenship rested.

Using the original mortuary reports I am able to give a description of the people whose bodies were recovered. I include part of the information available on what people, especially the unidentified, were wearing or what effects were found on their person. In most cases I am not including everything found as this would only list pants, shirt, etc. In some cases in the rush as people dressed in shared cabins they put on someone else's clothes. Some of the stewards who were found had the calling cards of passengers in their pockets and this led to confusion when identifying bodies. I list information that leads to a picture of who the person was. This includes the distinguishing physical features on the bodies that the recovery crews and mortuary workers noted in the official reports. It was the hope of the recorders that these descriptions would lead to later identifications. I list some of the amounts of currency that were found; this includes British pounds (£), American dollars ($), French francs, and coins. Shillings were listed as 's.' and pence were listed as 'd.'

From reviewing the original documents and comparing them with later information it becomes clear that the authorities recovering bodies were having difficulty giving age estimates, probably because of the amount of time a body had been exposed to the elements. For example a sixteen-year-old boy was originally estimated to be twenty-two years old. Some age estimates were out by twenty years or more. I have left an original estimated age in place if a real age could not be confirmed by using other sources. From newspapers and other accounts, details as to the occupation or interests of some of the dead and why they were travelling have been pieced together.

This book also provides useful information for those wishing to walk in our cemeteries. The addition of illustrations and photographs should help those not able to visit gain a feeling for the *Titanic* story and the impact it had on Halifax and the families of the victims around the world.

Olympic (top), dockside in Halifax Harbour during World War I, and *Titanic* (right). The notable exterior difference was that on *Titanic* the forward section of the promenade deck was closed in to shelter first-cabin passengers.

CHAPTER 1

THE MILLIONAIRES' SPECIAL

"These steamship men are hotel keepers rather than sailor men."

—Henry Sleeper Harper writing in Harper's Weekly, April 27, 1912. Mr. Harper, his wife, their Egyptian manservant, and Pekinese dog survived the sinking.

NEWSPAPERS COMPARED THE *OLYMPIC* AND *TITANIC* TO FAMOUS STRUCTURES AROUND THE WORLD. AFTER ITS SINKING, THE SIZE OF THE *TITANIC* WAS MEASURED AGAINST LOCAL BUILDINGS SUCH AS THE MASONIC TEMPLE. *THE CHICAGO DAILY TRIBUNE*, APRIL 16, 1912.

Titanic was the second of three sister ships built by the White Star Line to rival the ships of the Cunard Line and the Hamburg-Amerika Line. One common misconception was that *Titanic* was trying to best speed records set by other transatlantic liners. The White Star ships were in fact designed not for the fastest speed but to beat their rivals in luxury of accommodation. The standard of travel for first, second and even third class was to be set by these three ships.

The first of the three ships built was *Olympic*. From her performance, improvements were made to the design of *Titanic*, the second ship. For example, to shelter the first-class passengers from wind and wet, part of the promenade deck was enclosed. Interior spaces were redesigned and more first-class cabins were built to meet the demands of those who truly wanted to be pampered. A salt-water swimming pool, to be filled only in open sea to ensure clean water, complemented the squash courts and gymnasium. In first class, the furnishings were designed to represent the styles of different centuries. Cabins with sitting rooms were outfitted with twelve pieces of furniture. Special suites even had a room for a bath, something not available to all first-class passengers.

WIRELESS OPERATORS JACK PHILLIPS AND HAROLD BRIDE, PHOTOGRAPHED BY FRANCIS BROWNE IN SOUTHAMPTON PRIOR TO THE START OF THE MAIDEN VOYAGE. THEIR EFFORTS WOULD BRING THE CARPATHIA TO THE RESCUE. BOTH SURVIVED THE SINKING BUT PHILLIPS DIED OF EXPOSURE WHILE IN A LIFEBOAT.

Promotional advertising for *Titanic* listed the French à la Carte Restaurant, Turkish and electric baths, four elevators, a café, a palm court, and reading and lounge rooms. In New York, Wall Street gentlemen would proclaim *Titanic* the "Millionaires' Special." No mention was made of the fact that during construction the original sixty-four lifeboats

planned had been reduced to thirty-two and that after further discussion reduced to sixteen ordinary lifeboats and four smaller collapsible boats. The boats had been dropped from the design as it was thought they cluttered the boat deck and cut down on walking space. Twenty boats were more than was required by Board of Trade regulations.

'*TITANIC*, 45,000 TON MONSTER READY FOR SERVICE.'
— *Halifax Herald*, March 8, 1912.

Titanic was launched in Belfast without a formal christening ceremony. However the shores were lined with many people who worked for the Harland and Wolff yard. The years taken in the building of the ship represented a huge economic boost for the area. Everyone from architects to the families of the bathroom cabinetmakers wanted to see her touch water. After fittings were done and sea trials made, *Titanic* was taken to Southampton to be readied for its maiden voyage. One of the White Star Line's concerns was that the maiden voyage proceed as scheduled. *Titanic* was already delayed in getting into service as the Harland and Wolff yard had moved the ship to use the space for the *Olympic*, which needed repairs to a broken propeller. The new concern was caused by a coal strike across the United Kingdom that had limited fuel for sailings. White Star officials had to find a way to gather enough coal for the trip. The solution was to cancel the sailings of some smaller ships and shift the coal to the *Titanic*. This meant freight and passengers as well as some crew were also moved from other ships to *Titanic*.

Titanic was like a small town on the sea. There were sailors, stewards, waiters, officers, postal clerks, elevator operators, and even two window washers. Far below the passenger decks were the coal trimmers and firemen who would keep the boilers stoked. Among the passengers, there were the captains of industry, bankers, builders, ladies of leisure, teachers, clergy, authors, theatre people, valets, maids, and immigrants of many talents. In charge of it all was an experienced man of the sea, Captain E. J. Smith, formerly of the *Olympic*. As passengers boarded on Wednesday, April 10, they were greeted by a crew that had never worked together before and were, as much as the passengers, finding their way around the great ship. Like any small town there was gossip and secrets and occasional difficulties.

Some of the redirected passengers were not happy. The change in ship for some also changed their class of accommodation. First class on a smaller ship became second class on *Titanic*. For most passengers, however, even those who could only afford third class, the change was seen as an improvement. To be on the maiden voyage of the largest ship in the world would be something to tell the folks back home. Indeed, some of the passengers at Southampton and Cherbourg (the ship's first stop) had made their plans in order to be on the maiden voyage. For members of the crew, being on *Titanic* meant having work. The shortage of coal had limited sailings and for residents of Southampton who depended on ships

for employment, there had been great hardships. The chance to work *Titanic* was an opportunity for some crew to repay debts, for others to plan a future marriage.

The majority of the passengers on the voyage would board ship in Southampton, and included immigrants from across northern Europe. As *Titanic* gathered steam to leave Southampton Harbour for Cherbourg on the coast of France, an unfortunate incident occurred that was later considered an omen for disaster. Ropes securing the liner *New York* to another vessel along the docks broke as a result of the large displacement of water the *Titanic* made as it passed. Only the quick action of Captain Smith in having engines reversed and that of a tugboat nearby averted the smaller liner being pulled into the side of *Titanic*. This incident was noted by passengers in correspondence posted from stops in Cherbourg, France, and Queenstown, Ireland, its two stops before continuing to New York.

The *Titanic* was too large to dock at Cherbourg or Queenstown; passengers, luggage, and mail were brought alongside by small boats. Cherbourg would be where the last of the first-class passengers boarded. There was still room for almost three hundred more first-class passengers, but it was not yet high season for travel. Many immigrants from the Middle East boarded at Cherbourg.

Queenstown brought more mail, Irish immigrants, and a few second-class passengers. As in France, a few passengers disembarked. One of these was Francis Browne, candidate for the Jesuit priesthood and amateur photographer. A few

CHARLES JOUGHIN, CHIEF BAKER, THREW CHILDREN INTO LIFEBOATS. HE HAD DRINKS OF LIQUOR TO STEADY HIS NERVES. HE WENT DOWN WITH THE SHIP AND SURVIVED SWIMMING IN THE WATER UNTIL THERE WAS ROOM FOR HIM ON A LIFEBOAT. HIS SURVIVAL IS PORTRAYED IN A NUMBER OF MOVIES.

days later he would supply the world with some of the few onboard pictures of the ill-fated ship. At Queenstown, stewards of various services would know the final number of passengers they would be looking after, one even wrote home about gratuities received and anticipated. Crew and passengers posted letters through the onboard post office, which sent the mailbags to shore to wait a ship returning to Europe. Some families would receive this correspondence days after the sinking. Even after the call in Ireland on April 11th, the *Titanic* had capacity for another 1,100 passengers, so the tragedy that was to happen could have been worse. As *Titanic* headed out to open sea the wireless operators were receiving the first warnings of ice ahead.

Life on board was organized around meals, all other times were at leisure. First cabin would change for dinner and choose between the ship's dining saloon or the À la Carte Restaurant. Some in second cabin, like Baron von Drachstedt (who was really 20-year-old Alfred Nourney), would dress for dinner; passengers in third class for the most part would not change clothes for meals. Dining allowed one to meet new people, though first-cabin passengers tended to make up parties in advance. Such a formal arrangement would not happen in third class, where meal seating arrangements were based more on language spoken or country of origin. Comments were made on the food offered, not by the difference between first and third classes; that would have been expected. In third class the large quantity of food available would have attracted notice. For some of the immigrants it would have been better than what they had at home or on the journey to meet the ship. In all three classes, there were passengers who were never seen at meals as they were unwell and stayed in their cabins.

Music was a large part of the entertainment on board. Eight musicians were hired by a music agency to play for *Titanic*'s first and second cabins. Third class and crew members provided their own music. Some had instruments, including harmonicas, violins, and even one set of bagpipes, while others just sang songs of their country of origin. Recreational opportunities were available of various sorts. Seen at the gymnasium was Pierre Maréchal of France, an aviation pioneer, Karl Behr, tennis player, and others looking to keep fit.

Most passengers walked the outside decks for fresh air. After all, despite the luxury, ocean liners still had plenty of smells—coal smoke, cooking, and other things that could make the indoors stuffy. While taking exercise on the decks an opportunity arose to meet fellow travellers. There were libraries and writing rooms in both first and second cabin and smoking rooms for gentlemen.

Among first-class passengers, there were those who just liked to sit and people watch; others like Colonel Archibald Gracie or Margaret Brown, of Denver, Colorado, liked to engage in conversation. Margaret Brown was not well accepted by Denver society because she was one of the brash new rich and by all accounts somewhat loud. Her name appeared in the newspaper lists of prominent people who would be travelling on the maiden voyage of the *Titanic*. She enjoyed that type of notice, arranging her trip home with the Astors, who were in need of society. To make sure that Denver did not forget her, she was bringing home some artifacts for the local museum.

The cafe concession managed by Luigi Gatti, a popular London restauranteur, kept late hours, which was appreciated by those who wanted to gossip about those seen on board. Mr. and Mrs. Jacques Futrelle were sure to be there. He was the author of *The Chase of the Golden Plate, The Simple Case of Susan, The Thinking Machine on the Case*, and other detective stories. His wife, Lily May, was also an author. The couple had just secured publishing contracts while they travelled in Europe.

Henry B. Harris, one of America's foremost theatre owners and show managers, would be used to late night after hours, and was likely at the café with his wife. The café might also have appealed to sculptor Paul Chevré of France. He was on his way

MRS. JAMES J. (MARGARET) BROWN, AGE 44. HER SOCIETY IMAGE IMPROVED WHEN IT BECAME KNOWN THAT SHE ENCOURAGED THE OTHER WOMEN IN HER LIFEBOAT TO ROW. ON THE *CARPATHIA* SHE WORKED FOR THE COMFORT OF OTHERS AND TOOK UP A SUBSCRIPTION FOR THE DESTITUTE. TO THE PRESS, SHE SAID, "JUST THE BROWN LUCK, WE ARE UNSINKABLE." EVENTUALLY A BROADWAY PLAY WOULD MAKE HER THE UNSINKABLE "MOLLY" BROWN.

to Canada for the unveiling of one of his pieces at the new Chateau Laurier Hotel in Ottawa.

Among the people to keep a low profile during the voyage would be the Arthur Ryersons of Philadelphia, who were returning due to the death of a son in an automobile crash. There was also

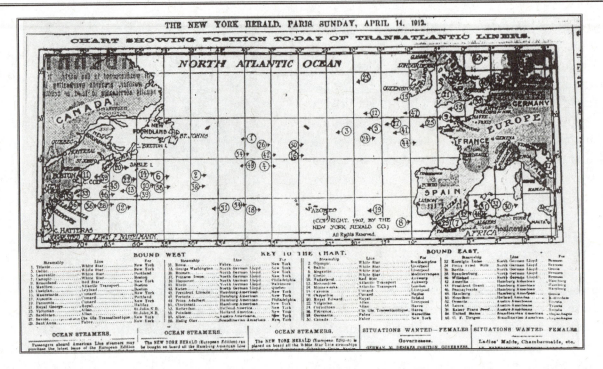

THE *New York Herald*, European edition, Paris, ran charts showing the positions of the transatlantic liners. On Sunday, April 14, the day before the sinking, the approximate positions of *Titanic* and *Olympic* are marked as No. 1 and No. 2. The *Carpathia*, the ship that would rush to rescue the survivors, is No. 18. A variety of vessels from fishing boats to freighters that carried passengers are not shown.

William Stead, who was travelling to the United States at the request of President Taft to speak at a peace conference. In his early life he had campaigned for the protection of children and was a respected journalist and peace advocate.

More reports of ice were received on April 12 and 13.

On Sunday morning, April 14, Captain Smith presided over Church of England divine service in the first-class dining saloon for passengers.

Servants of the first-class passengers and some crew would have also been in attendance. Three Roman Catholic priests and six Protestant ministers of various denominations were travelling in second class and were able to provide services for those interested. Most passengers had prayer books of their faith with them. Roman Catholics also carried strings of beads for the praying of the rosary in devotion to Mary, mother of Jesus; something they did every day of the trip. For the men

LEFT: DOROTHY GIBSON, ACTRESS, SAVED. MIDDLE: PIERRE MARÈCHAL, AVIATOR, SAVED. RIGHT: JAMES R. McGOUGH, TOY BUYER FOR GIMBEL'S DEPARTMENT STORE, SAVED.

who worked in the extreme heat of the boiler area, the kitchens, and the electrical rooms, Sunday passed like every other day.

The heat being generated throughout the ship was most welcome on that Sunday as the air outside was becoming colder. This was the day that the Marconi wireless operators received the most messages from other ships regarding ice. The operators, who were not employees of the ship, were very busy sending messages for the passengers that day. That was their main purpose on the ship, to generate income for their company. Ice reports were passed on but did not interest the operators. When the nearby *Californian* passed on a message saying that the ship was stopped because of ice, the *Titanic* wireless man, Jack Phillips, sent back "Shut up Shut up I am busy I am working Cape Race."

That evening Captain Smith attended a dinner party in the À la Carte Restaurant hosted by the Wideners of Philadelphia. He retired to his cabin around 9:30 p.m. In the first-class dining saloon, George Graham, a buyer for the Eaton's

department store in Winnipeg, Manitoba, signed a dinner menu along with the other men at his table. Noted on the back of the menu with the signatures was the date and distance from New York, 1,760 miles out. First-class passengers listened to music and made plans for the next day. Dog owners who kept their pets in their cabins or in the kennel were going to have an informal show to entertain their fellow passengers. The five young children in first class, fed by their nursemaids in the cabins, would be looking forward to the dog show. (The owner of the prized poultry on board would not be bringing them out to show.) Others made plans to meet at the gymnasium, squash court, or pool. As the ladies left the men, Colonel Archibald Gracie decided to retire early in order to be rested for his workout in the morning. He had just finished a conversation with Charles M. Hays, president of the Grand Trunk Railway, who spoke of the disaster that was destined to happen because of the rush for bigger and faster ships.

In second class, a hymn sing was held after

LEFT: NOELLE, COUNTESS OF ROTHES, AGE 27, TOOK THE TILLER OF HER LIFEBOAT AND COMFORTED THE NEWLY WIDOWED. HER HUSBAND, THE 19TH EARL OF ROTHES, WAITED IN AMERICA FOR HER. RIGHT: DOCTOR ALICE F. LEADER, FIRST-CLASS PASSENGER, SAVED. MOST REPORTS LIST HER AS MISS LEADER; IT WAS NOT SOCIALLY ACCEPTABLE FOR WOMEN TO USE THEIR PROFESSIONAL TITLES. SHE PRAISED THE COUNTESS OF ROTHES FOR TAKING CHARGE OF THEIR LIFEBOAT.

dinner by the Reverend Ernest Carter. An engineer travelling to Canada from Scotland, Robert Norman, played piano for one of the ladies who sang a selection of music. Others who had ventured outside quickly returned commenting on the increasing cold. In their cabin, Mrs. Ester Hart started her nightly vigil watching over her husband and their daughter, Eva, so convinced was she that something was not right with this large new ship. Not all of the twenty-five young children in second class were travelling with their mothers; indeed the two little boys of Louis Hoffman (actually Michel Navratil) may have been wondering when they would see their mother.

In third class, a good sleep was a struggle. The mothers of the eighty-four young children under the age of ten did their best to quiet fears with familiar stories and prayers. These children had enjoyed the different music played during the passing days, especially when Alma Palsson had used her mouth organ to entertain at the birthday party of one of her four children. She was herself looking forward to seeing her husband, who was waiting in Chicago. He had left the family two years earlier to establish a new life for them in America.

Throughout the ship, the crew performed its duties; the wireless operators received messages, the wait staff of Luigi Gatti's first-class restaurant concession did their final clean up. Shoes and boots had been collected for polishing. The barman was preparing drinks for those first-class passengers who were playing cards and others were just enjoying a good cigar.

High up in the crow's nest, the lookout spotted an iceberg. He rang the bridge; "Iceberg right ahead" was his message.

The ship struck the iceberg despite the efforts of the duty officer to veer away. At first it did not seem there would be much damage. Below decks the watertight doors had closed. The firemen and coal trimmers waited for their orders. Water came in from the rips in the hull made by the iceberg. Captain Smith was called from his cabin. Mr. Andrews, representing the builders on this maiden voyage, did a check on the damage and reported to the captain that the ship probably had two hours left. Valuable time had already passed. Finally the officers were told to prepare the

THE MEN THEY LEFT BEHIND THEM.

A DRAWING BY JOHN T. MCCUTCHEON FOR CHICAGO
NEWSPAPERS ILLUSTRATING A CHEERFUL PARTING SCENE.
SOME FEMALE SURVIVORS RECALLED THAT MEN WAVED
GOODBYE, SAYING THAT IT WAS JUST A PRECAUTION AND
EVERYONE WOULD BE BACK FOR BREAKFAST.

lifeboats. The captain asked the wireless operators to stand by to send a message for assistance.
As there was no public address system, stewards
started making their rounds to wake those passengers who had not noticed the collision or the
slowing of the ship. The engines were stopped,
but the electrical engineers continued to work to
keep the lights on. The captain gave the wireless
men the order to send the message asking for assistance. The only wireless operator on the nearby
Californian, after being told to "Shut up" earlier

in the evening by the *Titanic* operator, had by this
time retired for the night.

Some *Titanic* passengers were immediately
aware that something had happened. They noticed different sounds from people moving in the
corridors and the noise of the steam being released
as the fires in the boilers were raked. Those first-
class passengers already in bed got up and put on
the clothes and shoes that had been laid out for the
next day. Many passengers put clothing on over
their pyjamas. Even J. Bruce Ismay, the president
of the White Star Line, travelling with his own
valet, was on deck in his slippers. While the sea
post officers were desperately moving the mail up
and away from the flooding post office rooms,
passengers were calmly going to the purser's office
to reclaim valuables. Others decided to ignore the
commotion and returned to their cabins. Almost
an hour after the collision with the iceberg the first
of *Titanic*'s lifeboats was being loaded. Very few
sailors were among the ship's crew. Some of the
first-class men pitched in to help in order to have
something to do. As other passengers arrived from
second and third class there was a lot of milling
about waiting for direction. The musicians under
Bandmaster Wallace Hartley started to play.

"WE ARE PUTTING WOMEN OFF IN BOATS."
—*Titanic* operator's wired message to listening
stations.

At first there was reluctance on the part of
women to get into the lifeboats. Passengers

LEFT: DR. WILLIAM O'LOUGHLIN, SHIP'S SURGEON, WAS LAST SEEN STANDING WITH THE CHIEF STEWARD, THE PURSER, AND ANOTHER OFFICER. THE DOCTOR, WHO SERVED ON SHIPS FOR FORTY YEARS, WAS NOT WEARING A LIFE JACKET. THE CHIEF STEWARD WAS BURIED IN HALIFAX, THE PURSER WAS BURIED AT SEA. RIGHT: DR. ERNEST SIMPSON, JUNIOR SURGEON, WAS ALSO LOST.

thought it was safer to stay on the largest ship in the world then descend a great distance down in a small wooden boat to face being lost in the ocean. After all, a wireless onboard meant that a message asking for help could be sent. A light was visible in the distance that many people saw and thought to be a ship coming to the rescue. Who could blame the first-class women for being reluctant? They had enjoyed a ten-course dinner with wine a few hours earlier and were feeling sleepy. It would be noted that the gentlemen were calm and reassuring. The band was playing, the lights were on, and the thought of stepping out to the lifeboat while wearing a tight fitting hobble skirt or a heavy coat over a light nightdress was not very appealing.

The farther passengers were from the boat deck the longer it took to know of the danger. They then had to dress warmly and find the way up to the top of the ship. In third class, Alma Palsson had four children to dress warmly; Mr. and Mrs. Sage had nine children, ages four to twenty, to worry about. The widow Margaret Rice had five young boys to wake and dress. For some of the immigrants it was difficult to understand what was being said in English. All they owned was on the ship so there were those who took time packing cases or putting numerous pieces of clothing on. The ship had been built as required by American immigration law to physically divide the classes and this would slow the progress of those on the lower levels in reaching the upper decks. By the time many reached the upper decks the lifeboats were gone.

Despite the noise of steam being released from the boilers and rockets being fired, for many there was no sense of urgency. People were numb from standing out on the deck barely clothed. For some, hypothermia had already started to affect their actions. Time seemed to move very slowly. Due to the size of the ship it was not possible to see what was happening at all the lifeboats. On the port side the boats were being loaded with women and small children only. On the starboard side it was whoever was willing to get into the boats. The first boats were being lowered with many seats empty. In fact it was later estimated there were over four hundred empty places in the lifeboats; more than enough room for all the women and children who would be lost in the sinking.

CHICAGO AMERICAN

Registered in U. S. Patent Office.   Circulation Certified by the Association of American Advertisers.

MONDAY.   CHICAGO, APRIL 15, 1912.   MONDAY.

T DERS GATES

CHENEY SENT IN TO OPPOSE SPEEDY CARDS

The Batting Order.

CHICAGO.   ST. LOUIS.
Evers, 2b.   Huggins, 2b.
Sheckard, lf.   Ellis, lf.
Schulte, rf.   Oakes, cf.

TITANIC IS ON WAY TO PORT; 2,210

TIGERS HERE FOR OPENING OF HOT SERIES

The Batting Order.

CHICAGO   DETROIT
Rath, 2b   Vitt, lf.
Lord, 3b   Louden, 3b
Callahan lf   Perry, rf

THE *CHICAGO AMERICAN*, LIKE MANY NEWSPAPERS, ASSURED THE WORLD THAT THE *TITANIC* PASSENGERS WERE SAFE AND THE SHIP WAS BEING TOWED TO HALIFAX. LATER EDITIONS, ON THE SAME DAY, GAVE DESCRIPTIONS OF EFFORTS TO BEACH THE VESSEL. THE STORY WAS GIVEN PART OF THE FRONT PAGE ALONGSIDE BASEBALL NEWS.

The crew was hesitant to fully load the boats, fearing the boats would break in half from the weight of its passengers while being lowered. The crew had not done a drill to see how the boats worked and did not know the boats had been tested to be lowered when fully loaded. Some of the officers thought that once the boats were in the water they could come alongside and pick up more people. The sailors in the undermanned boats were more concerned with going down in the suction of the sinking ship and rowed away from the ship.

As *Titanic* sank, the water flowed over the watertight compartments into the next space. At one point the water rose into a corridor and poured down into the next stairwell. The ship took a list to one side and water started to pour into the opening for the anchor chains. Finally it became obvious to all but a few that the ship would not last until a rescue ship arrived. The distance from the boat deck to the water was shorter now and lifeboats were being lowered fully loaded. Men threw deck chairs into the ocean in the hope they would use them for survival. Others gathered in prayer looking for divine help.

For over 1,500 of the passengers and crew the early morning hours of April 15, 1912, would be recorded as their time of death.

CHICAGO EVENING AMERICAN

Registered in U. S. Patent Office.   Circulation Certified by the Association of American Advertisers

MONDAY.   CHICAGO, APRIL 15, 1912.   **MONDAY.**

...ATES ...IAMES ...E AXED

...of the Democratic ..., under the direc-

...rricaded doors to ... afternoon. The ... the city present. ...ffered the second ...ook County party

..., whose orders were ...en by the Sullivan ...on the Armory. At ...ea armed with axes ...ve of the convention

...ed down two doors ... militiamen took to

ZIM'S ERROR GIVES CARDS AN EARLY RUN

The Batting Order.

CHICAGO.	ST. LOUIS.
Evers, 2b.	Huggins, 2b.
Sheckard, lf.	Ellis, lf.
Schulte, rf.	Oakes, cf.
Zimmerman, 1b.	Konetchy, 1b.
Lennox, 3b.	Evans, rf.
Hofman, cf.	Mowrey, 3b.
Tinker, ss.	Houser, ss.
Archer, c.	Bliss, c.
Cheney, p.	Harmon, p.

Umpires—Eason and Johnstone.

National League Park, St. Louis, Mo., April 15.—Heine Zimmerman's wild throw in the first inning of to-day's game gave the Cardinals the first run of the game. The Cubs' new first baseman attempted to put the ball across the diamond, but instead of that hit the grandstand with it and the Cardinals went into the lead.

The Cubs evened the count, however, in the third.

Barring Chance, almost everybody in camp is in condition, the F. L. having a slight twitch in his head, although this morning he was much improved. The announcement that Chance has retired for-

BATTLE TO BEACH TITANIC; SAVE ALL

New York, April 15.—Efforts were being made late this afternoon to beach the Titanic at Cape Race because of the sinking condition of the mammoth steamer, according to wireless reports from Halifax.

Captain Smith's plan to reach Halifax, 600 miles from the scene of the collision, under the Titanic's own steam, was apparently abandoned because of the serious condition the steamer was found to be in after a more thorough inspection.

After transferring her passengers, the Titanic was taken in tow by the Allan liner Virginia. Later the Virginian left her ... she attempted to proceed under her

BODIE KNOCKS OUT A HOMER; SOX IN LEAI

The Batting Order.

CHICAGO	DETROIT.
Rath, 2b.	Vitt, lf.
Lord, 3b.	Louden, 3b.
Callahan, lf.	Perry, rf.
Bodie, cf.	Crawford, cf.
Mattick, rf.	O'Leary, 2b.
Zeider, 1b.	Gainor, 1b.
Weaver, ss.	Bush, ss.
Sullivan, c.	Stanage, c.
White, p.	Mullen, p.

Umpires—Evans and Egan.

BY BILL BAILEY.

Comiskey Park, April 15.—Ping B... put the ball into the bleachers in the th... inning of to-day's game with the Det... Tigers and scored Callahan ahead of ... on the home run drive.

Mattick doubled and Zeider singled a... this and the White Sox had a total ... three runs in the inning.

The White Sox scored in the oper... inning, but the Tigers evened this u... the second.

Callahan decided to send Doc Wh... his veteran southpaw, to the hill aga... the Tigers, White always having bee... tough one for Jennings' men to fathe...

CHAPTER 2

RECOVERY OF THE DEAD

They listened to wondrous music
In rooms that were planned for kings,
Beautiful notes from beautiful throats,
Sung as a songbird sings.
They reveled in baths of marble,
Like the baths of ancient Rome.
T'was a wondrous trip on a wondrous ship,
The ship that never came home.

—Verse from *The Voyagers* by William F. Kirk,
Chicago Evening American, April 22, 1912.

CAPTAIN SMITH, MASTER OF THE *TITANIC*. HE HAD PLANNED TO RETIRE AFTER THE RETURN VOYAGE. HIS BODY WAS NOT FOUND.

It took two hours and forty minutes from the time of the collision with the iceberg for the *Titanic* to sink. During that time people were able to witness the final moments of other people's lives. Those in the lifeboats reviewed those last hours on the ship. They would have to have been wondering if the people they left on deck had survived the awful crash thought to be the sound of the boilers ripping out of the ship. Were they safe or were they struggling in the water where terrible cries were heard for at least an hour after the sinking? The survivors would have to have been thinking if there was something they could have done to have seen their loved ones into the lifeboats. To believe that men had died heroically by choice helped to ease a feeling of guilt. It was too soon to know there were so many empty seats in the lifeboats. It was too soon to know that women and children had died.

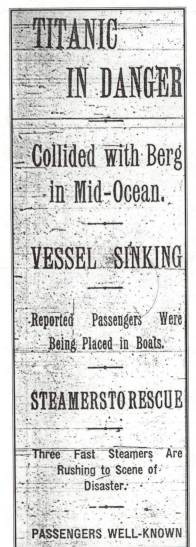

TITANIC IN DANGER

Collided with Berg in Mid-Ocean.

VESSEL SINKING

Reported Passengers Were Being Placed in Boats.

STEAMERS TO RESCUE

Three Fast Steamers Are Rushing to Scene of Disaster.

PASSENGERS WELL-KNOWN

ALL THE FIRST DAY, NEWSPAPERS REPORTED THAT THE *TITANIC* WAS STILL AFLOAT, INCLUDING *THE GAZETTE*, MONTREAL (ABOVE).

The shock of the situation, the difficulty in understanding such a dramatic change in circumstances, would be one reason survivors did not return to help rescue people out of the water. Another reason was self-preservation. To return to the mass of swimmers meant the risk of capsizing their own lifeboat. Eventually one officer did organize a boat to look for people in the water. He would be too late for most and would only find five people to pull into his boat. Cold, wet, and anxious, the survivors were left wondering if anyone would come to their rescue. Would they be doomed to drift in the Atlantic?

As the *Titanic* was sinking a number of ships received the calls for assistance, CDQ and SOS. The ship claimed by many survivors to have been visible from the decks of *Titanic* remains a mystery. Was there a ship or were people seeing the stars on the horizon on a very dark clear night? This is one of the questions that continues to generate debate. In 1912, the blame for not coming to the rescue was placed on the freighter *Californian* and its commander Captain Lord.

The ship that did speed to the rescue was a Cunard liner, the *Carpathia*. This ship, captained by Arthur Rostron, was bound for Naples, Italy, from New York City. The captain made the bold decision to turn his ship around and travel in darkness through the icefields. The firemen and coal trimmers worked furiously to stoke the boilers and the ship responded by exceeding her top speed. The captain ordered the other crew members to have the ship ready for any requirement. Preparations were made for the receiving of passengers and of the mails. *Carpathia* arrived in the area given in the *Titanic*'s SOS message two hours after the sinking. Imagine the thoughts of Captain Rostron on arriving just as light was beginning to break. The largest ship in the world was not there.

As the crew of the *Carpathia* scanned the waters, the first of the lifeboats was spotted. Slowly the *Carpathia* moved among the ice to reach the lifeboats. *Carpathia*'s passengers had been alerted to the situation by the vibration of the speeding ship. Some of those passengers went on deck, taking their cameras with them. Photographs were taken as the lifeboats came alongside and the survivors were hoisted onto the ship. The detail is not enough to see the faces or clothing of the people in the boats. It is obvious that many took off their life jackets as soon as it was clear they were rescued. This made it easier to board the *Carpathia*.

Some of the *Titanic* passengers were well bundled up for the cold, others were not. The last survivors were picked up five hours and thirty minutes after the sinking. While waiting rescue some clothing had been shared. Lawrence Beesley, a teacher from England, had dressed warmly but for some reason still had his dressing gown over his arm. When he was told to jump into a lifeboat he dropped it and another survivor put it on for warmth. (It was later returned on the rescue ship.) First-class passenger Robert Daniel had been pulled into a lifeboat wearing only woolen underwear. In the photographs it is impossible to distinguish what is being worn under bulky fur coats. Many of the ladies who had retired for the evening were in their night dresses; the newspapers would make more of those who had on elegant evening dresses. Dorothy Gibson, an actress, wore a satin evening dress. She would wear the same dress in a movie about the disaster. The young Mrs. Astor was well dressed underneath a cape coat suitable for going to the opera and also wore a string of pearls. (The pearls would gain a Halifax connection when they were later bought by Mrs. Izaak Walton Killam, wife of a Nova Scotian who made his fortune in the United States.) Scarves and travel hats were more common among the ladies than the large picture hats seen in the movies. One lady lost her

First-class passengers Ida Hippach and her fifteen-year-old daughter, Jean, were saved. Mrs. Hippach was a well known Chicago society woman who had lost two sons to the Iroquois Theatre fire in 1908.

straw hat as it was burned to attract the attention of the rescue ship.

A few small dogs were among the rescued, carried under the coats of their owners. It is believed that someone opened the kennels on the ship to

LEFT: CHRISTOPHER HEAD, BARRISTER AND EX-MAYOR OF BOROUGH OF CHELSEA, ENGLAND, LOST. MIDDLE: MARGUERITE FROLICHER, FIRST-CLASS PASSENGER, SAVED. RIGHT: KARL BEHR, NOTED TENNIS PLAYER WHO TWICE PLAYED FOR THE DAVIS CUP, SWAM FOR A LIFEBOAT AND WAS SAVED.

give the other dogs a swimming chance. Credit is sometimes given to John Jacob Astor, who always travelled with his dog, an Airedale named Kitty. One Newfoundland dog, Rigel, survived and was rescued as it was swimming alongside a lifeboat. The dog's bark had alerted the *Carpathia* crew to a lifeboat close to the bow.

A few people had their jewels and money; most did not. First-class passengers Mrs. Fortune and her daughters from Canada actually had handed their jewels back to the men on the ship as the lifeboat was being lowered. They felt it safer; the men did not survive. Other women did the same. Miss Edith Russell (Rosenbaum) had her steward retrieve her musical toy pig and left jewels behind. Major Arthur Peuchen of Toronto left over two hundred thousand dollars of securities and bonds in his cabin and grabbed three oranges and a favourite pin. Other survivors lost everything.

On reaching the *Carpathia* survivors were suffering from exposure to the cold North Atlantic waters. They had been outside for over seven hours. Many were wet from the water that was in the bottom of the lifeboats. Some people had injuries; four men would die after being rescued. Passengers that were able stayed on deck and waited for the other lifeboats to arrive. Some family members were reunited, giving hope to others. However, when all the boats were accounted for, many were missing. It was then that the final realization of what the crying, screaming, and moaning heard in the dark hours earlier had meant.

Other ships arrived to search for survivors who might be clinging to wreckage, including the *Californian*. The only survivors were those on the *Carpathia*. The Captain of the *Carpathia* had an Episcopal minister conduct a service for the comfort of the survivors with prayers for the dead before they left the wreck area. The White Star Line wired asking if the survivors should be transferred in mid ocean to the *Olympic*. This way they could be made more comfortable. Captain Rostron thought the sight of the sister ship of the *Titanic* coming out of the fog and the strain of the move would be too much for the grieving passengers to handle. The captain also considered taking the ship to the closest mainland port which was Halifax. He felt that travelling through more ice would be unsettling to all concerned. He tried to confer with Mr. Ismay about these plans but found the president of the White Star Line was willing to leave all decisions up to him. He ordered his ship to head to New York. *Carpathia* would arrive in New York on April 18. For 3 days

A COLLAPSIBLE BOAT, SHOWING THE CANVAS SIDES RAISED, NEARS THE *CARPATHIA*.

Captain Rostron had the task of providing for the survivors and his own passengers on a very small liner. There was enough food but accommodation was limited. Passengers had to sleep on tables and floors or in whatever chairs were available. The captain also had to deal with a great number of wireless messages.

Due to the number of wireless messages from newspaper men asking for lists of survivors, Captain Rostron ordered that no replies be given. Even a message from the president of the United States was ignored: William Taft wanted to know if his military aide, Major Butt, had survived. No reply would be sent to the White House. The work of the *Carpathia* wireless operator was limited to

sending out messages of passengers so that arrangements could be made for their journeys from the arrival pier. This lack of wireless cooperation was frustrating to the newsmen and added to the misery of waiting relatives and friends.

"REPORTED ALL PASSENGERS SAVED"
"*TITANIC* BEING TOWED TO HALIFAX"
"*TITANIC* SLOWLY STEAMING FOR HALIFAX"
"*TITANIC* TO BEACH ON SABLE ISLAND"
—From the newspapers, April 15, 1912

Communication of the news that the *Titanic* had hit an iceberg was published in newspapers

A lifeboat alongside the *Carpathia*. Photograph taken by a *Carpathia* passenger and featured in *Chicago Daily Tribune*, April 22, 1912.

on April 15, the day of the sinking. It took another day before the news that the ship had sunk was published around the world. Only the *New York Times* had got the story right in their first edition on the morning of the sinking. It was difficult even for the newsmen to believe that such an event had taken place. After all, they had used the promotional material that showed the *Titanic* as the largest ship in the world with all the latest safety features. Much faith was put into the boast that the watertight compartments would be keeping the *Titanic* afloat. When the first wireless messages were received it was assumed that *Titanic* would make for the closest port. The obvious choice seemed to be Halifax, Nova Scotia. In New York, P. A. Franklin, vice-president of the White Star Line, was quoted as saying it "could be definitely stated that no persons had been lost."

Unfortunately the wireless system was not a precise method of communication. This would be proven time and again during the weeks ahead. Wireless operators had to tap out a message, and the signals had to be heard over long distances. Sometimes the messages were relayed from ship to ship. The equipment on various ships was of different strengths. Not all wireless operators were experienced enough to pick up every detail. Weather and time of day had an effect on the distance a message would travel and the quality of the transmission.

One message received read "*Titanic* being towed to Halifax." But it was actually two messages that were mistakenly put together. One message stated that the *Titanic* had sunk. The other was that an oil tanker was being towed to Halifax. On the basis of this mistaken message, White Star officials in New York arranged for rail cars to travel to Halifax to pick up passengers. The trains consisted of coaches, dining cars, and optimistically, baggage cars for luggage and mail. When the correct message was known the trains were turned back. Harold Cottam, the wireless operator on the *Carpathia*, would tell the

American inquiry that he sent a message to the SS *Baltic* that the *Carpathia* was going to Halifax. This could have been picked up by other ships and relayed to shore. The *Chicago American* reported in a story dated April 15 "that Captain Smith had abandoned his plan to be towed to Halifax and was going to beach at Cape Race, Newfoundland." This report appeared many hours after Captain Smith and the *Titanic* had gone to a watery grave.

American newspapers printed many stories that were not accurate even after survivors arrived in New York on the evening of April 18. There was enormous competition for readers and any story was worth printing, especially if it mentioned the wealthy men who had gone down with the ship. The public demanded answers to many questions and the press was only too happy to be an ally to those demands. The Senate inquiry that was arranged soon after the disaster brought forward many of the issues raised in the newspapers. Questions such as whether survivors might be found clinging to icebergs or if the watertight compartments of the *Titanic* could hold people who would be running out of air were published in the papers. Along with these farfetched questions there were also practical ones, such as what was to happen to the bodies floating in the ocean.

HALIFAX IN THE NEWS

Until the *Titanic* sinking there had been a tradition for passing ships to give burial at sea for shipwreck victims. When a wreck was close to

LEFT: ELEANOR WIDENER, SAVED. RIGHT: THE BODY OF HER SON, HARRY E. WIDENER, AGE 27, WAS NOT RECOVERED, NOR WAS THAT OF HER HUSBAND.

shore, civilian or military authorities undertook the burial of the dead on land. The *Titanic* sinking, with almost 1,500 people dead, changed the recovery process. There was a demand for bodies to be given a proper burial. To meet that demand and to protect its reputation, the White Star Line arranged for its official agents, A. G. Jones and Company in Halifax, to charter a vessel to undertake a recovery effort. Halifax was chosen as the base of operations as it was the closest mainland port to the sinking and had the facilities and personnel to handle the situation.

The vessel that was available for the work was a cable laying ship, the *Mackay-Bennett*. The crew was asked if they wished to volunteer for work that would be unsettling. With the crew went undertakers from Snow's Funeral establishment in Halifax and the Reverend Kenneth C. Hines of All

Saints (Anglican) Cathedral. Included along with the supplies needed for any voyage were canvas and scrap iron for burials at sea. Also put onboard were 125 coffin boxes and all the embalming fluid available in Halifax. To help preserve bodies being taken to Halifax a large amount of ice was also put on the recovery vessel. Even as the *Mackay-Bennett* was preparing to leave Halifax Harbour, university men in the United States were reported stating that there would be no bodies to find. It was their scientific belief that everything would have been sucked down with the ship, never to return to the surface. Others agreed that many bodies were trapped in the tangle of wreckage of the broken ship. This is why only one vessel was at first contracted to do the recovery work. At the same time that doubts were being expressed as to the need for recovery efforts, reports were coming in of ships passing through great masses of wreckage and bodies.

One of the most "thrilling" accounts of the floating wreckage was related from the German liner *Bremen* on arrival in New York. The ship reported passing the wreckage of the *Titanic* on April 20; this was the same day that the recovery vessel *Mackay-Bennett* arrived in the area. A first-cabin passenger, Mrs. Johanna Stunke, stated:

> "It was between four and five o'clock on Saturday when our ship sighted off the bow to starboard an iceberg. We had been told by some of the officers that the *Bremen* was going to pass within a few miles of the position given by the *Titanic*

when she sank, so when the cry went up that ice was sighted we all rushed to the starboard rail. It was a beautiful afternoon, and the sun glistening on the big iceberg was a wonderful picture, but as we drew nearer and could make out small dots floating around in the sea a feeling of awe and sadness crept over every one, and the ship proceeded in absolute silence. We passed within one hundred feet of the southern most drift of the wreckage, and looking down over the rail we distinctly saw a number of bodies so clearly that we could make out what they were wearing, and whether they were men or women.

We saw one woman in her night-dress with a baby clasped closely to her breast. Several of the women passengers screamed, and left the rail in a fainting condition. There was another woman, fully dressed, with her arms tight around the body of a shaggy dog that looked like a St. Bernard. The bodies of three men in a group, all clinging to one steamer chair floated close by, and just beyond them were a dozen bodies of men, all in life preservers, clinging together as though in the last desperate struggle for life. Those were the only bodies we passed near enough to distinguish, but we could see the white life preservers of many more dotting the sea all the way to the iceberg. The officers told us that was probably the berg hit by the *Titanic*, and that the bodies and the ice drifted along together, but only a few miles south of their original position where the collision occurred. The scene moved everyone on board to the point of tears, even the officers making no secret of their emotions."

Mrs. Stunke also stated that a delegation of passengers approached the captain about stopping to recover the bodies but he declined to do so. He assured them that a recovery vessel, the *Mackay-Bennett*, was in the area. There is no way of knowing if any of the bodies sighted by the passengers and crew of the *Bremen* were picked up by the recovery vessels. And the iceberg spotted at that time may not have been the one hit by the *Titanic*. The captain of the *Bremen* was questioned by reporters in New York. "They were everywhere," the captain declared. "There were men, women, and children. All had life preservers on. I counted 125 and then grew sick of the sight. There may have been as many as 150 or 200 bodies. A short time before, about 50 or 60 miles north, we passed five icebergs in succession. Our lookout sighted them in time and we had no difficulty in avoiding them." Why didn't you slow down and take on some of the

WHILE THE WORLD WAITED FOR NEWS OF WHO SURVIVED THE SINKING, WHITE STAR LINE AGENTS CHANGED THE ADVERTISING MESSAGE "THE LARGEST STEAMERS IN THE WORLD" PUBLISHED ON APRIL 15 (THE DAY OF THE SINKING) TO "THE LARGEST STEAMER IN THE WORLD" IN APRIL 16TH EDITIONS. FROM THE *MONTREAL GAZETTE*.

THE *EVENING MAIL* OF APRIL 16 INCLUDED THE NAMES OF PASSENGERS WITH A HALIFAX CONNECTION.

bodies? he was asked. "It was absolutely useless, for the simple reason that we had no means of caring for them." He said he knew that the cable steamer *Mackay-Bennett* was searching for bodies and that he had communicated with its commander, informing him of where the bodies were.

The *Mackay-Bennett* left Halifax Harbour on April 17 and had to travel 700 nautical miles (1300 kilometers) to the site of the wreckage. It arrived at the site on the evening of April 20, five days after the sinking. The ship's crew waited until daylight on the 21st, to begin the recovery effort. It was their understanding that bodies would be buried at sea and each day that is what they did. They kept those bodies that were in very good condition, those that the undertaker thought might be shipped home and those that might still be identified. To the seamen aboard the *Mackay-Bennett* it would seem

perfectly reasonable that sailors be buried at sea. To Mr. Snow of the funeral home it seemed reasonable that the most likely bodies to be shipped home would be those of the first-class passengers and these he partially embalmed. No detailed record was kept as to the reason for burying a body at sea or taking it back to Halifax. It is known that the sheer number of bodies soon used up the supplies and that a passing ship had to be hailed to stop and provide more canvas. By April 26, *Mackay-Bennett* had recovered 306 bodies, of which 116 were buried at sea. By now bodies were being reported 30 miles away from the reported position of the sinking.

The work must have been incredibly difficult. With the sinking, a small town had been dumped into the ocean. Sea life would have been attracted to all the supplies on the ship. Even survivors on the *Carpathia*, like Mrs. Rose Abbott who had broken bones, were injured as the wreckage pushed to the surface. So there is no doubt that there were victims who died of injuries, some of which must have greatly disfigured the bodies. Add to that the time spent in the water with the rough weather and the crush of passing ice and ships. The captain of the *Mackay-Bennett*, Fred Larnder, said it looked as though the victims were standing in the water. While the life jackets kept the shoulders and heads out of the water, the recovery crew had a hard time estimating ages, often guessing a number that was more than the real age of the person, as the sea had aged the dead. It was said that the victims looked like they had simply gone to sleep, a likely result of hypothermia. Other victims would have died of heart attacks caused by hitting the cold water or from struggling in it. The undertakers and the newspapers of 1912 referred to all the victims as drowned. Despite the peaceful look on the faces of most of the dead, many crew members would comment how grateful they were to have a minister on the ship.

Each day the *Mackay-Bennett* was at sea the work went from early morning through to the late night. First the wreckage was spotted and small boats were put out with a crew to row and recover the bodies. While some men balanced on one side of the boat the others would reach in with hooks to bring the bodies closer. Then they would have to grab hold of the wet and very cold body. When six to nine bodies were picked up the men would return to the ship, unload, and go out again. As this was happening the groups of bodies in the water would often disperse due to the waves and the wind. Not

There was confusion on shore as to where the *Carpathia* was going with survivors. At Wanamaker Store, Broadway and 8th Street, New York, there was a Marconi Station directed by David Sarnoff. A message was received on April 15 at 9:55 p.m. from Cape Race, Newfoundland, to cancel special trains for passengers for Halifax. This meant the *Carpathia* was headed for Boston or New York.

The sons of Mrs. J. M. Brown (Caroline, not the famous Margaret) from Massachusetts did not know where they would find their mother. Murray and Robert Brown decided to split up, with one going to Halifax, the other to New York. Caroline arrived safely in New York. Other families had similar decisions to make.

all the bodies seen could be picked up before the light of the day faded so markers were put out so the work could resume the next day. It was not always possible to work on the water each day, depending on the weather. The problem caused by sending only one recovery vessel to the site meant that many bodies seen were not recovered.

As the bodies were delivered to the ship a number was tied to each body with the same number put on a small canvas bag. The undertakers and assistants made a detailed examination of the clothing and body. Physical details were recorded and any effects found were put into the numbered bags. These effects would be used in making further

CARRYING COFFIN UP GANGPLANK

CAPTAIN F.H. LARNDER

THE MACKAY-BENNETT

identifications at Halifax. After the work of the undertaker was as complete as possible a decision was made as to which bodies to keep for Halifax. Each person buried at sea was sewn in a canvas sheet along with the scrap metal necessary to weight the body down. The crew gathered around the minister for prayers. A final blessing was made as each body was dropped into the ocean. In some cases of people buried at sea, rings were left on their fingers. Religious items such as rosary beads and holy medallions were also not removed.

The wireless operator of the *Mackay-Bennett* would relay to other ships the names of those who had been found. Unfortunately relatives and friends waiting in Halifax did not know which bodies were buried at sea. Public opinion became so heated when it was learned that burials were taking place at sea that the White Star Line ordered the practice stopped. The list of the recovered dead indicates the last 106 bodies picked up by the *Mackay-Bennett* were all brought back to Halifax. This would seem to support the change in policy: It is unlikely that bodies drifting in the sea longer would have been in better condition than bodies found earlier.

THE LOADING OF COFFINS ON THE *MACKAY-BENNETT*; CAPTAIN LARNDER; THE SHIP; A MAP OF THE SEARCH AREA. BY THE TIME THIS APPEARED IN NEWSPAPERS, THE CREW OF THE *MACKAY-BENNETT* WAS ALREADY CONDUCTING BURIALS AT SEA. BEFORE LEAVING PORT, CAPTAIN LARNDER SAID: "THE BODIES WILL BE TENDERLY CARED FOR AND RETURNED TO HALIFAX AS SOON AS POSSIBLE." THE *MONTREAL DAILY STAR*, APRIL 24, 1912.

As the crew of the *Mackay-Bennett* carried out their work, reporters were anxious for stories to fill the public demand for information. When ships arrived in various ports after the sinking, crews and passengers would be questioned by newspaper reporters as to whether they had sighted wreckage of the *Titanic* or icebergs. Many stories were told, including that their own ships had almost run into icebergs. Others spoke of running through wreckage and seeing bodies tossed into the spray of the ships' bows. This led to calls to send more vessels to help in the recovery efforts. The White Star office in Halifax had already arranged for the cable ship *Minia* to leave Halifax with supplies, undertakers, and the Reverend Henry Cunningham of Saint George's (Anglican) Church. The *Minia* was to take over search duties while the *Mackay-Bennett* returned to Halifax. The first body found was that of Charles M. Hays, president of the Grand Trunk Railway. The *Minia* crew found seventeen bodies of which two were buried at sea. There was plenty of room and lots of supplies on the *Minia* so the two bodies buried at sea must have been badly disfigured. The *Minia* stayed in the area for six days.

The third vessel to search was the Canadian government vessel *Montmagny*. By this time the *Mackay-Bennett* and *Minia* had returned to Halifax. As the lists of those buried at sea were reviewed, it was noted that many were Roman Catholic. So along with the Reverend Samuel Prince from Saint Paul's (Anglican) Church went the Reverend Father Patrick McQuillan from Saint Mary's (Roman Catholic) Cathedral. The crew of the *Montmagny* worked the area for two

"THE ABOVE PHOTO WAS TAKEN BY THE SPECTATOR REPRESENTATIVE IN HALIFAX PREVIOUS TO THE DEPARTURE OF THE DEATH SHIP *MACKAY-BENNETT*...ON THE LEFT OF THE QUARTET IS DAVID McMURRAY, THE LOCAL (HAMILTON) BOY WHO IS AT PRESENT IN THE MARITIME PROVINCES REPRESENTING THE SEMMENS & FAEL COMPANY." THE *HAMILTON SPECTATOR*, APRIL 23, 1912.

weeks and only found four bodies, of which one was buried at sea. Again there was room on board to keep all the bodies; no reason is recorded as to why one body was buried at sea. The crew of the *Montmagny* reported that they sighted bedsteads, hats, an oak newel post, and painted wood drifting in the ocean.

The fourth and last official recovery ship was the sealing vessel *Algerine*, which steamed around the area for three weeks. In St. John's, Newfoundland, they loaded fifty coffins onto the ship. They found only one body, that of James McGrady, saloon steward, which was sent through the port of Louisbourg to Halifax for burial. The search for the *Titanic* bodies was officially at an

Paris, April 16: "Ambassador and Mrs. Bacon are in receipt of numerous congratulations on their fortunate decision not to sail." Ambassador and Mrs. Bacon of the United States were booked to return home on the *Titanic* from his posting in France but were delayed as his replacement had not yet arrived. Southampton, April 16: "Distressing scenes have been witnessed throughout the morning at the White Star offices here which have been thronged by relatives of the crew of the *Titanic*. The town is absolutely stunned by the news of the disaster, which is the greatest blow that Southampton has ever sustained." London, April 16: "I never thought there was such a thing as an unsinkable ship. The fact she sank in a few hours indicates her side was torn out," stated Alexander Carlisle, chief designer, Harland and Wolff. Mr. Carlisle was so affected during the memorial service at Saint Paul's Cathedral in London that he fainted and had to be carried out.

end. No more efforts would be made as the wreckage was considered too widely dispersed and that time, warming waters of the gulf stream, and sea life had eliminated human remains.

A list of the 119 bodies that were buried at sea by the crews of the four recovery ships is part of the official record prepared in Halifax in 1912. It is presented here in the same numerical order as the original. The missing numbers of the sequence were those bodies taken to Halifax. The information listed here is a combination of that found on the reports of the undertakers and that gathered from other sources. Not all the details pertaining to all the listed victims are included. What some of the people were wearing and some of the effects they were carrying is noted to give a picture of what was happening on the night of the sinking. At the end of the list is information on the nine bodies buried at sea by ships other than the official recovery vessels. Among the crew found were many firemen, sometimes called stokers. Their job was to shovel the coal into the fires to keep the boilers going. Those listed as coal trimmers were men who brought the coal from the piles and put it down next to the firemen.

THE CS *MACKAY-BENNETT*

The following bodies were buried from the *Mackay-Bennett*:

#6. Unidentified male, probably third-class passenger, estimated age 22. Blue serge coat and vest, black trousers, blue and white check shirt, no socks, black boots. Blue tattoo mark, and wore copper wire ring on thumb of right hand. Nothing else to identify.

#14. Leslie Williams, third-class passenger, embarked from Southampton, age 28. Fair hair. Green overcoat, blue serge suit, red striped shirt, two scarves, and effects. Address: 59 Primrose Street, Tony Pandy.

Leslie Williams was a Welsh bantamweight boxer, and had a wife and their only child at home. He was on his on way to America to work a twelve-month boxing contract. It was announced in the newspapers that his body would be buried in New York as per instructions from his wife but he had already been buried at sea on April 22.

PICKING UP THE BODIES WAS HARD WORK. IN THIS PHOTO, PART OF THE CREW LEANS TO ONE SIDE TO BALANCE THE BOAT WHILE OTHERS REACH IN THE COLD ATLANTIC WATER AND BRING THE BODY, WEARING A WHITE LIFE JACKET, ONBOARD.

#20. Unidentified male, probably a sailor, estimated age 28. Brown hair and moustache. Wore badge of Sailors' and Firemen's Union, blue coat and blue White Star jersey. No aids to identification.

#21. Unidentified male, steward, age 25 to 30. Dark hair, light moustache. Had paper reading "Dec. to Jan. 1911; First Saloon waiter S.S. Majestic," also keys marked "Locker No. 7 E Deck." Wore steward's jacket, vest, and trousers; laundry mark "E."

#23. L. Turner, saloon steward, age 25. Wore striped steward's coat marked W. A. Storr, steward's vest and apron, shirt marked L. Turner. Tickets for rooms 9 and 10. Address: 19 Terminus Terrace, Southampton, England.

There is no note in the records if "W. A. Storr" was the maker of coat. On the second list made of the bodies and disposition there are two listings for this body, one as A. H. Barkworth with the note that it is probably L. Turner, as Barkworth is listed by the White Star Line as a first-class passenger rescued. It might be that Mr. Barkworth gave his calling card to the steward. As the identity was thought to be L. Turner there were no further inquiries made.

#24. Unidentified male, probably a sailor, age about 20. Blue jersey, blue and red flannel shirt, green trousers, black boots.

#25. A. Hayter, bedroom steward, age 45. Identified from effects. Address: 10 Mayflower Street, Southampton, England.

#26. Unidentified male, probably an Italian cook, age about 32. Dark hair. Addresses found on body: "Mr. Freyer, Lawrence Villa, Stephenson Road, Cowes"; also "G. R. Barnes, 22 Sidney Street, Cambridge." Wore blue serge jacket and steward's white coat.

#27. Jean Monoros, assistant waiter, restaurant, age 19. Address: 27 Tension Street, London.

#28. Unidentified male, age about 30. Dark hair and complexion. Black coat, grey trousers, check shirt, black boots. No effects but table ticket and address "Shaking Bros., 155 Broad St., Ottawa." Italian.

In 1991, a society interested in *Titanic* victims identified this body as Joseph Caram of Ottawa, Canada, a third-class passenger who had gone home to Syria to find a bride. Many of the Syrian and Lebanese victims had been identified as "Italian type." His bride also perished in the sinking. Her body was not found.

#30. Unidentified male, probably a fireman, estimated age 22. Fair hair and moustache. Blue coat, dungaree trousers, grey flannel underwear. Wore Sailors' and Firemen's Union badge.

#31. William Evans, coal trimmer, age 35. Light hair and fair moustache. Brown coat and trousers, no socks, striped shirt, purple knitted tie. Envelope addressed to Mrs. Evans, 11 Ryde Terrace, Soton. He was originally listed as unknown and was identified in 1912 from the envelope.

#33. Unidentified male, estimated age 30. Brown hair and moustache. Nothing to aid in identification. Clothes indicated that he was an oiler from the engine department.

#36. Unidentified male, probably steward, estimated age 35. Dark hair. Steward's uniform. Left arm tattooed all over; right arm: clasped hands and heart; breast: Japanese fans. Gold ring on right little finger engraved "Madge." Gold watch and chain, seal, silver matchbox, keys, wine cards, gold and brilliant brooch, first-class steward No. 76. It

would seem that if this man's description had been published in the newspapers someone would have identified him.

#39. Unidentified male, estimated age 25. Dark hair. Wore evening dress trousers, black double-breasted overcoat, brown jacket and vest, no boots. Nothing else to aid identification. Silver watch, sovereign purse containing one sovereign, silver ring, coins for 4s. 3d., and keys. No marks on clothing or papers.

Who was this young man in evening dress trousers? Had he just started to undress for the night when the collision occurred? If so, he might have grabbed the jacket and vest that were laid out for the next day. Or maybe he dressed in a hurry and ended up wearing a mix of clothing. #40. Unidentified male, probably a sailor, estimated age 28. Fair hair and moustache. Nothing to aid in identification.

#41. E. J. Stone, bedroom steward, estimated age 22. Address: 105 St. Andrew's Road, Southampton, England.

#42. Unidentified male, probably one of the crew, estimated age 45. Black hair going grey. Lining torn from clothing was marked "Kinos Successors, 322-323 High Holborn, W. C. City Branch, 14 Cheapside, No. 4058. A217/5/10. Name, Mr. Mayer." Some of the clothes were left on the dead buried at sea. In the case of this body, the lining was kept because of the information marked on it.

#44. Unidentified male, steward, estimated age 21. Light hair. Steward's coat and trousers, white shirt marked "F. W. I.," keys marked "C Deck-Linen Locker."

#45. Edwin Keeping, valet of a first-class passenger, estimated age 32. Light hair. Grey overcoat marked "EK" inside pocket, black suit, striped shirt, black boots. Gold watch and chain, locket, pocketbook with diamond and ruby tie pin, one two-dollar bill, cigarette case, three pieces of twenty francs, one piece of 20f. Magyar, and three one hundred franc notes in purse, keys and lucky cent, 3 shillings, 3 dollars in coins, Paris address "Ritz Hotel."

Edwin Keeping was the valet of Mr. George D. Widener, a first-class passenger who was also lost. At first, wireless messages reported "G Widen" was found and newspapers guessed wrongly that it was George Widener, the multi-millionaire from Philadelphia. This wrong information delayed the Widener family from paying for private search boats. It was speculated that wealthy families would pay to have boats hired or would send private yachts to look for their missing relatives. Bodies of a number of millionaires were found so those plans were never followed. Mr. Widener and his son Harry were never found.

#46. Frederick Sutton, first-class passenger, importer, age 61. Brown hair, grey beard. Black coat, vest, and trousers; black boots. Gold watch and chain, tie clip, pocketbook, knife, three silver spoons with Norwich enamel crest, watch fob, gold seal ring with "F. S.," Freemason medal: sixty dollars in traveller's cheques; 2.10s in gold, 16s in silver, thirteen dollars loose coins in purse; circular letter of credit for one hundred pounds, Kountz Bros., N. Y., No. B. 18331; two silver thimbles; eyeglasses in case; silver whistle.

Halifax, April 17: "Not since April 1, 1873, when the White Star liner *Atlantic* crashed on the ledges of Terrance Bay and more than 500 souls perished have such scenes been witnessed in Halifax as this morning when wagon loads of rough wooden coffins were hauled through the streets to the cable ship *Mackay-Bennett*, at the cable slip wharf."

New York, April 18: "bodies of victims of the *Titanic* are at the bottom of the deep, never to leave it." Robert W. Wood, chair of experimental physics, John Hopkins University.

Frederick Sutton was from England with business interests in the United States. He was returning from a visit to his brother and sister in England. In Philadelphia he was president of the Sons of Saint George. His American friends travelled to Halifax to collect his body only to learn it had been buried at sea on April 21, six days after the sinking:

"A pathetic scene was witnessed at the morgue today when friends of Fred Sutton, of Philadelphia, who had long been waiting for his body, were told that Sutton was one of the identified who had been re-committed to the waters. At the identification room in the morgue all the satisfaction Mr. Sutton's friends had was to be shown his personal effects. Captain Larnder did his best, but in this case his act brought fresh pain to sorrowing hearts."—Halifax newspapers, April 30.

THE SAVED AND THE LOST

Mrs. Charlotte Cardeza, her son, maid, and manservant saved. Her fourteen trunks, four suitcases, and three crates of baggage lost. Samuel Ward Stanton, second-class passenger and noted American marine illustrator, lost. P. W. Fletcher, ship's bugler, lost. Mr. and Mrs. F. C. Goodwin and six children, travelling in third class, lost. They were immigrating from England to Niagara Falls, New York. Colonel Alfonse Simonius, president of Swiss Bankverein, saved. First-class passenger Mr. Thomas Pears of the soap firm lost, his wife Edith saved. Mr. Martin Rothschild lost, his wife saved. Third-class passengers Mr. Ling Hee and Mr. Chung Foo of Hong Kong saved. Mr. Len Lam and Mr. Lee Ling lost. Forty third-class passengers who embarked from Ireland saved, seventy-one lost. Masabumi Hosono, second-class passenger, an official with Japan's Transportation Ministry, saved.

#47. Leslie Gilinski, third-class passenger embarked from Southampton, age 22. Dark hair. Grey coat, vest, and pants; green shirt. Photographs, tickets, five-dollar bill, baggage insurance No. 73941 (B. Ins. Ass., Ltd.), £12 in gold; 60c.; 4p; keys; purse; primer on English language. Third-class ticket No. 14973.

The primer on English language would indicate that this man's first language was not English. For many third-class passengers, confusion as to what to do during the sinking was caused not by locked barriers but by language barriers.

#48. Unidentified male, steward, estimated age 35. Light hair and moustache. Steward's coat, vest, and trousers; flannel shirt. Nothing to aid identification.

#49. J. S. Gill, bedroom steward, age 40. Tattoo on left arm, "S. Gill" on Union Jack. Address: 111 Bedford Road, Bottle, Liverpool.

#50. Ernest Portage Tomlin, third-class passenger embarked from Southampton, age 30. He was from Notting Hill, London, England.

#51. Yosip Drazenire, third-class passenger embarked from Cherbourg, listed as Josef Drazenovic, age 33. Effects: pipe bowl, passport, set of beads, twenty-five dollars and five krones. The recovery ship list had him as Yosep Drazemoui; in Halifax they made it Yosip Drazenire. The differences in the last name could be from a typist's mistakes or as was often the case in the history of immigration, officials spelling names as they heard them and not how they were actually spelled.

#52. Mrs. Mary Mack, second-class passenger, age 57. Grey hair. Black coat and skirt, fur boa, striped cotton chemise, woolen singlet, black button boots, stockings. Wedding ring and seal keeper (chariot and horse), green stone ring on right hand, visiting card of Mrs. Wotherspoon, Ashbourne Rd., West Southborne, photo in frame. In purse, £15 10s. in gold, 10s. 4 3/4d. in silver and copper. Second-class Ticket E.77. Name in purse was Mrs. Mack, Millbrook Road, Southampton. Mary Mack was making her first trip to the United States and was to visit her daughter living in New York.

MRS. NEAL (EILEEN) McNAMEE, BODY #53.

#53. Mrs. Neal (Eileen) McNamee, third-class passenger embarked from Southampton, estimated age 23. Brown hair. Brown velvet coat; sailor blouse, white with blue anchor on front; blue flannel petticoat with "E. M. C."; blue corsets; blue skirt with black braid; black stockings and shoes. Wedding ring and keeper (turquoise and diamond) gold; bracelet on right wrist; two third-class tickets; one purse with 1s. 11d.; fountain pen; keys; cosmetic, etc. Address: Kingston House, Wilton Road, Salisbury.

Eileen was travelling with her husband, Neal, who was also among the lost. His body was never found. In Churchill Park, Salisbury, England, a memorial seat was placed near a tree planted in the couple's memory.

#54. Unidentified female, probably third-class passenger, estimated age 40. Brown hair. Wore wedding ring and keeper. Had one gold upper tooth.

#55. Unidentified female, possibly second-class passenger, estimated age 30. Brown hair. Had among effects, gold watch, marked on back "C. K. S." pinned on left breast. Opal and pearl ring, engraved "H. N. to D. S."; gold ring like rim of half sovereign; solitaire brilliant, and sapphire. Wedding ring engraved "A. L. to C. S., April 21, '09." Black coat and skirt; black underskirt; grey petticoat; camisole with violet ribbon threaded through; woolen singlet; black stockings with much darn at left knee; black shoes. No marks on body or clothing.

This lady was thought to be a second-class passenger because of all the jewellery she wore. She was buried at sea April 22, three years and one day after the date on her wedding ring. The undertaker noted that "all rings left on fingers." It is interesting that there were no marks on her clothing to identify the makers, which in turn could have identified where she was from, and no initials for laundry purposes, which could have indicated her name. In 1991, a group interested in *Titanic* victims pointed to this person being Mrs. Cordelia Stanlick Lobb, who was a third-class passenger. Mrs. Lobb's husband was also lost in the sinking. The Lobbs were returning to Stanton, Pennsylvania, from England.

#56. Unidentified male, probably third-class passenger, estimated age 40. Dark hair and moustache. Wore half hunter gold watch No. 5119, English make, and gold chain. False teeth, upper jaw.

#57. Unidentified male, steward, estimated age 35. Wore undervest and vest marked "H. L."; new black boots; letter in pocket to "Dear Humph," from "Dick," steward for Rooms No. 470 (first class). In 1991, a society interested in *Titanic* victims identified this body as Humphrey I. Lloyd, a steward.

#58. Catavelas Vassilios, third-class passenger embarked from Cherbourg, age 18. Dark hair and complexion. Dark mixture suit; check shirt; black boots.

#59. W. Vear, fireman, age 35. Dark mixture suit, striped flannel shirt, black silk muffler, black shoes. Address found on body: 1 Spa Gardens, Southampton. From the clothes this man was wearing it is obvious that he was not on duty.

#60. Unidentified male, probably a steward, estimated age 45. Dark hair and moustache. Wore company's uniform; steward for rooms 82, etc.; no other marks to aid in identification.

#61. Mary Mangan, third-class passenger embarked from Queenstown, age 32. Light hair. Green waterproof, black coat, skirt, blouse, red cardigan jacket, black button boots with cloth uppers. One gold watch, engraved inside "M. Mangan" and photo, and outside "M. Mangan"; gold locket with hair and photo as in watch, engraved "Mary"; gold chain; beads in pocket; brass belt buckle; medallion around neck; diamond solitaire ring; gold bracelet "MM"; wire gold brooch. She was returning to Chicago after going home to Ireland to show her mother her diamond solitaire engagement ring. While noted as being in the recovered effects the ring was not returned while the gold watch and other things were.

#63. Unidentified female, probably third-class passenger, estimated age 22. Dark black hair. Had purse with miniature photo of young man, photo locket, few coins. No other aid to identification.

#65. Unidentified male, fireman, probably on watch, estimated age 25. Light hair. Tattoo on right forearm, three dots.

#66. G. Hinckley, hospital attendant, age 50. Among clothes and effects were letters to G. Hinckley, 2 Oxford St., Southampton; matchbox with initials "G. H."

#67. Will Sage, third-class passenger, embarked from Southampton, age 11. Medium brown hair. Grey suit (Knickers), striped shirt, black boots, and stockings. No marks on body or clothing. Will Sage written on third-class ticket, list No. 20, berth 126.

The recovery team had estimated his age as 14. The Sage family of Peterborough, England, consisted of Mr. and Mrs. John Sage and nine children. Mr. Sage had sold his business and was moving the entire family to Florida to go into fruit farming. Of the eleven family members lost only the body of William, not yet old enough for long pants, was found.

#68. James Farrell, third-class passenger embarked from Queenstown, estimated age 40. Dark hair, light moustache. Dark suit, black boots, grey socks. Silver watch; two purses (one empty), the other with $10, 3s. 21/2d., and 10 kronor; two studs; cameo; beads, left on body. Name on ticket: James Farrell, Longford, No. B67233.

The remarks "beads, left on body" noted that rosaries carried by Roman Catholics for use in counting prayers said were buried with the dead.

#69. Henry Damgaard Hansen, third-class passenger embarked from Southampton, age 21.

He was travelling from Denmark to Wisconsin with Mr. and Mrs. Peter Hansen and Henrik Hansen. The three men were lost. Mrs. Hansen was saved.

#70. James Kelly, third-class passenger embarked from Queenstown, estimated age 34. Dark suit, vest and trousers; white socks; black boots. Beads left on body. He had been travelling to New Haven, Connecticut.

#71. Unidentified male, hospital attendant, estimated age 45. Medium hair, clean shaven. Blue uniform suit, coat marked "Hospital Attendant"; trousers marked "M. O."; black boots; key ring with address: Mrs. Van Push, 732 E.15th St., New York City. Clinical thermometer; keys; scissors; notebook; pouch and pipe; 5s. 91/2d.; knife.

In 1991 this body was identified, by a society interested in *Titanic* victims, as W. Durnford, Hospital steward.

#72. Mauritz Adahl, third-class passenger, age 30. Fair hair, light moustache. Among effects, ring marked 'M. A.'

He was going to find work in the United States to make money to build a home in Sweden. He had been shifted to the *Titanic* because of the coal shortage and wrote his wife of this change on April 9th.

#73. Herbert Jupe, third assistant electrical engineer, was originally listed as unidentified male. Estimated age 35. Dark

A letter was received in Halifax in May 1912 from the father of third engineer Herbert Jupe. With its spelling mistakes intact it reads:

Dear Sir I have been inform by Mr. F Blake Superintendent Engineer of the White Star Line Trafalgar Chambers on the 10th (May) that the Body of my Beloved Son Herbert Jupe which was Electrical Engineer No. 3 on the ill-Fated *Titanic* has been recovered and Burried at Sea by The Cable Steamer 'Mackey-Bennett' and that his Silver Watch and Handkerchief marked

HERBERT JUPE, BODY #73.

H. J. is in your Possession. He bought him a half doz of the same when he was at Belfast with the R. M. S. Olympic to have a new blade put to one of her Perpellors we are extremely oblidged for all your Kindness to my Precious Boy He was not married and was the Love of our Hearts and he loved his Home But God gave and God has taken Him Blessed be the Name of the Lord. He has left an Aceing Void in our Home which cannot be filled. Please send along the Watch and Handkerchief marked H. J.

Yours Truly C. Jupe. His mother is 72 Last april 4th. His father is 68 Last Feb 9th.

The items were returned to his parents.

LEFT: EDWIN H. PETTY, BODY #82, RIGHT: HENRY RUDD, BODY #86.

hair. Among effects, handkerchief marked "H. J."; silver watch. There is correspondence to the White Star Line from his parents requesting their son's effects.

#74. Unidentified male, probably third-class passenger, estimated age 36. Fair hair, light moustache. Dark trousers; pyjamas; jacket; black socks.

#75. Reginald Hale, second-class passenger, age 30. Address: Somerset, England.

#76. Unidentified female, probably third-class passenger, estimated age 24. Dark hair. Possibly Italian; name "Ethel" inside of watch; garnet ring on watch chain, originally two stones, one missing.

#77. W. Butt, fireman, age 30. Effects included National Service and Firemen Union Book. Address: 6 Cawte Road, Southampton, England. (See Body #10, R. Butt, Chapter 5 and Major Archibald Butt, Chapter 7.)

#81. Philip Joseph Stokes, second-class passenger, age 25. Address on ticket: 91 Hawstead Road, Catford, England.

#82. Edwin Henry Petty, bedroom steward, age 27. Among effects, letters and 2 pocket diaries with address: 25 Orchard Place, Southampton.

#84. Unidentified male, probably fireman, estimated age 25. Dark hair. Wore dungaree coat and trousers, and grey flannel shirt. Nothing to aid identification.

#85. William Hinton, coal trimmer, estimated age 31. Among effects were British Seafarers' Union No. 1037 and Royal Naval Reserve Stoker Papers, No. 288327. Address found: 26 Cumberland Street, Southampton.

#86. Unidentified male, probably storekeeper, estimated age 23. Light hair. Had keys marked "Engineer's Storekeeper."

In 1991 a society interested in *Titanic* victims identified this body from effects as Mr. Henry Rudd, engineering storekeeper.

#87. Unidentified male, possibly a fireman, estimated age 30. Light hair and moustache. Dungaree trousers, blue coat and vest, grey flannel shirt. Wore badge "Riverside and Dock Workers" Union.' No other aid to identification.

#88. Unidentified Male, probably a fireman, estimated age 50. Dark hair, light moustache. No aids to identification.

#89. Thos. Anderson, third-class passenger, estimated age 25. Listed as Thor. Anderson, embarked from Southampton.

#91. J. Smillie, saloon steward, age 25. Identified from effects. Address: 16 Malmesbury Road, Southampton, England.

#93. H. H. Roberts, bedroom steward, age 40. Wore black coat; steward's coat; 2 waistcoats;

brown and blue striped pyjamas; black boots; had false teeth, upper jaw. Identified from effects, address found: 39 Mary Road, Liverpool.

#95. Unidentified male, probably a fireman on watch, estimated age 20. Fair hair. Tattooed. Right arm: woman, butterfly, and anchor; left arm: butterfly, knight's head, and lady; no effects.

#98. Anders Wilhelm Gustafsson, third-class passenger embarked from Southampton, age 37. He was from a farm in Finland and was travelling to the United States with his brother. They were looking for construction jobs.

#99. Unidentified male, probably a fireman, estimated age 29. Tattooed. Right arm: clasped hands and heart, American flag and lady; left arm: "Dieu et mon droit." No other aid to identification.

E. J. Sjostedt, Sault Ste. Marie, Ontario, Canada, was lost. He was returning from Norway with a report for the Dominion government on treating copper sulphide ores. Annie Funk, 38, Methodist Episcopal missionary, returning to Boyertown, Pennsylvania, from India after five years, was lost. Herr J. von Reuchlin, of the Netherlands, a director of the Holland American line, was lost. Mrs. Edgar Meyer was safe, her husband was lost. Mrs. Meyer was returning to New York due to the April 9th death of her father, Andrew Saks, founder of Saks Fifth Avenue.

CYRIL S. RICKS, BODY #100.

#100. Cyril G. Ricks, assistant kitchen storekeeper, age 26. Among effects were keys marked "Superior Stewards." Address: 1 Hanley Road, Southampton, England.

#101. Joseph C. Nicholls, second-class passenger, embarked from Southampton, age 19. Among effects: boys' brigade belt, field glasses, and an account book.

Nicholls had been buried at sea as unidentified but was later identified in Halifax from his effects by the Carbines brothers of Calumet, Michigan. Joseph Nicholls was travelling to Michigan from St. Ives, Cornwall, England, with his mother and step-brother; both survived. Joseph also knew the Carbines's younger brother. The younger brother died in the sinking. (see chapter 3, William Carbines)

#102. Unidentified male, crew, estimated age 34. Wore uniform vest and white jacket. No other aid to identification.

#103. John Adams, third-class passenger embarked from Southampton, age 26. While listed as J. Adams, he was actually Richard May of Devon, England. A number of people travelling on *Titanic* had various reasons to use assumed names.

#104. Petro Ale, third-class passenger, estimated age 38. Dark hair. Grey suit, black boots, plain ring on left finger. Watch, gold engraved ring, memo book, 140 francs gold in purse.

When the official disposition of bodies list was typed up, this gentleman was included on the identified and unidentified list. The note of "plain ring on left finger" on the recovery ship list was typed on the second list as "plain ring, left on finger." In 1991 a society interested in the *Titanic* victims identified this man as Mr. Allesandro Pedrini, who worked as an assistant restaurant waiter. Obviously the effects of the deceased, some of which are still at the Nova Scotia Archives, need more review.

#105. Unidentified male, probably third-class passenger, estimated age 30. Dark hair and moustache. Wore blue serge suit and striped shirt marked "B. D."; black boots. No other aids to identification.

#106. Unidentified male, possibly a sailor, estimated age 35. Tattooed; right arm: "Aggie"; left arm: crossed hands and heart. No other aids to identification.

#107. W. Boothby, bedroom steward, age 42. Fair hair, prominent teeth. Uniform jacket and vest, White Star belt, pyjamas. Address: 31 Winchester Road, Shirley.

#108. Robert William Norman Leyson, second-class passenger, embarked from Southampton, age 25. He was from Wales and was living in London, England.

#111. George Alexander Chiswell, senior boiler maker, age 35. Effects included knife; pipe; rule; razor; shaving brush; pocket book; silver watch; book marked "C. Chisnell." Identified from effects. Address: 53 High Street, Itchen, Southampton River. Did this man grab a few things expecting to be rescued?

#112. Unidentified male, probably a steward, estimated age 45. Steward's uniform and ship's badge No. 42. No other aids to identification.

#113. Unidentified male, probably a fireman, estimated age 42. Tattooed; right arm: angel of love with thistle below; left arm: girl's head in centre of anchor, a ship, and flower with "Flo" in centre. Dungaree trousers, navy singlet. No other aids to identification.

#114. Unidentified male, possibly a fireman, estimated age 40. Dungaree trousers; grey flannel shirt and drawers. No aids to identification.

#115. Abele Rigozri, on crew list as A. Rigozzi, victualing department, estimated age 25. Hair dark (Italian type). Grey overcoat, blue coat, white waistcoat, striped shirt, wearing truss, black band on arm, patent shoes.

This man was thought, at first, to be a third-class passenger because of the clothes he was wearing. He may have been off-duty and grabbed his street clothes. The "black band on arm" was a sign of mourning for a recent death in the family. Black arm bands were found on a number of the bodies.

#116. J. Butterworth, saloon steward, age 26. Address found: 270 Priory Road, St. Dennis, Southampton.

#117. Unidentified male, estimated age 40. Dark hair, probably Italian. Rough blue coat, grey tweed vest and trousers, grey wool socks, black boots. Effects included silver watch and chain, and purse of French gold. No marks to aid in identification. No guess was as to whether this man was a passenger or member of the crew.

The only guess was "probably Italian," which is not necessarily a valid choice for identification.

#118. Unidentified male, possibly an oiler, estimated age 52. Fair hair. Dungaree suit. No aids to identification.

#120. Charles Humblen, third-class passenger, embarked from Southampton, age 42. Brown hair and moustache. He was from Norway.

#121. Charles Louch, second-class passenger, a retired saddler, age 50. Black beard and moustache. Fawn waterproof coat, grey mixture suit, pyjamas underneath, money belt. Address found: Weston-super-mare, England. His wife survived the sinking.

#123. Frederick Tamlyn, mess steward, deck department, estimated age 24. Address in discharge book: 20 Southampton Street, Southampton.

#125. Unidentified male, second-class steward, estimated age 17. Brown hair. Steward's uniform, white and green striped pyjamas, black button boots, washing mark "G. V. N." Wore badge No. 37, wedding ring.

#127. W. G. Robertson, assistant steward, estimated age 18. Identified from effects. Address: 36 Mount Street, Southampton, England.

#132. Unidentified female, probably third-class passenger, estimated age 40. Dark hair. Very dark complexion, probably a foreigner. Black skirt and blouse, no boots. No other aids to identification.

"Foreigner" was meant to signify not Anglo-Saxon.

#146. Walter J. Anderson, bedroom steward, estimated age 40. Address: 12 Queen's Terrace, Southampton, England.

#151. J. M. Robinson, saloon steward, estimated age 32. Address: Vine Cottage, Carlisle Road, Southampton. Effects: plain ring left on finger, heart-shaped locket (empty), knife, empty purse.

At first this body was reported as going to the mortuary, while a later report says buried at sea April 24. The body was not taken to Halifax.

#152. J. C. Hill, saloon steward, estimated age 32. Address: 64 Padwell Road, Southampton, England. The name that was recorded on the first report was J. C. Hell.

#153. Edward Lockyer, third-class passenger, embarked from Southampton, age 21. Brown hair. In effects were scissors, keys, silver watch and chain, R.S.P.C.A. medal, etc. Address found: London, England.

Edward also had gold-rimmed eyeglasses in his pocket, which belonged to Miss Emily Badman, who survived. She recalled that she had handed the glasses to him while playing tennis earlier in voyage.

#154. Unidentified male, estimated age 32. Brown hair and moustache, false upper teeth. Wore blue jacket, grey vest, and black pants. No other aids to identification.

There was no guess made as to whether this was a crew member or passenger.

#155. John William Gill, second-class passenger, estimated age 31. Address found: 2 Griffen Road, Clevedon, England.

#156. Erik Johansson, third-class passenger, embarked from Southampton, age 22. He was from Sweden.

Left: Hugh McElroy, Body #157, Right: Oscar Woody, Body #167.

#157. Hugh W. McElroy, chief purser, age 37. Dark hair. Wore ship's uniform. Keys, one tagged "Linen Locker No. 1 C Deck." Address found in effects: Miss McElroy, Layton, Spottisbury, Dorset.

This body was originally marked down as that of a steward, D. Lily. In Halifax, the review of the crew list revealed that there was no D. Lily onboard. It was decided to list the body as unknown. In further reviewing this man's effects the address of a Miss McElroy pointed to the identity of the chief purser. However, it should be noted that the description of clothing said ship's uniform, white jacket, but did not specifically mention an officer's uniform, which is what the chief purser is seen to wear in photographs. Even the white jacket should have had some mark of quality to it. As chief purser he was a man of great importance on the ship. The burials at sea left many unanswered questions. (Body was originally listed as "Herbert" McElroy.)

#158. W. Watson, fireman, estimated age 25. Address found: Olden Lane, Manchester.

#159. Ernest T. Barker, saloon steward, age 37. Address: 4 Grand Parade, Harringay, Southampton, England.

#160. Unidentified male, possibly a sailor, estimated age 42. Wore bracelet. No other aids to identification.

#162. Unidentified male, possibly a fireman, estimated age 42. Dark hair, light moustache. No aids to identification.

#164. Unidentified male, possibly a fireman, estimated age 34. Dark hair, light moustache. No aids to identification.

#167. Oscar S. Woody, United States mail clerk, estimated age 38. Address: Washington, D. C. (see Chapter 3, story on ship's post office.)

#168. H. T. Hewett, bedroom steward, estimated age 35. Address: Southampton, England.

#170. Unidentified male, possibly carpenter's mate, estimated age 25. Carried key No. 73, marked "Carpenter's Locker." Silver watch and chain, memo book. No other aids to identification.

#171. Patrick Connors, third-class passenger, embarked from Queenstown, estimated age 70. White hair.

#173. Henry Olsen, third-class passenger, embarked from Southampton, age 28. Fair hair. He was from Bergen, Norway.

#176. Thomas Theobald, third-class passenger, embarked from Southampton, age 34; the recovery crew estimated he was age 46. Pepper and salt suit, brown knitted waistcoat, purple tie, green striped flannel shirt, grey socks, no boots.

#177. W. Mayo, leading fireman, estimated age 40. Address: 24 Cable Street, Southampton, England.

#178. Unidentified male, estimated age 25. Brown hair, light moustache. Tattooed right arm: "anchor and rose," wife's name "Madge." Effects included a gold ring, knife, nickel watch. Six pawn tickets in possession, and following addresses: Henry Murray, Sailor's Home, Southampton, and 45 Fir Grove Road, Southampton; Sidney Sedunary, 47 Fir Grove Road and 98 N'land Road, Southampton; John Sedunary, 47 Fir Grove Road, Southampton.

In 1991 a society interested in *Titanic* victims confirmed the identity of this body as Mr. Sidney Francis Sedunary, third-class steward.

#180. Unidentified male, estimated age 40. Dark hair. Wore steward's white coat, black coat, and dungaree pants, no effects. No other aids to identification. No guess was made as to this man's occupation.

#181. Mansor Novel, third-class passenger, embarked from Cherbourg, estimated age 28. Black coat and pants, blue waistcoat, cotton shirt, four shirts, black boots. This man seems to have wanted to take all of his shirts with him. He was travelling from Lebanon to his home in Canada. He was a Syrian who became a British subject in Canada.

#182. Unidentified male, possibly a fireman, estimated age 45. No aids to identification.

#184. W. Saunders, coal trimmer, estimated age 30. Address: 13 Dukes Road, Southampton, England.

#185. Unidentified male, probably second-class steward, estimated age 25. Fair complexion.

Scar on right lower jaw. Wore blue coat with brass buttons, trousers, steward's white coat, pyjamas, green singlet, green football jersey with white bands. Second class steward No. 20 on badge.

#190. Rossmore Abbott, third-class passenger, estimated age 22. Very fair. Brown overcoat, grey pants, green cardigan, blue jersey, black boots. Watch, chain, and fob, with medal marked "Rossmore Abbott," empty pocket book, two knives.

Rossmore Abbott was not 22 years old, but just 16. He had embarked at Southampton with his mother Rose (Rosa) and younger brother Eugene, age 9.

Rosa Abbott had taken the boys to her family in England to start a new life after her marriage breakup. The boys were homesick for their friends left behind in Rhode Island, and their mother made the decision to return to the United States. Due to the coal shortage in England, they were transferred to the new ship, *Titanic*, from another vessel. They had a cabin in third class. On the night of the collision they would only have been awakened by a steward after some time had passed. More time was taken to dress and then find their way on deck. "Women and children first" would exclude the boys who were of working age and considered men. Their mother would not leave her sons to get into a lifeboat so the family of three awaited their fate. When the ship sank Rosa and the boys were separated. Rosa Abbott was the only woman to go down with ship and to survive in the water. She was pulled into Collapsible A. Many of the people clinging to the collapsible died and drifted away. Others died of the cold and were put

ON THE *MINIA*, A BOTTLE OF EMBALMING FLUID IS PLACED TO OBSCURE THE FACE OF THE VICTIM FOR THIS PHOTOGRAPH.

overboard. Finally those who remained, including Rosa Abbott, were transferred to another lifeboat.

Rossmore's body may have been too disfigured to bring to shore; Eugene's body was not found. Friends in Rhode Island held a memorial service for the boys. Rosa did not attend as she spent many weeks in hospital in New York recovering from the physical injuries sustained in the sinking and being hit by wreckage. Rosa Abbott married again but did not have any more children.

#194. Unidentified male, estimated age 35. Light hair. Grey overcoat, Artex singlet, night-shirt, dress trousers. Wore gold ring marked "H. B." or "B. H."

In 1991, a society interested in *Titanic* victims tentatively identified this body as William Hull Botsford, a second-class passenger from New Jersey. He had graduated from Cornell University's College of Architecture and worked in the New England area for a railway company. In 1910 he was the YMCA lightweight wrestling champion. He was returning from a study trip of European architecture.

#199. Unidentified male, probably a steward, estimated age 30. Scar on right hand; dark. Green overcoat, steward's uniform, no shirt, grey singlet. Knife, key, £1, 11s. 4d. No marks on clothing.

#200. John James Davies, extra second baker. Address: 19 Eastfield Road, Southampton, England.

THE CS *MINIA*

The *Minia* crew numbered bodies 307 to 323. One crew member, Francis Dyke, wrote his mother about the experience: "I can tell you none of us like this job at all but it is better to recover them and bury them properly than let them float around for weeks." The following bodies were buried from the *Minia*:

#310. Unidentified male, probably a fireman. No aids to identification.

#318. Unidentified male, probably a fireman. Blue eyes, brown hair, smooth face. Wore brass watch and chain. No other aids to identification.

THE *MONTMAGNY*

When the *Montmagny* took over the search, the numbers 324 and 325 were not used. This may have been in case the *Minia* picked up other bodies on the way home. It could have been that the wireless message was not read properly or received correctly due to the dense fog. The *Montmagny* used numbers 326 to 329. The following body was buried from the *Montmagny*:

#326. Unidentified male, possibly a steward, age about 50. Height: 5 feet, 9 inches; weight: 150 pounds. Light complexion, partly bald. Wore steward's white coat, light check overalls, coat-maker's mark: "Baker & Co., Southampton." No further aids to identification.

THE *ALGERINE*

The *Algerine* found only one body, #330 James McGrady, which was sent to Halifax for burial.

OTHER SHIPS

The following bodies buried at sea were not recovered as part of the Halifax effort and were never assigned body numbers. Four male survivors died after they were taken aboard the *Carpathia* and were buried at sea. They were:

William Fisher Hoyt, first-class passenger. He was from New York City.

A fireman who could not be identified.

Sidney C. Siebert, bedroom steward, age 29. Address: 8 Harold Road, Shirley, England.

H. W. Lyons, able seaman, age 26. Address: 27 Orchard Place, Southampton, England.

On May 13, the SS *Oceanic* found a lifeboat containing the bodies of three men. These men had died before they could be rescued by the *Carpathia*. There was no time for the crew of the *Carpathia* to retrieve the bodies on the morning of April 15, as the other lifeboats were arriving. The three men were buried at sea from the SS *Oceanic*. They were:

Thomson Beattie, a first-class passenger, age 37. He was in evening dress and was identified from papers found in his pockets. He had been travelling with a large party of friends from Winnipeg, Manitoba.

A fireman, who could not be identified.

W. F. CHIVERTON, BODY FOUND BY SS *ILFORD* AND BURIED AT SEA, JUNE 8, 1912.

A steward, who could not be identified.

On June 6, 1912, the crew of SS *Ottawa* committed to the sea one body, male, thought to be William Kerley, 28, assistant saloon steward.

On June 8, fifty-four days after the sinking, the SS *Ilford* found a body drifting in the ocean. He was identified as W. F. Chiverton, a saloon steward. He was buried at sea. Address: Mill Street, Newport, England.

After almost two months of recovery work, 128 bodies were recommitted to the ocean to join the 1,160 passengers and crew members of the *Titanic* whose bodies were never found.

Roll on thou deep and dark blue Ocean roll!
Ten thousand fleets sweep over thee in vain;
Man marks the Earth with ruin—his control
Stops with the shore.
—Lord Byron

THE UNLOADING OF THE *TITANIC* DEAD FROM THE *MINIA* AT THE NAVAL YARD, HALIFAX.

CHAPTER 3

HALIFAX RECEIVES THE DEAD

"The picture that inevitably presents itself, is of men like John Jacob Astor, master of scores of millions; Charles M. Hays, the great railway magnate; Isidor Straus, merchant prince; Major Archibald Butt, soldier; H. Markland Molson, banker…any or all of these stepping aside and bravely and gallantly remaining to die, that the place he might otherwise have filled could perhaps be taken by some sabot shod, shawl enshrouded, illiterate and penniless peasant woman of Europe."

—Commentary printed in many newspapers,
April 18, 1912.

"The Last Boat" drawn by Hal Coffman for the *Chicago Evening American*, April 22, 1912.

On April 30, the *Mackay-Bennett* returned to the port of Halifax with 190 of the bodies recovered. The city was ready for the arrival of what the press termed "the death ship." As the ship entered the harbour, church bells tolled and flags were at half-mast. "Halifax was in funeral garb" and many of the business windows were draped in black; some contained framed photographs of the *Olympic*, which was labeled "*Titanic*" as no pictures of the new ship were available. Undertakers from around the Maritime provinces (Nova Scotia, New Brunswick, and Prince Edward Island) had been called in by Snow & Company, a local undertaking establishment, to handle the embalming. Of the 43 undertakers present, one was a woman. Mrs. Mary Walsh from Saint John, New Brunswick, would look after the female remains.

Announcements were made in the churches on Sunday that it would be unseemly to gather by the docks to watch the unloading of bodies. As the day the ship arrived was a working day, most people were forced to follow that advice. The undertakers and authorities, taking no chances, arranged for the *Mackay-Bennett* to dock at the naval yard where the high stone wall would be a barrier to idle on-lookers and members of the press who had arrived to cover the story. The vehicles for transporting the dead were checked as they entered the yard to make sure unwanted visitors had not tried to sneak into the restricted area. Not all the wagons were funeral hearses as there were not enough of those in the city. There was not enough time to embalm the bodies while at sea and there were not enough coffins for the bodies so some were carried off the ship covered in canvas.

Years later, people trying to make a point about class discrimination would state that only the first-class passengers were in coffins. This is not true. There were 125 rough wood burial boxes taken on the voyage by the *Mackay-Bennett*. There were only twenty-nine first-class gentlemen brought to Halifax. Mr. Snow, the undertaker, and the Reverend Canon Hind would not have felt it proper to leave the bodies of the women covered in canvas when boxes were available. Using all the boxes for the men, women, and two young boys found still left 84 bodies that needed covering. The bodies already buried at sea had used up most of the canvas. It was impossible for the men on the recovery ship to sew up in canvas all the bodies buried at sea and

The Wednesday, April 17, edition of the *Chicago American* ran this composite drawing with the caption: "Famous Men Missing in Wreck of *Titanic*. From top to bottom: Colonel John Jacob Astor, New York scion of Astor fortunes. Benjamin Guggenheim, millionaire smelter magnate. Isidor Straus, reputed world's richest merchant prince. Major Archibald Butt, personal aide to President Taft. Henry B. Harris, theatrical producer and manager. William T. Stead, noted London journalist and correspondent of the Hearst newspapers. Francis D. Millet, noted artist."

also the ones being taken to Halifax. The lack of time and supplies was the reason some bodies were brought off the *Mackay-Bennett* covered in sheets, not class discrimination.

Sailors, soldiers, teamsters, and others unloading the ship treated the bodies with great care irrespective of the place in society the deceased persons had held. It would take all day to move the bodies. The wagons were driven up the steep hill of North Street, passing the railway station where some coffins would later be shipped from, to the Mayflower Curling Rink on Agricola Street.

"Halifax, April 30. Strangely solemn and profoundly impressive is the interior of the Mayflower Curling Rink, which became a morgue today. This structure, which has on more than one occasion been the scene of all that represents life and gaiety, has been completely transformed for the silent sleepers gathered from the deep. Never before in the history of Halifax has such a spectacle been witnessed. All this afternoon and late tonight more than a score of embalmers, with a large number of assistants, were engaged in embalming the bodies at the Mayflower morgue brought in from the scene of the *Titanic* disaster. Orders were given by the White Star line that all bodies should be embalmed and properly clothed and prepared for burial…The bodies so far examined present no mark of mutilation. Most others are frozen and many slightly decomposed. As a result of the frost, the work of the undertakers has been of necessity much retarded." *The Gazette*, Montreal, May 1, 1912.

The rink where the game of curling was played on ice surfaces was an ideal temporary mortuary.

The Mayflower Curling Rink was divided into cubicles to give dignity to the bodies and those who were searching for lost ones.

There was ample space for tables where the clothing and effects of the deceased could be examined. The large floor surface was cleared and divided into curtained spaces. This allowed the undertakers a place to embalm the bodies. After this the bodies were placed in groups of three for viewing. This was done so that visitors coming to make identifications would not be overwhelmed by the large number of dead. There was a nurse on duty in case anyone needed assistance. Unfortunately for Frank Newell, an undertaker from Yarmouth, Nova Scotia, he would be the first to collapse in shock. When he uncovered body #121 to prepare it for viewing he saw that it was his uncle, Arthur W. Newell of Boston.

With the announcement that the bodies of the *Titanic* victims would be brought to Halifax, the city hotels filled with relatives and friends of the deceased. Strict arrangements were put into

TELEGRAMS OF SYMPATHY

New York, April 16. "The officials of the White Star line here sent the following answer to the Duke of Connaught's telegram of sympathy: 'We beg to sincerely thank His Royal Highness, the Governor General of Canada for his message of sympathy with the relatives and friends of the passengers on the *Titanic*, who lost their lives in this most deplorable calamity and will convey his expressions to all concerned through the medium of the public press.'" H. R. H. Prince Arthur, Duke of Connaught and his wife, the Duchess, took a personal interest in the tragedy as many onboard were known to them.

Messages to President Taft from, Sandringham, King George V: "The Queen and I are anxious to assure you and the American nation of the great sorrow which we experience at the terrible loss of life that has occurred among the American citizens as well as among my own subjects by the foundering of the *Titanic*."

Belgium, King Albert: "I beg Your Excellency to accept the deepest condolence on the occasion of the frightful catastrophe to the *Titanic* which has caused such mourning in the American nation." Messages of sympathy were also received from King Victor Emmanuel of Italy and other heads of state and governments.

place so that only these people were allowed into the rink to identify the dead. The fear was that publicity seekers and the curious would try to gain entrance. The newsmen were also thought to be unscrupulous in their attempts to gain access to a sensational story. Members of the press were disappointed that a number of wealthy families had sent representatives and were not in the city themselves. Vincent Astor, the son of multimillionaire John Jacob Astor, was followed constantly while in Halifax. Other families wired instructions as to what to do with the bodies of their loved ones if found and brought to Halifax. This meant that shortly after being embalmed, bodies were sent by train to other parts of North America for burial or for shipping overseas.

The following list of the fifty-nine people sent away from Halifax for burial is presented in alphabetical order. This allows for a wife and husband, bodies #7 and #119; and a son and father, bodies #1 and #255, to be together. It is noted with the person found if a wife or family member was lost. Also mentioned is if a wife or family member survived the sinking. In some cases husbands were on business and their families were at home or a father was just travelling with children.

#135. Hudson J. Allison, first-class passenger, age 30. Was wearing leather coat, blue suit, grey silk muffler. Effects included: keys; letters; photos; stock book; three pocket diaries; one Canadian Pacific Railway ticket book; two pocket books; card case: $143.00 in notes; chain with insurance medals; £15 in gold; $100.00 Thomas Cook & Sons travellers' cheque; £35 in notes; gold cuff links; diamond solitaire ring; gold stud; knife; silver tie clip; $4.40 in odd coins; traveller's ticket.

The body of Hudson Allison was forwarded to Montreal on May 1st, care of G. E. Clark. Burial took place in Ontario, Canada. Allison was lost along with his twenty-five-year-old wife, Bessie, and their young daughter, Lorraine, age 2 years and 9 months. Lorraine was listed in first-class as Miss Allison to reflect her social standing. This led to reports that no children were lost in first-class. The couple had an eleven-month-old son with them. They also were bringing a nurse, a maid, a cook, and a chauffeur back from their London house. At the time of the collision, Hudson left their cabins to see what was going on. Mrs. Allison was separated from her baby boy and would not leave the ship

Hudson Allison, Body #135.

Mr. Allison was with the financial house of Johnson, McConnell & Allison. He had been married for six years to the former Bessie Daniels of Cincinnati. The couple had been at their London home for four months and were returning to their main residence in Montreal. They were taking with them a cook, a maid, a children's wet nurse, and a chauffeur. The wet nurse who took Trevor Allison into a lifeboat gave a false name. Her real name was Alice Cleaver and she had been found guilty of throwing her own baby off a train years earlier. Her sentence was reduced as it was found she was suffering from mental stress. There is no record to know if Mr. and Mrs. Allison knew of her background. Once the story became known in Montreal, the relatives of the baby dismissed Alice from her duties.

At the memorial service at Douglas Methodist in Montreal "Death March in Saul" was played as it was at many memorial services. After Mr. Allison's funeral, the twenty-five horses that he had bought in England arrived by freighter and were delivered to his farm.

Trevor Allison, having lost his parents and sister, would die seventeen years later of food poisoning while visiting in Maine.

Survivor Trevor Allison with nurse who took him into lifeboat.

TUESDAY.   CHICAGO EVENING AMERICAN, APRIL 16, 1912.   TUESDAY.

JOHN JACOB ASTOR PERISHES; MRS. ASTOR SAVED

DIAGRAM SHOWING WHERE AND HOW TITANIC SUNK AND RESCUES WERE EFFECTED

AT 9.30 MONDAY MORNING THE TITANIC SANK 500 MILES OFF CAPE RACE; ABOUT 670 WOMEN AND CHILDREN HAD BEEN PUT OFF IN THE LIFE BOATS AND WERE PICKED UP BY THE CARPATHIA, WHICH ARRIVED SHORTLY AFTER THE TITANIC HAD SUNK WITH THE REMAINING 670 PASSENGERS AND CREW OF 860

AT 10.25 SUNDAY NIGHT THE TITANIC STRUCK AN ICEBERG, PUNCHING A GREAT HOLE IN BOWS AND IMMEDIATELY SENT OUT WIRELESS CALLS FOR HELP. THESE WERE HEARD BY THE STEAMSHIPS CARPATHIA, PARISIAN AND VIRGINIAN WHICH STARTED TO THE RESCUE THE TITANIC STARTED A DASH FOR CAPE RACE

NEW FOUNDLAND

CAPE RACE

NOVA SCOTIA

HALIFAX

SOUTHAMPTON ⟶

COMPLETE CABIN LIST OF TITANIC

$15,000,000 LOSS ON LINER AND CARGO; TWO-THIRDS INSURED

Astor, Titanic Victim, One of 5 World's Richest Men

For days after the sinking, the fate of John Jacob Astor featured in the headlines. *The Chicago Evening American*, April 16, 1912.

without him. The couple did not know that their children's nurse had already taken the baby into a lifeboat. Whether the Allisons ever decided to seek a lifeboat is not known but they were seen on deck by a number of survivors. If the couple did finally make the decision to leave there were no more boats available. The bodies of Mrs. Allison and little Lorraine were never found.

#259. Owen G. Allum, third-class passenger, age 17. Dark hair. Grey tweed suit. Effects included a gun metal watch and chain, hair brush, two knives, cigarette case, pocketbook, Ticket No. 1223. for Owen George Allum, 7 Gerrold Villas, Vansittart, Windsor. Instructions from White Star New York office by wire, May 2nd. Forwarded May 4th to Boston, to connect with the SS *Arabic*

bound for Liverpool, May 7th. Burial took place near Windsor, England.

#22. Ramon Artagaveytia, first-class passenger, age 71. Grey hair, bald. Blue overcoat, blue suit, white dress waistcoat, black boots and purple socks, two vests marked "R. A." pink drawers also marked "R. A." Instructions received from the White Star New York office by letter April 23rd. Claimed in Halifax by Alfred Metz Green, Uruguayan Consul, to be forwarded to South America, via New York, for burial in family plot, Montevideo, Uruguay.

#142. Carl Oscar Asplund, third-class passenger, embarked from Southampton, age 40. Hair and moustache fair. Brown coat and vest, striped trousers, black boots. Gold watch, two

Nineteen-year-old Vincent Astor travelled to Halifax from Harvard University to claim his father's body. In background are messenger boys at the telegraph office and a policeman in "bobby" helmet. Was it his initials on the handkerchief found on John Jacob Astor's body?

memo books, gold charm and locket broach marked "F of A," keys, knife, plain gold ring. Third class (seven tickets). This man was travelling with his wife and five children. They had lived in the United States, returned home to Sweden, and this trip was bringing the family back to Massachusetts. The night of the sinking the family was able to come up from the third-class area to the promenade deck. There Mrs. Asplund was put into a lifeboat with her three-year-old boy and five-year-old daughter. The twin brother of the girl and two other boys, ages nine and thirteen, were left on the ship with their father. The three boys were not found. The body of Carl Asplund was forwarded to his wife, Mrs. Selma Asplund at Worcester, Massachusetts, May 3 for burial.

#124. Colonel John Jacob Astor IV, first-class passenger, multi-millionaire, age 47. Light hair and moustache. Blue serge suit, blue handkerchief with "A. V.," belt with gold buckle, brown boots with red rubber soles, brown flannel shirt with "J. J. A." on back of collar. Gold watch, cuff links, gold with diamonds, diamond ring with three stones, £225 in English notes, $2440 in notes, £5 in gold, 7 s. in silver, five 10-franc pieces, gold pencil, pocketbook. Legend has it that Mr. Astor might have been in the group of swimmers hit when the forward funnel of the *Titanic* toppled. His body was delivered in Halifax to Mr. N. Biddle and was forwarded to New York, May 1st, in the private rail car "Oceanic." His son Vincent (from his first marriage) returned to New York with the body. Was buried in the family mausoleum, Trinity Cemetery, New York City.

John J. Astor was one of the world's five richest men. He was the greatest real estate owner on Manhattan Island—an inventor of patented items, like a bicycle brake—which he gave over to public interest—and an author of science fiction. He was the leading male in American society until his divorce from his first wife. His second wife was a woman less than half his age and the scandal sheets referred to her as a "child bride." To get away from such comments, he took his new wife on a tour. He had been returning from his honeymoon after many months as his wife was expecting their first child. The handkerchief with the initials "A. V." has always raised speculation as to what the initials stood for. John J. Astor was the fourth man to carry that name in his family. A cousin already was the fifth to have that name. It may be that the young Mrs. Astor wanted her husband to know in a touching way that she was expecting a child. She could have embroidered those initials "A. V." on the handkerchief to indicate an heir was expected. The couple was known to give each other little gifts; at the stop at Queenstown, Ireland, John Jacob had bought a lace shawl for her from a woman in the small boats that had pulled up alongside the great ship. An explanation for the initials was never asked of Madeleine Astor.

Mr. Astor's valet went down with the ship. Mrs. Astor and her maid survived. Four months after the sinking, Madeline Astor gave birth to a son who was named John Jacob Astor VI.

#174. Reverend Robert J. Bateman, second-class passenger, age 51. Black overcoat, black frock coat, vest and trousers, gold watch and chain, Masonic pin, gold mounted eyeglasses, gold links, four gold studs, cigar holder, pipe lighter, knife, photo, fountain pen. Address found: Robert J. Bateman (per) Pendennis, Staple Hill, Bristol. He was travelling alone. In accordance with a May 2 wire from his wife, his coffin was forwarded May 6 to Mrs. R. J. Bateman, Jacksonville, Florida.

#148. Jacob Birnbaum, first-class passenger, age 25. Light grey overcoat, blue pyjamas, and effects. Address found: Jacob Birnbaum, San Francisco. Instructions from White Star New York office by wire, May 2nd. Forwarded May 3rd to Joachim Birnbaum, Red Star Line, Pier 60, N. Y. City. Returned to Belgium for burial.

#208. Emil Brandeis, first-class passenger, department store owner, age 48. Grey hair and moustache. Dark suit, brown shirt with blue stripe, black shoes, silk socks. Diamond cuff links, gold knife, platinum and diamond watch chain, gold pencil case, gold ring, gold cigarette and matchbox with initials, pearl tie pin, gold watch, small amount of money. Instructions from White Star New York office by wire, April 29th. Body forwarded to Mrs. Brandeis, Omaha, Nebraska, May 2nd.

#299. Katherine Buckley, third-class passenger, embarked from Queenstown, Ireland, estimated age 18. False teeth, top teeth dark. Long blue overcoat, blue serge jacket and shirt, white blouse, blue corsets, grey knickers, 10s in silver, £1 in gold, five-dollar note in purse, satchel, third-class ticket No. 32994. Instructions from White Star Boston office by letter, April 29th. Forwarded to Boston, May 3rd, at request of her sister, Margaret, 71 Montview Street, Roxbury, Massachusetts, for burial in Roxbury.

Tyrrell Cavendish, Body #172.

William Carbines, Body #18. Identified from this photograph and a letter found on body.

#18. William Carbines, second-class passenger, age 19. Dark suit, white shirt with green stripe, knitted socks, black boots. Name found on letter, Mr. W. Carbines, Higher Stennack, St. Ives. His body was claimed in Halifax by his brothers who travelled from Calumet, Michigan. The coffin was forwarded May 10th, to St. Ives, Cornwall, England, via New York, at request of his brothers.

#172. Tyrell W. Cavendish, first-class passenger, age 30. Black striped flannel suit, boots.

Instructions to White Star New York office by wire, May 1st. Body forwarded, May 3rd, care of Simpson, Crawford and Co., to Mrs. T. W. Cavendish. Burial of his ashes was in London, England. He was the son of the Honourable Charles Cavendish. Mrs. T. W. (Julia) Cavendish was the only child of Henry Seigel, a wealthy American; she and her maid were saved. In memory of her husband she had a village hall built in Thurston, Suffolk, England.

#130. Charles H. Chapman, second-class passenger, age 52. Dark suit, abdominal belt. Silver cigarette case, garnet tie pin, garnet ring, papers, gold mounted cuff links, $200, two gold studs, fountain pen, knife, pipe, £2 10s. gold in purse. Forwarded, May 2nd, care of J. J. Griffin, 2282 7th Avenue, New York. Burial in the Bronx, New York.

#269. Captain Edward G. Crosby, first-class passenger, veteran Lake Michigan navigator and president of the Crosby Transportation Company of Milwaukee, age 70. Grey tweed suit

CAPTAIN EDWARD G. CROSBY, BODY #269.

and overcoat; $500, £80 in notes; £6 in gold in purse; 8s. 6d. in silver; pipe; memo book. He was a well-known shipping man and a friend of Charles Hays (Body #307). His body was delivered in Halifax to Howard G. Kelly, vice-president, Grand Trunk Railway, for shipment to Milwaukee, Wisconsin, May 3rd. "Better dress, all the other passengers are doing it" were Captain Crosby's last words to his wife and daughter, who survived the sinking.

#197. E. Gilbert Danbom, third-class passenger, embarked from Southampton. The recovery crew estimated his age as 46, he was only 34. Very fair with moustache. Black overcoat, dark suit, white pleated shirt, black boots. Wedding ring marked "S. B. T. E. G. D., June 6, 10," gold watch and chain, knife, keys, jewel case, pin, opal and ruby ring, fountain pen, bracelet, lady's watch and chain, knife, three memo books, solitaire diamond ring, scissors, U. S. A. naturalization papers, cheque for $1315.79, Security Bank, Sioux City, Iowa, pocketbook, $266.00 in notes, $30.00 in gold. Third-class ticket for three. Gilbert Danbom was returning from an extended stay in Sweden with his wife and four-month-old son. Travelling with them was his wife's sister, husband and five young children. All ten members of this group were lost in the sinking. Only Gilbert's body was found. The amount of money found on Gilbert gives a good example as to why taking third class did not necessarily mean the passenger was poor. The initials on his wedding ring stood for: Sigrid Brogren to Ernst Gilbert Danbom and the date was their wedding day. His wife may have handed him the jewellery case to pocket as she dressed their son. Gilbert's body was forwarded to Alfred Danbom, Stanton, Iowa, May 3rd, where his mother, family, and community attended his burial at the Lutheran cemetery.

#295. Sebastiano del Carlo, second-class passenger, age 29. Fair hair, light moustache. Grey overcoat, dark tweed suit. Gold watch and chain, diamond and gold pair of earrings, gold chain locket, silver watch and chain, knife, pin, pocketbook and papers, 5 dollars in notes, 37 francs. Forwarded to Boston April 30th for shipment to Italy by Cretic, May 18th, which was the request of his widow who survived the sinking. The couple had been on their way to Chicago, Illinois. Mrs. del Carlo was taken in by the Sisters of Charity as she was destitute. She returned to Italy and on her death fifty-eight years later, she was buried beside her husband.

#62. Walter D. Douglas, first-class passenger, multi-millionaire manufacturer of starch, and a director of the Quaker Oats Company, estimated age 55. Grey hair. Evening dress, with "W. D. D." on shirt. Gold watch, chain, sov. case with "W. D. D.", gold cigar cutter, gold pencil case, gold knife "WDD," gold cigarette case "WDD," five gold studs, wedding ring on finger engraved "May 19th, 84," pocket letter case with $551 and one £5 note, cards. Forwarded May 1st to G. C. Douglas, his son, Minneapolis, Minnesota, for burial in Cedar Rapids, Iowa. Walter's wife and her maid survived the sinking.

#133. William C. Dulles, first-class passenger, attorney and broker, age 39. Green suit, grey sweater, and overshoes. Among effects were gold watch and chain, gold plated knife and chain, gold tie clip "W. C. D.," four memo books, gold stud. Forwarded to R. R. Bringhurst, Philadelphia, Pennsylvania, May 1st, for burial.

#286. Harry Faunthorpe, second class passenger, salesman, estimated age 36. Dark hair, going bald. Green raincoat, grey coat and vest, blue pants, white waistcoat with stripe, purple and green flannel shirt, brown drawers, black boots. Six gold and diamond rings, sovereign case, £3 10s., George sovereign, spectacles, gold watch chain and seal, silver watch, silver chain, two knives, papers, 12s. 6d. in silver, 1s. 2d. in copper. Forwarded to the lady who was travelling as his wife, care of Mr. William Stringfield, Philadelphia, Pennsylvania. Instructions from White Star New York office by wire, May 3rd.

#236. Stanley H. Fox, second-class passenger, salesman, age 38. The crew of the recovery ship estimated Stanley's age as 60. This mistake could indicate that the crew was simply rushed

New York, April 16th: The German Kaiser wired from Corfu to his cousin King George V of Great Britain expressing sympathy at the loss of the *Titanic*. The German press blames the sinking on British inefficiency and the American craze for speed. April 24: The White Star Line pays the transportation cost for Americans to go to Halifax to view bodies. One hundred mourners and the members of the press fill Halifax hotels.

with inspections at sea. Grey hair. Grey suit; grey overcoat. Letter credit case, two memo books, card case, £2 in gold, $65 in notes in case, watch and chain, pen, nickel watch, 11 shillings, 25 cents. Address found: Stanley H. Fox, 38 Gregory Street, Rochester, New York. Forwarded May 3rd, to Rochester to widow. Order of Mrs. Emma Fox.

The words "instructions from" usually appear in the lists recording the dispositions of bodies of those sent home. In the case of Stanley Fox, it is noted as "Order of Mrs. Emma Fox." There is nothing in the record to explain the use of the word "Order." However, the newspapers of the day did give great detail regarding the claims over the body of Stanley Fox.

Among the mourners who had arrived in Halifax were a man and woman from Rochester, New York; she gave her name as Lydia Fox. Lydia made herself known to the authorities at the Mayflower Curling Rink. She claimed that her sister-in-law, Stanley's widow, was too distraught to

FAMILIES AND FRIENDS OF THE DECEASED ARRIVED IN THE CITY AT THE NORTH STREET railway station.

travel to Halifax. For that reason she would accompany the body back to Rochester. Her identification papers proved who she was. On the same day, a telegram arrived in Halifax from the widow asking authorities not to give the body to Lydia Fox. There was another telegram, care of Snow, the undertaker to Lydia, which stated she had no right to claim the body. Lydia Fox denied any knowledge as to why this telegram was sent. This caused a great commotion in Halifax. The body was already on a train and Lydia Fox, and the man she was with, left Halifax. The authorities sent word to the station in Truro, ninety-four kilometres from Halifax, to have the coffin removed and sent back to the city. Lydia Fox was not told of this. The small amount of money and effects found on Stanley Fox had not been given to the sister-in-law so she was allowed

to continue on her way. The body of Stanley Fox was later shipped to Rochester after the mayor of that city contacted Halifax authorities on behalf of the widow. The newspapers speculated that there may have been a family dispute over insurance money. Others, aware that fake survivors were starting to show up in New York to take advantage of public sympathy, felt it may have been an attempt to seek publicity. It is now thought that family disapproval of Stanley's marriage choice may have been the cause of the dispute.

This was a situation that was found in many families concerned about social standing. The Fox family had been in Rochester for three generations. Stanley was the grandson of a wealthy merchant. Stanley's older brother, Morton, was married to Lydia but it does not appear that he was the mysterious escort that came to Halifax. The unnamed man may have been present to protect Lydia on her mission to a port city in another country. Stanley also had a sister who does not seem to have been involved in the Halifax dispute.

Stanley worked for a machine tool company, the Gleason Works of Rochester. The company had patents on gear-making machines that were in demand in North America and Europe. Stanley was one of the company salesmen who was able to demonstrate the machines on offer. If a sale was made he would help install and train staff in the use of the equipment. As an important employee of such a respectable company, it is doubtful if his marriage choice could have been a cause for public comment despite any family reservations. Stanley and his wife Cora had two sons, and the oldest boy had the same name as Stanley's brother. Stanley had left Rochester for six weeks of sales calls in Europe. In correspondence to his company he stated that he was returning to the United States on the steamship *Titanic*.

Nothing is known of Stanley's actions during the last hours of his life on April 15th. The only unanswered question is with the "Order of Mrs. Emma Fox" recorded on the mortuary records. The name of Stanley's wife was "Cora Fox." What caused such small errors and discrepancies?

#322. Joseph J. Fynney, second-class passenger, age 35. He was a rubber merchant from Liverpool, England, who was going to visit his mother and sister in Montreal. He was travelling with a young man from Liverpool who also perished in the sinking and was not found. Joseph's body was delivered in Halifax to his brother-in-law, Mr. Hoseason, C. N. S. S. Co., to be taken to Montreal for burial. Inscribed on his stone in Montreal is Psalm 77, verse 19: "Thy way is the sea, and Thy path in the great waters and Thy footsteps are not known."

#275. Arthur Gee, first-class passenger, textile merchant, age 47. Dark hair and moustache. Brown overcoat, dress pants, tuxedo suit. Silver watch, gold chain, silver cigarette case, knife, pen, pipe, glasses, case, pocketbook, two rings, one left on, cuff links, £15 in notes, initials on shirt "A. G." Forwarded to New York May 9th, to be sent to Liverpool, per "S. S. *Baltic*." For burial in Manchester, England. A coincidence occurred in that Harold Bride, the wireless operator who survived the sinking, also travelled back to England on the *Baltic*, arriving there on May 18th.

#147. George E. Graham, first-class passenger, age 38. Black overcoat, blue serge suit. Memo book, cheque for three hundred dollars, pocketbook, credit book T. & Eaton & Co., and other effects. Address found: 91 Dundurn Place, Winnipeg, Manitoba. Graham was a buyer for the toy department, Eaton's store in Winnipeg. The T. Eaton Company was a family-owned business that had two large department stores and a thriving catalogue order division that served all of Canada.

GEORGE E. GRAHAM, BODY #147.

The Eatons took great pride in looking after their employees, so it is no surprise they closed both stores to mark the passing of their employee. Mr. John C. Eaton, the president, attended a memorial service in Winnipeg. Other members of the Eaton family attended a service at the Broadway Methodist Tabernacle in Toronto where Mr. Graham's father and other family members were present. The choir

COVER OF DINNER MENU, T. EATON CO. ARCHIVES. THE MENU—3 1/2 INCHES WIDE BY 4 1/4 INCHES HIGH—MADE A POCKET-SIZED SOUVENIR. LIFTING THE COVER REVEALED THE MENU CHOICES FOR APRIL 14, 1912.

in Toronto was made up of Eaton store employees who sang "One Sweetly Solemn Thought."

When George Graham's body was found, the company handled all the arrangements. His body was forwarded April 30th, to Toronto care of T. Eaton & Co., with Mr. Matthews, undertaker, as the escort. For the funeral in Harriston, Ontario, a special train from Toronto brought fifty representatives of the company.

In the T. Eaton Co. archives is an April 14, 1912, menu for the *Titanic*. In the first-class dining room George Graham had dinner with four other gentlemen. The men signed the menu. It reads: "S V Silverthorne, 5855 Vou Verseu Ave., St. Louis; Geo G. Graham, 31 Dundurn Place, Winnipeg, Can.; Edward P. Calderhead 561 West 180th St, New York; James McGough, 708 York St., Phila. Pa.; J. Irwin Flynn, 635 West St, Brooklyn. 1760 miles out." Only George Graham was lost in the sinking. Silverthorne, Calderhead, and Flynn ended up in the same lifeboat.

THE STORE WILL CLOSE AT 1 P.M. TO-DAY

AS A TOKEN OF OUR SORROW and sympathy with the widow, family and friends of the late Mr. George E. Graham, and as a mark of honor and respect for his heroic end on the S.S. "Titanic," our Toronto and Winnipeg Stores will close at one o'clock to-day.

Mr. Graham was our associate in Toronto for six years before going to Winnipeg at the opening of the Store there, since when he has been one of our most trusted lieutenants, and a buyer and manager of important departments; honored and loved by all who knew him.

Our heartfelt sympathy is also extended to the bereaved ones in this international calamity.

THE **T. EATON C**o. LIMITED
TORONTO AND WINNIPEG

TO MARK THE PASSING OF GEORGE GRAHAM, THE EATON STORES IN WINNIPEG AND TORONTO CLOSED FOR A HALF DAY. NOTICE APPEARED IN *THE GLOBE*, TORONTO, APRIL 20, 1912.

#19. Samuel Greenberg, second-class passenger, estimated age 50. Grey hair, partly bald, moustache. Dressing gown, grey coat, green ditto, blue trousers. Greenberg had been travelling alone. His coffin was forwarded May 3, to Mrs. Greenberg, Bronx, New York City.

#35. William H. Harbeck, second-class passenger, moving picture operator, age 44. Black coat, grey mixture tweed trousers and vest, red tie, black boots. Cheque books, traveller's cheques, lady's bag, gold watch and chain, two lockets, gold time meter, fountain pen, diary, false teeth, pencil, knife, diamond ring, union card for Moving Picture and Projecting Machine Operators' Union, £15 in gold, £15 6s. in silver, 10s. in purse in lady's bag, wedding ring in bag, pearl and diamond pin. Address found: 114, 24th Avenue.

This list of what William was carrying certainly shows a wide assortment of effects was found on the bodies. His wife was not with him but he was accompanied by a young lady from France who survived the sinking. On May 4 his body was forwarded to Mrs. Harbeck, 733 Michigan Street, Toledo, Ohio.

#224. Wallace Henry Hartley, bandmaster, age 33. Brown hair. Wore uniform with green facing, brown overcoat, black boots, green socks. Effects included: gold fountain pen marked "W. H. H.";

The menu from the first-class dining room for April 14, the night of the collision, signed by the men George Graham had his final meal with. The men noted that the *Titanic* was 1,760 miles out from New York.

WALLACE HARTLEY, BODY #224.

diamond solitaire ring; silver cigarette case; letters; silver match-box marked "To W.H. H. from Collingson's staff, Leeds"; telegram to Hotley, bandmaster *Titanic*; nickel watch; gold chain; gold cigar holder; stud; scissors; 16s.; 16 cents; coins. Address: Surreyside West Park Street, Dewsbury.

Hartley's name was at first reported incorrectly because of a misspelling on the telegram. The wireless was not a precise method for correct spelling as many words were processed quickly. His body was forwarded May 4th to Boston for shipment to Liverpool. He was interred on May 18, 1912. It was estimated that forty thousand people showed up for his funeral in Colne, Lancashire, England. His grave has an elaborate marker unlike those of the two band members who are buried in Halifax. The question remains regarding the last music played on the ship. (See Chapter 6 for music played.)

#307. Charles Melville Hays, first-class passenger, president of the Grand Trunk Railway, age 55. Delivered in Halifax to Mr. Howard G. Kelley, vice-president, Grand Trunk Railway, and taken to Montreal on the private rail car "Canada." The Halifax Board of Trade provided a beautiful wreath for the car that carried Mr. Hays's body. It was noted that the train carrying Honourable

C. M. HAYS, BODY #307.

Frank Cochran, Minister of Railways, was one of many that pulled over, his on a siding in Bathurst, New Brunswick, to allow for the passing of the funeral train of Charles M. Hays. Mr. Hays was buried in Montreal.

Colonel Archibald Gracie, a survivor, stated that before the collision he had a long chat with Charles Hays, who predicted that with the race between shipping companies for luxury and speed a disaster was sure to happen. Colonel Gracie commented, "Poor fellow, a few hours later he was dead." After the collision Mr. Hays would have been able to size up the situation. His keen eye would have known the lifeboats were few and chances of being rescued from the water slim. His wife and married daughter along with their

cont. on p. 61

10 P.M. | *The Montreal Daily Star.* | **10 P.M.**

VOL. XLIV • N° 91. Weather Forecast: COOL. MONTREAL, TUESDAY, APRIL 16, 1912. PRICE ONE CENT.

ABANDON HOPE FOR C. M. HAYS

| Little Hope That Others of the More Than 2000 Persons Aboard The Titanic Have Been Saved---Virginian Arrived at Scene Too Late---Possibility That Parisian May Have Picked up Additional | Grand Trunk Officials Receive Word from Star Line Office in New York Late This Evening That They No Longer Have Hope for Any Additional Survivors than Reported | Leading Centres Astounded at Complete Loss of Largest Vessel Afloat With the Terrible Toll of Human Life---London and New York Offices of the White Star Line Besieged by Anxious |

"A Montreal telegram states that a wireless message has been received there announcing that Mr. Charles M. Hays, president of the Grand Trunk Railway, is among the *Titanic* survivors onboard the *Carpathia*. His wife and daughter have already been reported as saved." Reuters, April, 17, 1912. This story of Hays's survival, printed in European newspapers, was to prove false. A message making travel arrangements for Mrs. Hays was transmitted and wrongly interpreted by others.

Mrs. Hays survived, as did her daughter and their maid. Mrs. Hays recalled that after the collision there appeared to be no confusion and the men stepped aside for the women. The last she saw her husband he was standing with their son-in-law, Thornton Davidson, and Montreal banker H. Markland Molson. Thornton was the son of Mr. Justice Davidson of the Superior Court and in his younger years was a member of the famous Victoria hockey team. Other

MRS. CHARLES (CLARA) HAYS, WIDOW OF RAILWAY MAN, WITH SURVIVORS MR. AND MRS. GEORGE A. HARDER OF BROOKLYN, NEW YORK, ON THE *CARPATHIA*. MRS. HAYS MAY HAVE BEEN ANNOYED BY THE AMATEUR PHOTOGRAPHERS ON THE SHIP. THIS PHOTO WAS TAKEN BY MISS BERNICE PALMER OF GALT, ONTARIO, A PASSENGER ON THE *CARPATHIA*.

survivors remember that during the night as the lifeboats came together Clara Hays would call, "Charles Hays, are you there?" Mrs. Thornton Davidson stated to the press that the women never thought the men were in danger by staying on the ship. "We did not even think of kissing them goodbye."

Mr. Hays's private secretary, Mr. Vivian Payne, was also lost. Monsieur Paul Chevré, the French sculptor who was travelling with the Hays party, survived. He was asked to get into a lifeboat to give example to women who were reluctant of getting into the boats for fear of being lost in the ocean. Earlier the women had been told there was nothing to worry about and to go back to their cabins.

NOT FOR THESE ALONE, BUT FOR THE LIVING, ALSO, WHOSE BRAVE ENDEAVORS MAKE THAT SACRIFICE WORTH WHILE.

THIS ILLUSTRATION APPEARED IN *THE GLOBE*, TORONTO, APRIL 24, 1912. IT SIGNIFIED THE STOPPING OF WORK (11:30 A.M. MONTREAL TIME) IN EVERY DEPARTMENT OF THE GRAND TRUNK SYSTEM IN CANADA, BRITAIN, AND THE UNITED STATES.

Mr. Hays was widely known and respected in transportation circles around the world. He was described by Sir Wilfred Laurier in 1911 as the "Greatest Railroad Genius in Canada." His promotion of Pacific trade brought the honour from the Emperor of Japan of the Order of the Rising Sun (third class). Mr. Hays was prominent in social and charitable organizations. It was decided by Grand Trunk Railway officials that Charles Hays's body might not be found so memorial services to be held around the world on Thursday, April 25, were planned. At 11:30 a.m. Montreal time, there was a five-minute period of silent devotion. This was observed in Grand Trunk offices in England, Canada, and the United States. As well, thousands of employees of the entire service of the Grand Trunk, affiliated railways, and hotels stopped work for the five minutes. So too did the steamboat service on the Great Lakes and Pacific Ocean. Offices were draped in black and purple. Mr. Hays's body was found Friday, the day after this huge memorial tribute.

Rev. Cunningham was quoted in the Halifax newspapers saying that when the body of Charles Hays was found by the crew of the *Minia* they thought they had found a group of first-class passengers. The Reverend had hoped that they would find the body of George Wright of Halifax.

cont. from p. 58

maid survived and were taken from New York to Montreal in a private railway car. Both his son-in-law, Thornton Davidson, and his private secretary, Mr. Vivian Payne, were lost.

PROPHECY OF MR. HAYS

"Before I retired," said Colonel Gracie, U.S.A., one of those saved, "I had a long chat with Charles M. Hays, president of the Grand Trunk Pacific Railway. One of the last things Mr. Hays said was this:

"The White Star, the Cunard and the Hamburg-American lines are devoting their attention and ingenuity in vieing with one another to attain the supremacy in luxurious ships and in making speed records. The time will come soon when this will be checked by some appalling disaster.

"Poor fellow, a few hours later he was dead."

PROPHECY OF MR. HAYS REPORTED IN *THE GAZETTE*, MONTREAL, FRIDAY, APRIL 19, 1912.

#256. Lewis Hickman, second-class passenger, age 32. Fair hair and moustache. Green overcoat, fancy vest, dark suit. Keys, razors, scissors, silver watch and chain, amber cigarette holder, cigarette case. Forwarded May 4th to Mr. Honeyman c/o Simpson, undertaker, Neepawa, Manitoba. There were three Hickman brothers on the *Titanic* as they had been transferred from another ship that was laid up for lack of coal. Leonard, Lewis, and twenty-one-year-old

LEWIS HICKMAN, BODY #256. BURIED IN NEEPEWA, MANITOBA.

Stanley were all lost. Only Lewis's body was found. Leonard, age twenty-four, had worked for a farmer in Manitoba and went home to Fritham, England. Leonard and his brothers were going back to Manitoba to work. The farmer did not want the man he knew to be buried in Halifax and arranged for the body to be shipped to Manitoba. It was discovered to be Lewis and not Leonard but that did not matter. A full funeral took place and all three brothers' names were inscribed on the gravestone in Neepawa.

#38. Alexander O. Holverson, first-class passenger, age 42. Black overcoat, grey suit, black and grey necktie, blue shirt, green pyjamas with black stripe, underclothes, patent leather shoes, four gold teeth top left, and five below left. Gold watch with black beetle in case; silver card case; fountain pen; trinket case containing five scarf pins, watch chain, gold tie clip, gold and mother of pearl cuff links and studs to match, solitaire diamond ring, one other set cuff links; one unmounted stone; smoked glasses; pocketbook; 12s., two keys; knife; two £5 notes; letter of credit for $5000, No. 7710, by Kountze Bros., New York; business card, A. O. Holverson, Cluett Peabody & Co., New York. Holverson's wife survived the sinking. His coffin was delivered in Halifax to H. T. Holverson of Alexandria, Minnesota and forwarded May 1st to New York for burial there.

#80. Charles C. Jones, first-class passenger, age 46. Evening dress, grey leather-lined overcoat, black boots. Delivered in Halifax to Dr. James H. Donnelly on May 1st, for forwarding to Bennington, Vermont. Buried in the Colgate family plot. Charles Jones was escorting a Mrs. Mellenger and her daughter to Vermont where a new job awaited her. The two women survived.

#283. Cenai Kantor, listed as S. Kantor, second-class passenger, estimated age 36. Very fair hair and moustache. Grey and green suit, green overcoat, blue shirt, check front marked "F," black boots, "C" on singlet. Pocket telescope, silver watch, pocketbook with foreign notes, letter case, empty purse, purse, £1 10s. in gold, ten shillings in silver, and other coins.

Mr. Kantor was originally from Moscow. He was one of a number of people found that had glasses in their possessions that could be used for seeing distances. There is no record of what he did in his last hours but it is interesting to speculate if he was one of those who thought they could see a ship in the distance. His wife survived the sinking. Instructions were received from the White Star New York office by wire, April 29th. His body was forwarded to 1735 Madison Avenue, New York, care of Spieler, for burial in Queens, New York.

#258. Edward Austin Kent, first-class passenger, a prominent architect of Buffalo, New York, age 58. He had spent two months in Europe. Fair hair, grey moustache. Grey coat, dress suit pants. Silver flask, two gold signet rings, gold watch, gold eye glasses, gold frame miniature of "Mary Churchill Hungerford," knife, two pocketbooks, 48 francs, two studs, one link. His body was delivered in Halifax on May 1st to H. K. White of Boston, for shipment to Buffalo, New York. The gold frame miniature found on the body belonged to passenger Mrs. Helen Churchill Candee, an interior designer. It was a treasured possession and like many of the women going into lifeboats, Mrs. Candee thought the men had a better chance of surviving, so she gave it to Mr. Kent for safekeeping. It was returned to her by the White Star Line.

#90. Arthur Lawrence, saloon steward, age 35. Black rainproof coat, dark mixture suit, white steward's coat marked "A. Lawrence," knitted vest, green and pink pyjamas. Gun metal watch and chain; button hook; bundle letters; two fountain pens; pocket knife; keys; book of stamps; empty purse. His coffin was forwarded May 4th, via Boston to Liverpool on S.S. *Arabic*, May 7th. On instructions of his widow. He was the only crew member sent home for burial. His burial was in Rockford, Essex, England.

#126. Milton Clyde Long, first-class passenger, age 29. Dark hair. Black clothes; flannel vest, and black and white vest; white shirt marked "M. C. L"; handkerchief marked "M. C. L." (monogram); brown boots; and effects. His father, Judge Charles L. Long, sent letters to the White Star Line on April 23rd and 24th. Milton's body was forwarded to Springfield, Massachusetts, for burial April 30, care of J. H. Shepherd as per his father's instructions. Milton was Judge and Mrs. Charles Long's only child.

#292. Thomas F. McCaffry, first-class passenger, banker, age 46. Bald head, light moustache. Dress suit, brown overcoat, "T. C. Mc." on drawers, etc. Delivered in Halifax to E. E. Code, May 2nd, for forwarding to Montreal, Quebec, for burial. Thomas McCaffry was western superintendent with the Union Bank in Vancouver, British

LEFT: EDWARD A. KENT, BODY #258. RIGHT: MILTON C. LONG, BODY #126.

Columbia. He was travelling on holiday with a party of friends from Winnipeg, Manitoba.

#175. Timothy J. McCarthy, first-class passenger, stationery buyer for Jordan Marsh, age 51. Grey hair and moustache. Grey overcoat, black striped suit, purple knitted tie, prayer book, and effects. Delivered in Halifax to Mr. J. V. Finn, April 30th, for forwarding to Boston. As a stationery buyer for Jordan Marsh, he had made twenty-one trips across the Atlantic. He left a wife and five children, ages ten to twenty-two, in Dorchester, Massachusetts, to mourn his loss.

#225. John S. March, U. S. Mail Superintendent, 57 Emmet Street, New York, estimated age 45. Dark clothing, vest, blue pants, striped shirt. Gold watch and chain, fountain pen, diamond tie pen, gold ring with letter "M." Forwarded to Newark, New Jersey, May 3rd care of Smith & Smith undertakers for burial.

LEFT: FRANCIS D. MILLET, BODY #249. RIGHT:
DOCTOR W. E. MINAHAN, BODY #230.

#249. Francis David Millet, first-class passenger, Secretary of the American Academy, Rome, age 66. Grey hair. Light overcoat, black pants, grey jacket, evening dress. Gold watch and chain with "F. D. M." on watch, glasses, two gold studs, silver tablet bottle. Delivered in Halifax, May 1st, to Mr. Lovering Hill for forwarding to Boston, Massachusetts.

Francis Millet was an internationally known artist and had been director of decorations for the Chicago Exhibition. He was a drummer boy for the Union Army during the American Civil War and had been a war correspondent during the Spanish-American War. He was travelling with Major A. Butt. The trip had been Millet's suggestion to get Major Butt away from the political intrigue of the upcoming presidential election. (see Chapter 7, Archibald Butt)

#271. Jacob Christian Milling, second-class passenger, age 48. Dark beard, light hair, partly bald. Dark tweed suit, leather vest. Gold watch and chain, silver name plate, two pocket knives, comb, one cuff link, gold ring marked "AP 29 98," two pairs glasses, purse, toothpick, key, £26, 100 kroners, photos, railroad passes. Instructions from White Star New York office by wire, May 4th. Forwarded on May 6th to Boston for cremation. Ashes sent to Clausen, Copenhagen, Denmark.

#230. Doctor W. Edward Minahan, first-class passenger from Fond du Lac, Wisconsin, age 44 (if he had lived five more days he would have been 45). Grey hair. Black suit and overcoat. Pocketbook, papers, gold watch inscribed "Dr. W. E. Minahan," keys, knife, fountain pen, clinical thermometer, memo book, tie pin, diamond ring, gold cuff link, nickel watch, comb, check book, American Express, $380, one collar button, £16 10s. in gold, 14 shillings, nail clipper. Delivered in Halifax May 2nd, to his brother, Victor Minahan, for burial in Green Bay, Wisconsin. Doctor Minahan's wife and daughter survived the sinking.

#309. Sigurd H. Moen, third-class passenger embarked Southampton, age 25. Instructions from White Star New York office, May 10th. Coffin forwarded to New York, May 10th, for shipment to Norway by Scandinavian American Line. When this body reached its destination, the coffin was opened for viewing. Photographs taken at the viewing show the face of Sigurd looking very peaceful.

#43. Nicholas Nasser, second-class passenger, estimated age 32. Black hair, Italian type. Blue serge suit, white shirt with black spots, brown boots. Watch and chain, purse with £7, belt round waist with £160 in gold. Forwarded May 3rd, to J. J. Cronin, undertaker, Brooklyn, New York.

Nicholas was in fact not "Italian type" but a Syrian. He was with his new, fifteen-year-old wife on their way to Cleveland, Ohio. His wife survived the sinking.

#122. Arthur Webster Newell, first-class passenger, banker, age 58. Grey imperial and moustache. Black suit, white shirt, black boots, and effects. President of the Fourth National Bank of Boston.

He had been travelling in the Holy Land, Egypt, and Europe with his daughters. His body was forwarded to Boston, May 1st, according to wire from Mrs. Mary A. Newell. Burial in Cambridge, Massachusetts. His two daughters survived the sinking.

#263. Arthur S. Nicholson, first-class passenger, age 64. Grey hair and moustache. Light tweed suit, brown waistcoat, pearl scarf pin, "N" on book, gold watch and chain, gold pencil case, horseshoe cut diamond pin, glasses, gold cuff links, three gold studs, £9 in gold in pocketbook. Forwarded May 6th to F. E. Campbell, 214 West 23rd Street, New York. Buried Bronx, New York.

#234. Engelhart C. Ostby, first-class passenger, head of the jewellery manufacturer Ostby & Barton, age 64. Gold-filled teeth. Effects: gold watch and chain, knife, glasses, diary, two pocket books, and papers. Instructions in letter of H. W. Ostby, April 24th. His coffin was delivered in Halifax to David Sutherland for forwarding to Providence, Rhode Island, for burial.

Ostby and his daughter were returning from Egypt. He was still being reported as saved a week after the sinking. His daughter, who survived the sinking, had to ask the press to correct this mistake.

#166. Austin Partner, first-class passenger, stockbroker, estimated age 45. Blue suit. Cigar case, silver cigarette case marked "A. P.", cigar cutter, gold hunter watch, keys, gold links, 3 gold studs, 9s. 32d., $50 in gold, £3 in gold, £5 note, pocketbook with $71. Instructions from White Star New York office by wire, May 1st. Body forwarded to New York, May 7th, for shipment per S. S. *Minnehaha*, sailing May 11, for burial in Surrey, England. A stockbroker from Tolworth, Surbitan, England, Austin Partner was travelling to inspect Canadian business operations.

#207. Walter Chamberlain Porter, first-class passenger, manufacturer of shoes, age 46. Light moustache and hair. Green overcoat, dark suit, blue cardigan, blue silk pyjamas. Gold ring on right hand, gold with diamond on left, glasses in case, etc. Address found, 10 Lennox Street, Worcester, Massachusetts. Porter had prolonged his stay in England to travel on the *Titanic*. He left a wife and four children to mourn his loss. Delivered in Halifax to Mr. E. Sessions, April 30th, for forwarding to Worcester, Massachusetts, for burial. Instructions of widow.

#232. Sante Ringhini, manservant, estimated age 33. Dark hair, slight moustache. Black pants, grey overcoat, a ring marked "Sante." Ring insribed "R. S." left on finger. Mr. F. W. Wender

POSTAL CLERKS

There were five mail officers working the postal facilities on the *Titanic*. The two British men, John Jago Smith and James Bertram Williamson, were called sea post officers. There were three Americans working in the office. In charge was John S. March, United States mail superintendent of the *Titanic*. He was a widower who lived with his daughter, Miss Nellie March, at 59 Emmet Street, Newark, New Jersey. He had been crossing the ocean for nine years and was on the *Olympic* prior to starting on the *Titanic*. The other Americans were Oscar S. Woody, Washington, D. C., formerly of North Carolina, who was buried at sea, and William L. Gwynn of Asbury Park, New Jersey. The men were employees of their respective governments.

Contracts were awarded to shipping lines for the carrying of mails. The passengers and crew on the ship could also take advantage of the facilities. Letters left at Cherbourg, France, and Queenston, Ireland, give us a view of the first days of the voyage. Passengers were eager to use *Titanic* stationary in letters to friends and relatives. Crew members wanted to keep in touch with home. They wrote that letters were short as they did not have much paper. One crew member wrote on the back of a discarded menu. After the collision, water reached the mail storage area. All five men began the task of moving the registered mail up to higher decks to await a rescue ship. Their struggle was noted by surviving passengers who praised them for their devotion to their duty. The five men were lost in the sinking. The United States Postmaster General asked that the $2,000 maximum payment for death on duty be awarded to the families of the American men. It was estimated that 7 million pieces of mail were lost in the sinking. Of the 3,423 sacks of mail about 200 was registered mail. The post office issued orders regarding lost international mail orders:

Among the millions of pieces of mail matter carried on the lost steamship *Titanic* there were doubtless thousands of dollars worth of international money orders. It is the earnest desire of the department that postmasters give careful attention to the inquiries made and promptly report the facts to the third assistant postmaster general, division of money orders, to the end that every effort may be made to insure early payment to the intended beneficiaries.

escorted the body to New York May 11th for widow. The request came not from the widow but from Mrs. J. Stuart White of New York, as Sante was her manservant. Mrs. White and her maid had survived the sinking.

#7. Mrs. Charity L. Robins, third-class passenger, estimated age 60 (she was really age 47). Grey hair. Blue waterproof, black skirt and undershirt, white undervest and chemise, black lawn shoes and black stockings, set false upper teeth. One gold ring, one wedding ring, and one diamond ring; purse "A Robins"; second-class passenger ticket *Olympic*; gold watch and chain; two receipted accounts and excess luggage ticket, Plymouth, Great Western docks; £60 in five notes and other coins.

#119. Alexander A. Robins, third-class passenger, embarked from Southampton, age 49. Dark hair and moustache. Black overcoat, grey trousers and vest, blue vest, black boots. One gold watch, chain, and seal; one gold watch chain and locket; one silver watch; works of one Waltham watch; three knives; two pipes; one cigarette holder; cigar ditto; keys; gold ring marked "R"; hair comb; two pocket diaries; papers; Int. Mercantile Marine Co. Cheques $2,500; £41 in gold; 37s. 6d. in purse.

The bodies of Mr. and Mrs. Robins were forwarded May 4th to Yonkers, New York. Request of Mrs. Curtin, their daughter, 24 Garfield Street, Yonkers, New York. Mr. Robins was a contractor and a native of Wales. The Robins were travelling as third-class passengers, returning from a trip to Wales, but as can be seen from the money they carried, the couple were frugal, not poor. Mrs. Robins was carrying a second-class ticket for the *Olympic*, sister ship to the *Titanic*. This ticket shows how she travelled to England. It may be the couple felt that a cabin in third class on their return to the United States was sufficient.

#16. George Rosenshine, first-class passenger, age 46. Dark grey overcoat, black suit, black gloves, underclothing marked "G. R." and effects which included letter of credit and $430. Address found: 57 & 59 East Eleventh Street, New York. There was also a letter and affidavit of personal property for Mrs. G. M. Thorne of New York.

It seems Mr. Rosenshine was travelling as the husband of Mrs. Thorne while his own wife was in New York. His "friend" Mrs. Thorne survived the sinking. His body was delivered in Halifax to A. A. Rosenshine, for forwarding to New York. This victim was listed in newspaper reports as a retired member of the manufacturing company Rosenshine & Sons Company, New York. He retired on February 17, 1912, and had been travelling in Europe. His company imported ostrich feathers. Interestingly, newspaper reports noted that with all the lost cargo on *Titanic* there would be many claims on insurance and also mentioned that luckily there was not a large quantity of ostrich feathers onboard as these were very expensive.

#109. Alfred Rowe, first-class passenger, estimated age 50. Brown suit, grey suit pyjamas, "R. F." on singlet. Gold ring, £15 in bank notes. Address 6 Peterson Terrace, London, S.W. Forwarded May 4th from Halifax via *Empress of Britain* to Liverpool, England, for burial.

#9. Nihl Schedid, third-class passenger. When he embarked from Cherbourg he was listed as Daher Shedid. He was nineteen years old and was returning from Turkey. His description: "Dark hair. Scar under right side of chin. Grey mixture suit, handkerchief with blue border. Name found, Nahil Schedid (on health certificate); probably Southern French or Italian." Instructions from New York office by wire, May 2nd. Forwarded, May 4th, to Mrs. Schedid, Mt. Carmel, Pennsylvania.

ISIDOR STRAUS, BODY #96.

#96. Isidor Straus, first-class passenger, age 67. Grey hair and moustache. Front gold tooth (partly). Fur lined overcoat; grey trousers, coat, and vest; soft striped shirt; brown boots; black silk socks. Pocketbook, gold watch with platinum and pearl chain, gold pencil case, silver flask, silver salts bottle, £40 in notes, £4 2s. 3d in silver. The coroner's report listed the following information regarding Mr. Straus. Occupation: gentleman; cause of death: accidental drowning; length of illness: suddenly. Delivered in Halifax to Mr. Maurice Rothschild and forwarded May 1st to New York for burial in the Bronx. As per instructions of Mr. Percy S. Straus, New York. (See Chapter 4.)

#1. Walter van Billiard, third-class passenger, age 9. The recovery crew estimated his age as 10–12. Light hair. Overcoat, grey; one grey coat; one blue coat; grey woolen jersey; white shirt; grey knickers; black stockings; black boots. Purse containing few Danish coins and ring, two handkerchiefs marked "A." Later identified from effects.

#255. Austin van Billiard, third-class passenger, embarked from Southampton, age 35. Dark hair; red imperial and moustache. Grey suit, green flannel shirt, brown boots. Pipe, £3 5s. in purse, gold watch "J. B." on back, twelve loose diamonds, one pair cuff links. Austin van Billiard was originally from North Wales, Pennsylvania. He left to travel and work in Europe, met an English girl, and they married and had children. For a time the family lived in Africa and found work in diamond mining. Austin decided to return to the United States with his family. While stopping in England to visit her relations, Mrs. van Billiard decided to remain there with her two youngest children to recover her own health. So only the father and two boys were on the *Titanic*.

The first body found by the recovery ship *Mackay-Bennett* was later identified as nine-year-old Walter van Billiard. Nothing in his effects seems to have provided the means for identification other than the handkerchiefs marked with the letter "A." These could have belonged to his father. The Danish coins have led some to believe this boy might have been another child. The case could be made that the boy wanted some coin for his purse as little boys often do. Austin van Billiard was identified from his effects. The "J.

MR. W. VAN DER HOEF, BODY #245.

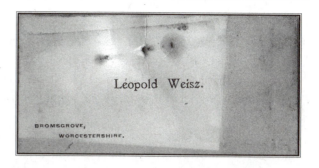

THE CALLING CARD OF LEOPOLD WEISZ, BODY #293, WITH HIS ADDRESS IN ENGLAND. THE CARD IS HELD IN THE COLLECTIONS OF THE NOVA SCOTIA ARCHIVES, HALIFAX.

B." on the back of his watch may have referred to Austin's own father, James. The twelve loose diamonds were probably part of Austin's plan to become a diamond merchant as announced in letters to his parents in Pennsylvania. The elder van Billiards had never met the two boys lost in the sinking.

James, age ten, was not found. The bodies of Austin and Walter were forwarded on May 4th to North Wales Depot, Pennsylvania. Austin's wife and two remaining children would move to North Wales the next year.

#245. Wyckoff van der Hoef, first-class passenger, age 61. Grey hair and beard, bald on top. Evening dress, "W. V." on drawers, black boots. Two false teeth (top), gold ring marked "L. E. N. to V. W.", gold watch and fob with gold medallion, five studs, gold links, keys, knife, glasses, $62 in case. His body was delivered from Halifax to Mr. D. C. Chauncey for burial in Brooklyn, New York. Wyckoff was secretary of the Williamsbury

Fire Insurance Co. He was a bachelor who lived in Brooklyn, New York.

#293. Leopold Weisz, second-class passenger, age 33, owner of a successful stone-carving business. Dark hair, fair moustache. Black coat, fur-lined Astrachan collar, grey suit, "W. L." on shirt. Key chain and keys; gun metal watch; cigarette case, two pocket books; bank book; gold watch; silver wrist watch; two cuff buttons; one gold ring; one pin; one gold chain; £56 in gold; one dollar and coins; £30 in notes; $26 in notes. When his clothes were checked it was found that he had $30,000 cash sewn into the lining of his coat. Instructions from White Star Line Montreal office by wire, April 30th. Forwarded to E. Armstrong & Co., Montreal for burial. His wife survived the sinking.

#169. Richard Fraser White, first-class passenger and a senior at Boudoin College, age 21. Very fair. Brown suit, white shoes. Keys, matchbox, gold watch, blood stone ring. Address found: The Pines, Brunswick, Maine.

Richard White was the son of cotton manufacturer Percival W. White, who was also lost. Richard's body was delivered to F. A. Smith, and forwarded, April 30th, to Boston, Massachusetts, for burial in Winchenden Springs. Instructions from his mother.

#131. Albert Wirz, third-class passenger, embarked from Southampton, age 26. Dark hair, fair moustache. Dark suit, woolen socks, buckle shoes. Travelling from Switzerland to Wisconsin. His body was forwarded, May 8th, to Mrs. T. M. Brown, Beloit, Wisconsin.

When the fifty-nine bodies were delivered to their destinations, the funeral services attracted large crowds. The largest single gathering of people was probably for Mr. Wallace Hartley, the bandmaster, who had the courage to play while the ship went down. Not only was his funeral a huge demonstration of public emotion for him but also for the other musicians. There were many musical tributes to these brave men around the world.

For many of the first-class gentlemen their passing was marked by minutes of silence or the closings of their business establishments on the day of the funeral. The largest of these tributes would have to be the five minutes of silence held for Charles M. Hays, president of the Grand Trunk Railway.

The fifty-nine sent home included thirty first-class passengers and one manservant; fourteen second-class passengers, the bandmaster, and a mail supervisor; eleven third-class passengers and one crew member. It had been announced that bodies would be transported free of charge. Victims from England and the continent were to be sent where the relatives designated. The relatives and friends that travelled to Halifax looked at all the bodies and claimed those they knew. There has always been the legend that photographs were taken of the bodies and that these were distributed to White Star offices around the world. No copies of these photographs have ever been found. The White Star Line did distribute a list of descriptions of the dead to White Star agents, and various White Star offices did receive instructions as to the disposition of bodies. The authorities eventually decided that time was running out for identifications to take place.

There remained 150 bodies to be interred in three Halifax cemeteries. The first body committed to a grave in Halifax was William Harrison, who was buried on May 1st, sixteen days after the sinking of the *Titanic*. Most requests for shipping of bodies were carried out, but in the case of William Harrison this was not done. His wife had requested his body be sent back to England for burial. But as he was the private secretary of the president of the White Star Line, it was thought it would be good to set an example and have him buried in Halifax. After all, there was no telling how many bodies would be found or what condition they would be found in. It could quickly become undignified to be sending bodies all over the world in various states of decomposition. It was also bad public relations that first-class passengers were being sent home for burial while the unionized crew members were not.

There were instructions from a few families to bury their loved ones in Halifax, but for the most part, burials were done because the bodies could not be kept any longer. The first mass burial on May 3rd was for the unidentified. Most were thought to be crew members or third-class passengers and there was little possibility that their families would be able to afford to travel to make an identification. Burials of the remaining unidentified and identified followed over a period of nineteen days. The last *Titanic* victim was buried in Halifax on June 6, 1912. Later on, instructions would be received from some families regarding the gravestones and what was to be inscribed on them. The temporary mortuary was closed after most bodies were buried with the remaining taken to a funeral home.

The White Star Line agent in Halifax received 245 canvas bags of effects from the medical examiner. These were delivered to the agent's office on Hollis Street by the chief of police. The clothing the deceased were wearing was not used for their burial as it was damaged from the salt water and often had to be cut off the body to allow for embalming. Many travellers carried valuables sewn into the lining of their clothes so the inspection in Halifax required tearing the material to make a thorough check. The authorities decided that all discarded clothing would be burned rather than being carted to the city dump. There was concern that the rumours of great wealth found in the clothing would cause an unseemly spectacle. There was also the possibility that publicity seekers would try to salvage the clothes.

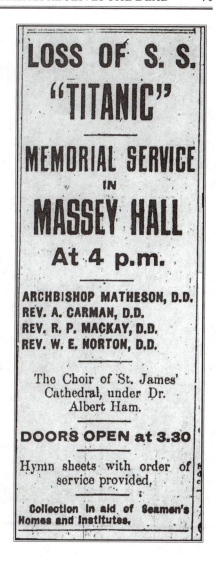

LOSS OF S. S. "TITANIC"

MEMORIAL SERVICE IN MASSEY HALL

At 4 p.m.

ARCHBISHOP MATHESON, D.D.
REV. A. CARMAN, D.D.
REV. R. P. MACKAY, D.D.
REV. W. E. NORTON, D.D.

The Choir of St. James' Cathedral, under Dr. Albert Ham.

DOORS OPEN at 3.30

Hymn sheets with order of service provided.

Collection in aid of Seamen's Homes and Institutes.

ADVERTISEMENT FOR ANGLICAN MEMORIAL SERVICE IN MASSEY HALL, TORONTO, ONTARIO.

THE EVANGELICAL ALLIANCE ORGANIZED A PROTESTANT SERVICE AT BRUNSWICK STREET METHODIST CHURCH, HALIFAX, ON FRIDAY, MAY 3RD, 1912.

As Halifax prepared to bury the dead, clergy in the city planned services for the churches. At a few funeral services, coffins of the *Titanic* victims were in the church. Due to the number of bodies found and given that identified victims had no family members in the city individual funerals were not practical. Most of the coffins were taken directly to the cemeteries from the temporary mortuary. As the religious affiliation of many of the victims was unknown, the Evangelical Alliance organized a Protestant service at Brunswick Street Methodist Church. It had a capacity for over 1,000 people and was packed for the service on Friday, May 3rd. In front of the pulpit was the flag of the United States of America and the flag of Great Britain and its Empire. Flowers for the service included those provided by Mrs. Hugh Rood of Seattle, Washington. Mrs. Rood had been on holiday in Europe with her husband, Hugh. Mrs. Rood decided to stay longer in England and cancelled her passage on the *Titanic*. Her husband continued on home and was in first class on the *Titanic*. There is no record of what he did during the last hours of his life. After the sinking, Mrs. Rood sent a message through her lawyer saying she had not sailed on the ship. (The lawyer informed the press and at the same time told them that he had lost a cousin, Mr. Edward Kent, in the sinking.)

Mrs. Rood had hoped that the recovery ship would have her husband's body. Like so many who came to Halifax, she was to leave with the disappointment that he was not found. At the very least, providing flowers for the services in Halifax was a way for Mrs. Rood to feel she had taken part in a final remembrance. Many of the families who lost loved ones on the *Titanic* could not afford to travel to Halifax even if a body was found. When one reviews the lists of the *Titanic* victims in three Halifax graveyards it is still possible to understand their feelings of loss.

RABBI JACOB FINEGOLD (CENTRE) AND WORKERS FRANK FITZGERALD (LEFT) AND FRED BISHOP (RIGHT), AFTER THE STONES HAD BEEN PLACED AT THE *TITANIC* VICTIMS PLOT IN THE HEBREW CEMETERY.

CHAPTER 4

BARON DE HIRSCH CEMETERY—10 VICTIMS

"Think of it! A few more boats, a few more planks of wood nailed together in a particular way at a trifling cost, and all those men and women whom the world can so ill afford to lose would be with us today."

—Lawrence Beesley, survivor, 1912.

In reports published in newspapers around the world in 1912, the Baron de Hirsch Cemetery was referred to simply as the Hebrew Cemetery. The Baron de Hirsch Hebrew Benevolent Society was founded in September 1890 by a small group of Jews in Halifax who recognized the need for a house of worship. The name was chosen to honour the Jewish philanthropist Baron Maurice de Hirsch of Munich. The urgency of having a Jewish cemetery became apparent when one of the founding members of the society, Morris Levy, died suddenly in March 1892. The body had to be taken by train to New York for burial. To prevent this from happening again, the society made arrangements to purchase a plot of land on what was then the outskirts of Halifax. The land was part of the Culvie Farm and was purchased from William A. Hendry in June 1893 for the sum of three hundred dollars. The land was prepared for use as a burial site and consecrated on Sunday, July 30, 1893, by Reverend Simon Schwartz.

The charter for the Baron de Hirsch Hebrew Benevolent Society was obtained in 1895 by a private members bill in the Nova Scotia Legislature. Thus the first Jewish Orthodox congregation in Canada east of Montreal was formally incorporated. Reverend Smolovitz was the first man engaged to cater to the religious and spiritual needs of the community of seventeen families. As a small community the Jews in Halifax could not afford a rabbi but were able to meet their needs with learned local men who could lead them. A former Baptist

"ENTREAT ME NOT TO LEAVE THEE."
"WHITHER THOU GOEST I WILL GO;
WHERE YOU DIEST, I WILL DIE AND THERE
I WILL BE BURIED."
—Book of Ruth, Old Testament.

ISIDOR AND IDA STRAUS

Body #96. Isidor Straus had travelled across the Atlantic many times. He had been a blockade runner for the South during the American Civil War. He became part owner of Macy's Department Store in New York and for a time served as a United States Congressman. He was a director of many New York banks. Isidor and his wife, Ida, age 63, with an estimated worth of fifty million dollars, were contributors to many Jewish charities and to public subscriptions. They were also campaigners for social reform.

Married in 1874, the couple was returning from a winter holiday at Cap Martin on the French Riviera. They mingled with other first-class passengers and exchanged wireless messages with family members who were passing on a ship bound for Europe.

It is well recorded that as the *Titanic* was sinking there were a number of opportunities for Mrs. Straus to board a lifeboat. A number of officers and first-class gentlemen urged her to go. She refused to leave her husband. Isidor was urged to take a seat on the basis of his age, but he declined to go while other men stayed. He wished his wife to go with the other women. Again she said no and was remembered as saying

"Where you go, I go." The couple did find a place for Mrs. Straus's maid, Miss Ellen Bird. Mrs. Straus gave her fur coat to the maid to keep her warm saying she no longer needed it. There is no recorded comment as to whether Mrs. Straus put her life jacket back on; her body was never found. Mr. Straus's manservant was also lost in the sinking.

Various survivors would claim they saw the couple stand back hand in hand, others said they sat in deck chairs, still others said they went back inside. Six days after the sinking Mr. Straus's body was found and was taken back to Halifax as Body #96. His body was taken by train to New York for burial.

MOURN ISIDOR STRAUS' LOSS.

Sixty Thousand Jews in Jerusalem Weep—Poor Fast Out of Respect to Memory.

[BY CABLE TO THE CHICAGO TRIBUNE.]

JERUSALEM, April 20.—When the news of the fate of Isidor Straus and his wife reached here 60,000 Jewish inhabitants went into mourning. The poor Jews who have been getting their food from a soup kitchen established by Isidor Straus resolved not to touch food that day and kept a solemn fast in memory of their benefactor.

At the service in Temple Beth-El, Fifth Avenue and 76 Street, New York, Rabbi Samuel Shulman stated "God Blessed him and gave him Ida Straus...they were two persons with one thought. Beloved and adored of each other in life, in death they were not separated."

The couple was praised for their devotion to each other in newspapers, churches, and at temple services. A public memorial service in New York had to be canceled as thousands of people wanted to gain admission to the building. Newspapers also reported that sixty thousand Jews wept in Jerusalem for the loss of this generous husband and wife. The employees of Macy's Department Store collected for a memorial that was erected in New York City. The Strauses' three children gave ten thousand dollars to Harvard University as a memorial to their parents.

Church building was purchased on the corner of Starr and Hurd Streets in downtown Halifax. To help the congregation pay for the property, contributions were made by non-Jewish residents of Halifax, confirming that the Jewish community was well established by 1912. They waited for the dead of *Titanic* to arrive in the city to ensure those of their faith received a proper burial.

Notable Jewish passengers on *Titanic* other than Isidor and Ida Straus (see sidebar) was multimillionaire Benjamin Guggenheim, who with his valet, is remembered as having changed into his finest evening clothes on the night of the disaster. Having travelled the world, Mr. Guggenheim realized there was no hope of rescue. He asked a crew member to tell his wife he had done his duty and went down as a gentlemen. There are a number of variations given of his final words, but what is known is that his body was never found. His wife was in New York; his female travelling companion survived the sinking.

On Tuesday, April 30, the *Mackay-Bennett* arrived in Halifax Harbour with 190 bodies on board and most were taken to the Mayflower Curling Rink, which was established as a temporary morgue. This gave the rabbi, Reverend M. Walter, only three days to examine the dead to determine how many were Jews and to prepare for burial before sundown on Friday—the beginning of the Sabbath. The rabbi saw that a number of Jewish male victims were being taken by train for burial in their hometowns. This left him with many unidentified, who he thought on inspection looked Jewish. His actions were reported in newspapers across North America, including the *Montreal Gazette*:

Saturday May 4, 1912. "Bodies Missing At Halifax Graveside, Jewish Rabbi Had Claimed Ten From Protestant Cemetery….A sensation was created at Fairview Cemetery…it was found that ten bodies were missing….the bodies had been taken away…by the Jewish Rabbi with some of the principal Hebrews of the city and had been deposited in the mortuary room of the Jewish cemetery. The Rabbi had been given nine bodies at the morgue after his report to the registrar of deaths that he found them to be Hebrews. The Rabbi said he had had no opportunity of examining the other bodies…which had been taken out previously to his investigation…He therefore repaired to the cemetery, opened the coffins…satisfied himself that they were the bodies of Hebrews and forth with…had them taken away to the Jewish burying ground… Nothing was said to any of the officials about his intention, but the Rabbi acted thus promptly, he says, because if he had waited the burial would have taken place and it would have been too late. What the authorities will do about the matter is still to be seen. The burial permits issued by the registrar of deaths distinctly states that the interment was to be in Fairview Cemetery…

Monday, May 6, 1912. "Were Not All Hebrews Bodies Taken To Cemetery, Returned To Morgue…A new development transpired regarding the bodies taken from the Fairview cemetery by Hebrews while awaiting interment. The Hebrews were required by the authorities to return them to the morgue. This was done. It now appears that the bodies taken were not all Hebrews. Since the order for internment some of them have been identified…The Attorney General, it is understood, will take steps to secure payment for damage to the coffins in the changes to which they have been subjected. The matter will come up again tomorrow."

Tuesday, May 7, 1912. "Were All Christian, Hebrews Relinquish Claims to Disputed Bodies, Halifax…It developed at the *Titanic* morgue that the ten bodies taken by Hebrews from the Fairview Cemetery… were all Christians, either Roman Catholic or Protestant. The White Star line had telegrams from friends regarding all of them and the fact that they were Christians was established to the satisfaction of the local Hebrew Association. The bodies will now be sent back to Fairview Cemetery."

Rabbi Walter had the best of intentions in trying to bury those who he thought were of his faith. He was working on a tight schedule as were the other people involved in caring for the dead. The rabbi would bury only ten men in the Hebrew Cemetery, of which eight have never been identified. Of the two identified men it was later learned that one man, Michel Navratil, was a Roman Catholic, the other, Frederick Wormald, was a member of the Church of England. The ten bodies were laid to rest in two rows of five, with identically sized gravestones.

FIRST ROW LEFT TO RIGHT:

#15. Michel Navratil, who was travelling under the name of Louis M. Hoffman. He was a second-class passenger, age 32. Black hair and moustache. Grey overcoat with green lining, brown suit. Pocketbook, one gold watch and chain, silver sovereign purse containing £6, receipt from Thomas. Cook & Co. for notes exchanged, ticket, pipe in case, revolver (loaded), coins, keys, etc., bill for Charing Cross Hotel, Room 126, April 1912. (See sidebar.)

#264. Unidentified male, probably steward, age about 30. Height: 5 feet, 9 1/2 inches; weight: 150 pounds. Dark hair. Wore steward's white coat, blue coat and trousers, uniform vest, blue jersey, black boots, drawers marked "H. Lyons."

cont. on p. 82

ORPHANS OF THE *TITANIC*

The man known as "Louis Hoffman" travelling in second class with two boys was Michel Navratil, a Catholic. He was a tailor by trade and had moved to Nice, France, where he met and married Marcelle Corretto, ten years his junior. Their first child was born in 1908 and named Michel, but was known by the nickname "Lolo." In 1910, their second child, Edmond, was born and nicknamed "Momon." The couple had marriage difficulties and separated. In April 1912, Michel decided to take the boys away. It was this decision that placed him—as Louis Hoffman, a name assumed from a friend—and the two boys on the maiden trip of the *Titanic* to New York. Once in New York he planned to disappear into an ever-growing country. He kept to himself on the ship but his two young sons were noticed. Younger passengers wanted to play with the "adorable" French boys.

The events of April 14, 1912, ended all Michel Navratil's plans. His last act of

cont. on p. 80

MICHEL NAVRATIL, BODY #15.

MICHEL NAVRATIL GRAVESTONE IN THE BARON DE HIRSCH CEMETERY, HALIFAX.

cont. from p. 79

life was to save his sons. With the help of another man he warmly dressed the boys and made his way to the lifeboats. There he placed three-year, ten–month-old "Lolo" and, witnesses said, dropped two-year-old "Momon" into the descending collapsible boat D, then stepped back to await his fate. The one question remains, what did Mr. Navratil intend to do with the loaded revolver found in his pocket? Was he expecting trouble from authorities as he made his way across Europe and to America? Or was he afraid of being robbed of the money he needed to carry out his plans?

When the boys arrived in New York on the *Carpathia*, the press dubbed them the unknown orphans of the *Titanic*. Their story was followed with great interest by the press.

The children only knew their nicknames and spoke French. They were looked after by a New York woman, first-class passenger Miss Margaret Hays, who shared the lifeboat with them. She called them "Louis and lump" because the younger boy was almost as large as the older one. The boys' photographs appeared in major newspapers around the world and were seen by their mother in Nice. She described her boys as "large" and that the younger one was "strong" for his age. Mrs. Navratil sailed on the SS *Oceanic* for New York to regain her sons. During that voyage the ship stopped on May 13 to recover a lifeboat drifting in the ocean. In the lifeboat were the three victims of the *Titanic* sinking that the crew of the *Oceanic* buried at sea. Of Mrs. Navratil's arrival in New York there is this story:

Ocean Waifs are in Mother's Arms. Mme. Navratil arrives in New York. Was met at the Depot by Miss Margaret Hayes. Lolo and Momon, the little waifs of the *Titanic* disaster, snatched from the sea and kept for a month in a big strange land, today were clasped in the arms of their mother, Mme. Marcelle Navratil, who arrived from France on the White Star liner, Oceanic. Hurrying down the gangplank after kindly customs officials had facilitated her landing, Mme. Navratil, who is an Italian woman, 24 years old, of remarkable beauty, rushed to Miss

Margaret Hays, the rescuer of the two little boys, who, with her father, was waiting on the pier. They took her in a cab to the Children's society rooms, and there she was reunited with her children.

The little boys, four and two years old, were thrust into one of the last lifeboats to leave the sinking *Titanic* by an excited Frenchman, who asked that they be cared for. A steward told him he could not enter the boat, and he said he did not want to, but must save his boys. Miss Hays was in the boat, and she at once took the children under her protection. Arriving in New York on the *Carpathia*, Miss Hays at first could learn nothing of the children's identity, and she planned to care for them.

THE NAVRATIL CHILDREN WERE DESCRIBED AS "TWO WAIFS OF THE SEA" BY THE NEWSPAPERS.

Then developed another chapter of the weird story of the disaster in the ice fields. The Frenchman's body was recovered and taken to Halifax, where it was found that he was booked on the passenger list under the name Hoffman. Cable messages to France brought the information that Mme. Navratil's husband, from whom she was separated, had kidnapped her children...He sometimes used the name Hoffman. Photographs of the boys were sent to Mme. Navratil in France and she identified them as her children....

—The *Spectator*, Hamilton, Ontario, May 17, 1912.

It was then that the full story of "Louis Hoffman" became known. Michel had often spoken of going to America to open a dress-making establishment. He took the children from her cousin's home where the children were staying pending divorce proceedings. A few days later she had received a letter from Austria informing her that he was taking the children back to his home country. This proved to be a false lead and she discovered he had gone to England. The next time she knew of the whereabouts of her children was when she saw the newspaper photographs.

The body of "Louis Hoffman" was picked up five days after the sinking. He was buried in the Hebrew Cemetery in Halifax, based on his assumed name and appearance. Despite

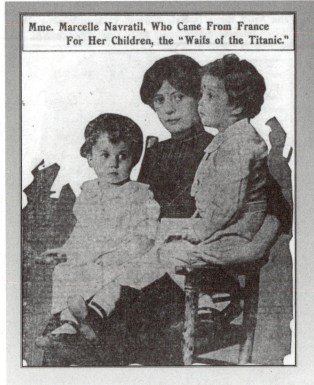

Mme. Marcelle Navratil, Who Came From France For Her Children, the "Waifs of the Titanic."

man was left in the Hebrew cemetery and his real name, Michel Navratil, was inscribed on the gravestone. The mother and the boys had free second-class passage on the SS *Oceanic* and made their way back to France. The younger of the boys, Edmond ("Momon"), later married and was an architect and builder. He served in the French Army during World War II, was captured, and sent to a prisoner of war camp in Germany. From there he escaped and returned to France. He died in 1953 at age forty-three. Mrs. Marcelle Navratil died in 1974. The older boy, Michel ("Lolo"), became a professor of philosophy, married, and fathered three children.

He finally visited Halifax in 1996 and had a Roman Catholic priest say a blessing at his father's grave. He said to those around him in the graveyard that "I heard the angels sing." The last known male *Titanic* survivor, Michel Navratil died in Montpellier, France, on January 30, 2001 at the age of ninety-two.

the new information discovered with his wife's arrival in New York, the body of this Catholic

cont. from p. 79

Effects included brass watch with "Evening Times" stamped on face, gold-rimmed spectacles, ship's key and tickets for second staterooms D 51 to D 89.

From the clothing and tickets it is likely this man was a steward. The "H. Lyons" on his drawers does not match any name among the stewards. There was a "W. H. Lyons," an able seaman, who survived the sinking but died from exposure and was buried from the rescue ship, *Carpathia*.

It would be difficult for a clothing mix-up such as this to take place onboard ship as stewards and able seamen would have separate quarters. It may be that the men lived in the same building in Southampton. Unfortunately no assignment list for stewards on *Titanic* exists. Surviving passengers were not asked for their cabin numbers or the names of their bedroom stewards.

#144. Frederick W. Wormald, first-class saloon steward, age 46. Dark hair and moustache. Steward's

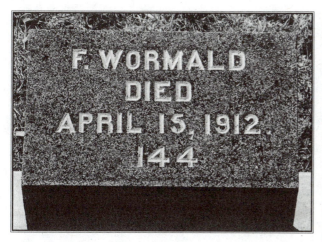

FREDERICK WORMALD GRAVESTONE IN THE BARON DE HIRSCH CEMETERY, HALIFAX.

uniform, white coat marked "A. Wormald," overcoat. Gold watch, keys, gold snake ring, gold chain and charm, sovereign purse, knife. First saloon No. 74. Address: 5 Testwood Road, Southampton. It was later discovered that Mr. Wormald was a member of the Church of England.

Wormald left a wife and five children to mourn his loss. His wife booked passage from England so the family could visit Frederick's grave in Halifax. On arrival in New York immigration officials turned the family away as they had no visible means of support. On returning to Southampton the family discovered they had been evicted from their home for non-payment of rent. Mr. Wormald's name appears on a memorial plaque to *Titanic* victims in his parish of Holy Trinity, Southampton.

#214. Unidentified male, age about 26. Height: 5 feet, 8 inches; weight: 165 pounds. Brown hair,

ADVERTISEMENT IN MONTREAL NEWSPAPERS FOR A BENEFIT PERFORMANCE FOR THE *TITANIC* FUND.

CHILDREN ON THE *TITANIC*:

"Oh Muddie, look at the beautiful North Pole with no Santa Claus on it." Douglas Spedden, age six, to his mother in lifeboat #3 on the morning of April 15, 1912. An only child, Douglas would die in 1915 as the result of being run down by an automobile.

Chicago Tribune, April 19: "Miss Georgette Madill saved. Miss Madill is 15 years of age and one of the great heiresses of St. Louis. A year ago she was awarded $7,500 a year 'pin money' by the Probate Court. She is the principal heir of George A. Madill, president of the Union Trust Company of St. Louis. She went to Europe last year."

Coming up with the final number of children on the *Titanic* is problematic. The generally accepted figure of fifty-three victims is based on the age of eleven as the cut-off age. Young boys were refused entry to the lifeboats based on the consideration of whether they were of working age. This age would have been very low in 1912, especially among the poorer classes. There are stories of mothers who would not leave their male children on the ship and so gave up their own chance for a seat in the lifeboats. Other mothers saw their families divided, with the boys staying with their fathers to face certain death. There were parents travelling with children who were in their late teens and early twenties. There were also teenage brides on the ship; one married woman was only fifteen years old. Would a girl who was married at that age be any less a child than a well-to-do heiress in first class?

In first class there was a three-year-old girl whose name appears in many lists of the dead as "Miss Allison." She has often been mistaken for a woman victim because of her title. But she was given this courtesy because of her station in life and not her age. Even some of the crew lost, while listed as the "brave men" of the *Titanic*, were only in their teens. By today's standards they would be considered children. The *Titanic* story will always have unanswered questions. The true number of "children" lost is one of them.

light eyebrows, clean shaven. He wore steward's badge No. 41. Nothing else to aid in identification. This man was probably a steward but this was not noted in the official record.

#278. Unidentified male, possibly a fireman, age about 21. Height: 5 feet, 6 1/2 inches; weight: 165 pounds. Sandy hair. Two large prominent front teeth. Wore dungaree coat and trousers, grey flannel drawers. No aids to identification.

2ND ROW LEFT TO RIGHT:

#78. Unidentified male, fireman probably on watch, age about 45. Height, 5 ft. 6 in.; weight, 170 lbs. Hair slightly grey, red moustache, long and red eyebrows. Wore dungaree coat and trousers, flannel singlet, no boots or socks. Tattoos: girl and anchor on right arm; sailor, "E. G.," and hands crossed over heart on left arm.

#248. Unidentified male, probably member of cook's department, age about 35. Height: 5 feet, 7 inches; weight: 155 pounds. Very black hair, brushed back from forehead; brown moustache. No upper teeth. Wore dungaree trousers and grey striped jacket. Nothing to aid in identification.

#136. Unidentified male, possibly a fireman, age about 38. Height: 5 feet, 8 inches; weight: 185 pounds. Black hair, close cut black moustache. Fine set of teeth, slightly discoloured. Shirt, pants, jumper, no boots. No aids to identification.

#291. Unidentified male, age about 33. Height: 5 feet, 6 inches; weight: 155 pounds. Sandy hair, thin sandy moustache. Very bad teeth, only four upper teeth. Wore two pairs pants, pyjamas, blue suit, dark overcoat, uniform with buttons on vest, blue striped woolen vest, wrist watch. No other aids to identification.

No guess was made as to whether this man was a passenger or crew. This man certainly dressed for warmth or was trying to save some of his clothes. It is unfortunate that none of the clothing contained any aids to identification.

#289. Unidentified male, probably a steward, age about 24. Height: 5 feet, 3 inches; weight: 140

DRAWING FROM STORY OF THE WRECK OF THE *TITANIC*, REPRESENTING THE WEALTHY AND THE POOR WOMEN WHO WAITED AT THE WHITE STAR OFFICES FOR NEWS OF THE SURVIVORS.

pounds. Black hair. Large front upper teeth. Wore steward's uniform, green raincoat, gold ring with green stone, corkscrew, ship's key, No. 37. Tattooed left arm: anchor, cross, and heart (all in one).

"Civilization
Mourns," the
Montreal Daily Star,
April 20, 1912.

CHAPTER 5

FAIRVIEW LAWN CEMETERY—121 VICTIMS

"Are you saved? Believe in the Lord Jesus Christ and you shall be saved!"

It was said that second-class passenger Reverend John Harper, age 39, a Baptist minister from Surrey,
England, swam among the dying asking this question. His body was never found and these words of
popular legend were used in religious pamphlets. His six-year-old daughter, Annie, survived.
Four other Protestant ministers went down with the ship: Reverend Robert Bateman from
Jacksonville, Florida; Rev Ernest Carter, who had led the Sunday evening hymn sing in second
class, and his wife, Lillian, from London, England; Reverend Charles Kirkland from Old
Town, Maine; and Reverend William Lahtinen
and his wife, Anna, from Minneapolis, Minnesota.
Only Reverend Bateman's body was found; it was
sent to Florida for burial.

Fairview Lawn Cemetery was established in 1893 as a non-denominational burial ground. A private company, Fairview Lawn Cemetery Limited, managed the grounds from 1894 until 1944. Unable to continue operating due to financial difficulties, the company handed over cemetery responsibilities to the City of Halifax. In 1912, the White Star Line commissioned land surveyor E. W. Christie to design the *Titanic* plot on what was then the northwest edge of opened gravesites. The curve of the line of the fourth row of gravestones creates the effect of the bow of a

MR. WILLIAM HARRISON'S (BODY #110) FUNERAL WAS HELD AT ALL SAINTS (ANGLICAN) CATHEDRAL, HALIFAX. HE WAS THE FIRST *TITANIC* VICTIM BURIED IN HALIFAX.

ship. Between the top of the first row and the top of the fourth row, a gap has been left that some suggest is to represent the gash that the iceberg had made in the side of the *Titanic*. Is this a coincidence or the deliberate design of the surveyor?

As yet there is no documentation uncovered that would support this being done for artistic purpose. Due to the large number of bodies to be buried, long trenches were dug to accommodate the coffins, which ended up side by side. There was no attempt to bury in numerical order or to separate passengers from crew members.

The last *Titanic* victim was buried here June 12, 1912, and by the end of the year gravestones were being placed. The White Star Line paid for one size of stone. If the family wanted a larger stone or an inscription, they had to pay for it. Fairview Lawn Cemetery is the only one of the three cemeteries that has different sized stones. It is also the only cemetery where the *Titanic* gravestones have more than the listing of name, date of death, and the assigned body number.

Row 1 Left to Right:

#212. Percy Deslands, saloon steward, age about 40, was originally listed as unknown male. Height: 5 feet, 6 1/2 inches; weight: 145 pounds. Dark hair, moustache very thin. Steward's uniform; effects: first class saloon steward's badge, No. 73; knife; corkscrews; empty purse. Address: 405 Portswood Road, Southampton.

#8. Vendla Maria Heininen, third-class passenger, age 23, was at first listed as an unidentified female. Height: 5 feet, 7 inches; weight: 160 pounds. Wore chemise marked "V. H." in red on front. Wore boots, size 8. Sum of 150 Finnish marks sewed in clothing. In 1991 a society interested in the *Titanic* victims used research of effects to identify Vendla as a woman travelling from Finland to find work in New York and had her name inscribed on her gravestone.

#281. Unidentified female, age about 35. Height 5 feet, 4 inches; weight: 175 pounds. Light brown hair. Large wart on index finger of left hand. Wore black coat, blue skirt, red jersey, green blouse, woolen singlet, grey underskirt, black boots and stockings. No other aids to identification.

No guess was made as to whether this lady was a passenger or one of the few stewardesses lost. In May 2001, this grave was opened to take samples for DNA testing. However, after eighty-nine years only the lid of the coffin was intact—the body had completely deteriorated. (See Chapter 7.)

#240. Unidentified male, age about 24. Auburn hair. Wore grey overcoat, blue serge suit, and white sweater. Effects included nickel or silver box purse for coins; silver Maltese Cross of Coronation of Edward VII, 1902, attached to watch chain; silver watch with three photos enclosed in back thereof, of two women and a boy with cap on, maker of watch, J. B. Yabsley, 72 Ludgate Hill, London; watch key attached to chain engraved "Panny," 2 Richmond Street, Brighton.

No guess was made as to whether this man was passenger or crew. In May 2001 this grave was opened to take samples for DNA testing. However, it was discovered that after eighty-nine years only the lid of the coffin was partially intact—the body had completely deteriorated. (see Chapter 7)

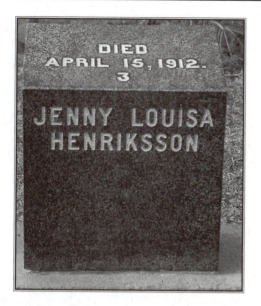

BODY #3. THE INITIALS ON HER CHEMISE HELPED TO IDENTIFY JENNY.

#329. Charles E. Smith, second-class bedroom steward, age 38. Address: Portsmouth Road, Woolston.

#3. Jenny Lovisa Henriksson, third-class passenger, age 28. Was originally listed as an unidentified female. Height: 5 feet, 6 inches; weight: 150 pounds. Brown hair. Wore chemise marked "J. H." in red. Grey cloth jacket, red jersey jacket, blue alpaca blouse, blue serge skirt, woolen combinations, black stockings, black boots, grey cholera belt. One grey suede glove.

Henriksson was heading for Iron Mountain, Michigan, with a cousin and friends. In 1991, a society interested in the *Titanic* victims identified Jenny from her effects and had her name engraved on her gravestone.

#137. Unidentified male, possibly a fireman, age about 50. Height: 5 feet, 9 inches; weight: 175 pounds. Dark brown hair, long reddish moustache. Tattooed right arm with British and American flags. No other aids to identification.

#303. Unidentified male, age about 25. Height: 5 feet, 3 inches; weight: 130 lbs. Sandy hair, clean shaven. Tattoos: right arm—clasped hands across heart, girl's bust with wreath beneath; left arm—life belt with "Good Hope" ship in centre.

This man carried no effects in his dungaree coat and pants. No guess was made as to his position on the ship.

#129. Unidentified male, probably a fireman, age about 25. Height: 5 feet, 9 inches; weight: 145 pounds. Brown hair, clean shaven. High forehead, good teeth, tattooed right arm: girl's bust with "Cissie" below. No other aids to identification.

#92. Unidentified male, probably a fireman, age about 36. Height: 5 feet, 6 1/2 inches; weight: 160 pounds. Light brown hair; red moustache rather long. Good set of coarse teeth. No aids to identification.

#296. Unidentified male, possibly a fireman, age about 25. Height: 5 feet, 2 1/2 inches; weight: 150 pounds. Sandy hair, short sandy moustache. Tattoos: right arm—ship on back of hand, girl and snake on arm; left arm—girl's bust. No other aids to identification.

#274. Leslie N. Bogie, second-class bedroom steward, age 46. Address: 100 Crescent, Eastleigh.

Leslie Bogie was originally listed as unknown with estimated age 25. Then the undertakers in Halifax did a more detailed report: "Height 5 ft. 10

1/2 in.; weight 180 lbs. Age about 45. Light brown hair, tinged with grey; light moustache. Wore blue suit; pyjamas and drawers marked 'L. B.' Effects included key with tag marked 'second staterooms F 1 to F 14'. No further aid to identification."

#220. Unidentified male, probably a fireman, age about 35. Height 5 feet, 8 inches; weight 160 pounds. Light hair, clean shaven. Large scroll, girl's head, and a heart tattooed on right arm. "Bird and Plant" with "Jamaica" under and "Rose" tattooed on left arm. Wore black coat, flannel singlet, and dungaree trousers.

#223. Unidentified male, probably a steward, age about 20. Height: 5 feet, 5 inches; weight: 145 pounds. Brown hair. Eye teeth extra long. Wore steward's uniform. Nothing to aid in identification.

#203. Unidentified male, probably a fireman, age about 45. Height: 5 feet, 9 inches; weight: 180 pounds. Brown hair and moustache. Wore blue serge suit, union cable belt, and striped flannel shirt. Tattooed right arm—snake around coconut palm, hand with bouquet of roses; left arm—woman's bust over wreath and dagger.

#94. Unidentified male, probably a fireman, age 45 to 48. Height: 5 feet, 9 inches; weight: 165 lbs. Auburn hair and moustache. Somewhat receding chin, hazel eyes, robust, bridge of nose somewhat sharp. No aids to identification.

Each undertaker had his own way of recording information. When age was guessed at, it was sometimes listed as estimated. Other undertakers would use the word "about" in front of the age; others would give a range, as in this case. The words "probably" and "possibly" were also

guesses as to employment on the ship or class of passenger.

#237. Unidentified male, age about 20. Height: 5 feet, 11 inches; weight: 145 pounds. Sandy hair, clean shaven. Shoulders very square. Wore dark grey suit, letters "F. H." on shirt. Effects included open face nickel watch and silver chain with matchbox attached; tortoise shell tobacco pouch; two little pictures: one of Town Hall, Portsmouth, and one of Portsmouth Coat of Arms.

No guess was made as to whether this man was a passenger or member of the crew.

#198. Unidentified male, possibly a fireman, age 35 to 40. Height 5 feet, 5 inches; weight: 175 pounds. Brown hair, sandy moustache. Nail on index finger, left hand, broken. No aids to identification.

#128. Unidentified male, probably steward, age about 24. Height 5 feet, 8 inches; weight 135 pounds. Sandy hair, clean shaven. False upper teeth. Ship's uniform, grey overcoat, pyjamas under. Silver watch and pocketbook. No marks on clothing. Carried open face watch made by Thomas Howard, 157 Kirkdale Road and 200 Rice Lane, Liverpool; stamped "German make." Had postcard with picture of four little girls on reverse side. Also one-inch by two-inch instantaneous snapshot of boy or young man.

#254. Unidentified male, probably a sailor, age about 45. Height: 6 feet; weight: 180 pounds. Sandy hair and moustache. Tattoos on right arm: two sailors holding English flag, man's head (cowboy), clasped hands and heart (true love), and flower. Tattooed on left arm: girl's bust, with

A. Maytum, chief butcher, Body #141.

English flag under, under which is girl; woman's bust and Union Jack; also woman in kilts. Wore dark mixture suit, grey flannel singlet. Nothing else to aid in identification.

It would seem all the tattoos led the recovery crew to believe this man was a sailor. He may have been travelling as a passenger or may have been one of the *Titanic* crew.

#229. Unidentified male, probably a fireman, age about 26. Height: 6 feet, weight: 170 pounds. Brown hair, light brown eyebrows. Upper teeth widely separated, high protruding forehead, clean shaven. Grey shirt and drawers. Nothing to aid in identification.

#141. Arthur William Maytum, chief butcher, age about 50. Was originally listed as "unknown male." Height: 5 feet, 3 1/2 inches; weight: 158 pounds. Sandy hair, very thin on top of head, very light moustache. Second and fourth upper teeth on left side missing. Wore striped coat, white coat marked "A. May," striped flannel shirt, blue trousers. Carried keys marked "Butcher." Effects include plain gold ring, six pence, picture postcard, addressed Mrs. Kempsey, 83 Antrim Place, Antrim Road, Belfast.

There was speculation that this body might be an engineering department mess steward. The recovery crew estimated his age as 30; the Halifax undertakers estimated age as 50. There is no record that there was a dispute over the identification in 1912 and the gravestone was inscribed A. Maytum. Mr. Maytum, of 12 Stafford Street, Southampton, left behind a wife and three children. The name on the white coat might have been embroidered to save time so the last name was shortened. A. May, the mess steward, would not have dressed as well as the chief butcher and they would not have known they would be on the same ship. They certainly would not have been in the same crew quarters.

#243. Edward T. Stone, second-class bedroom steward, age about 24. Was originally listed as unknown. The undertakers in Halifax described him as being 5 feet, 7 inches tall, with a weight of 145 pounds. Dark brown hair, clean shaven. Wore black cloth overcoat, steward's vest, and trousers marked "Stone," pyjamas. Effects included gold double-headed snake ring, ship's keys marked second staterooms E 99-107. Tattoos: on left arm—Chinese dragon; on right arm—American flag and clasped hands. The men on the recovery ship had described his estimated age as 30, his hair as dark, and his tattoo on left arm as a "Japanese" dragon. They also included in the effects two knives and a button hook, which were left off the second list as it was probably thought these items to be too ordinary to be recognized by anyone. Address: 91 Shirley Road, Southampton.

#213. Unidentified male, age about 30. Height: 5 feet, 8 inches; weight: 160 pounds. Light red hair,

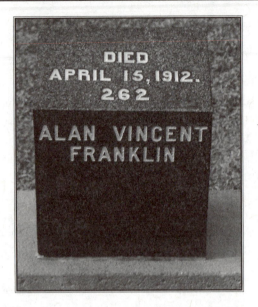

clean shaven. Freckles on face and forearms. Two prominent upper front teeth. Wore mixture suit, green shirt, no coat. Effects include keys, pocket scissors, knife, and about forty-five dollars in American and Canadian bills.

This person is one of the few to be listed as carrying Canadian money and the only unidentified person to be mentioned as having freckles. Many undertakers had come to Halifax to prepare the bodies for viewing. Each undertaker recorded features of the dead that they thought would lead to identification. No guess was made as to whether this man was a passenger or crew member.

#262. Alan Vincent Franklin, second-class saloon steward, age about 21. Address: Egremont, Newton Road, Southampton. This man was originally listed as unknown. Height: 5 feet, 7 inches; weight: 180 pounds. Hair very light, no moustache. Prominent nose, receding chin. Wore steward's coat, vest trousers, green overcoat with tag "Miller & Son, Southampton," shirt marked "A. Franklin." Effects included nickel watch stamped "Joe Meyer's Special" on face. Bunch of keys, including key of stateroom 38; wire spring belt with anchor buckle, stamped inside with a wreath surmounted by a crown; second class steward badge No. 9; small card printed "Mr. W. Harris" with "Jun" added in writing.

It is possible the card was from a passenger Alan Franklin had served before and June might be a return passage date. There was in fact a Mr. Walter Harris in second class from England; he also died in the sinking. Stewards often kept track of passengers so as to meet them on another voyage. In 1991 a society interested in *Titanic* victims identified Alan Franklin, age 29, and had his name inscribed on his gravestone. It does seem odd that with the name printed on the shirt that this man would not have been identified in 1912.

#265. Unidentified male, probably a steward, age about 28. Height 5 feet, 6 inches; weight: 165 pounds. Dark hair; light moustache. One lower tooth missing. Wore steward's uniform. Effects included silver watch; keys marked Nos. 7 and 9. Nothing to aid identification. The original list said he carried a book. Details of what type of book it was are not mentioned.

#233. Unidentified male, age 24 to 26. Height: 5 feet, 8 1/2 inches; weight: 140 pounds. Black hair, black eyebrows, looks like Japanese. Low forehead, prominent eyebrows, very large head. Grey pants, print shirt. No aids to identification.

Originally listed on the recovery vessel records as "probably Greek." No guess was made as to whether he was a passenger or member of the crew.

#216. Unidentified male, probably a steward, age about 35. Height: 5 feet, 6 inches; weight: 165 pounds. Red hair, thin moustache. Wore steward's uniform, truss, and black boots. Nothing to aid in identification.

#29. Unidentified male, probably one of the crew, age about 30. Height: 5 feet, 7 inches; weight: 150 pounds. Hair very fair, very faint tattoo mark on left forearm, looks as though attempt was made to have same obliterated. Blue jersey, blue trousers, grey flannel underwear, black boots, and socks. No marks on clothing, no effects. Nothing to aid in identification.

#257. Unidentified male, possibly an engineer, age about 38. Height: 5 feet, 7 inches; weight: 185 pounds. Dark brown hair, light eyebrows, clean shaven. Very large forehead. Wore boiler suit, double breasted uniform jacket, green striped flannel shirt. Nothing found to aid identification. While this man may never be known, the engineers on the *Titanic* won high praise for their work in keeping the lights on until a few minutes before the ship broke up.

#193. John Law Hume, "Jock," bandsman, first violinist, age 21. Was originally listed as unknown male. Height 5 feet, 9 inches; weight: 145 pounds. Light curly hair, clean shaven. Wore light rain coat, uniform jacket with green facing, and vest; purple muffler. Carried cigarette case, silver watch, knife with carved pearl handle, brass button marked "African Royal Mail," English lever watch. Address: 42 George Street,

Dumfries, Scotland. (See Chapter 6 for story of the musicians.)

#179. Unidentified male, possibly a fireman, age about 26. Height 5 feet, 10 inches; weight: 190 pounds. Very light hair, small light moustache. No aids to identification.

#217. O. W. Samuel, second-class saloon steward, age 41. Steward's uniform, gold stud, glasses, corkscrew, scissors, name on knife: O. W. Samuel.

#97. Reginald Fenton Butler, second-class passenger, age 25. He was travelling alone. The recovery crew estimated his age as 42. He was listed as wearing a black suit. Effects: gold watch and chain, silver cigarette case, gold matchbox, knife, fountain pen, memo book, Oddfellows' stud, letter case, and pocketbook with £60 2s. His family had the name of his hometown and his age inscribed on his gravestone. The inscription reads "Reginald Fenton Butler, of Southsea, England. Died April 15, 1912. Aged 25 yrs."

#270. Alfred A. Debble, first-class saloon steward, age 29. Wore black pants, white coat with buttons, green rain coat, no shirt. Identified from effects. Address: 81 Atherley Road, Southampton.

#110. William H. Harrison, first-class passenger, age 40. Green overcoat, dark suit, white shirt with blue stripe, purple socks. Fountain pen, cigarette holder, three memo books, pair cuff links, gold stud, bill book, pipe, keys, silver knife, £10 in gold, £1 18s. 8d. in bag, and £10 in notes.

The body number is not on the large gravestone. William Harrison was the private secretary to Mr. J. Bruce Ismay, president of the White Star Line. Mr. Harrison's wife had requested that his body be shipped home to England but her wishes were not followed. His was the first body buried at Fairview Lawn after a service on May 1st, at All Saints (Anglican) Cathedral, Tower Road. It is possible the White Star Line officials wanted to set an example so that every family did not request that bodies be shipped around the world. The job of private secretary was an important one. It is interesting to wonder if those memo books contain notes as dictated by Mr. Ismay on improvements to the *Titanic* or changes for the 3rd ship being built. On the large stone is inscribed that he was the "beloved husband of Ann Elizabeth Harrison." There are also the words "In the midst of life we are in death."

#4. Gosta Leonard Palsson? At first this boy was listed as:

"Male, estimated age two. Fair hair. Grey coat with fur on collar and cuffs; brown serge frock; petticoat; flannel garment; pink woolen singlet; brown shoes and stockings. No marks whatever. Probably third class."

IN 2001 BONE FRAGMENTS WERE TAKEN FOR DNA TESTING AT THIS GRAVESITE. THE ONLY ITEM FOUND IN THE GRAVE WAS A FUNERAL DECORATION THAT READ "OUR DEAR BABE." FOR EIGHTY-NINE YEARS THIS GRAVE WAS THOUGHT TO BE THAT OF GOSTA PALSSON, PICTURED AT LEFT.

This was the only body recovered that did not have a life jacket on. From the amount of clothing worn it is obvious that his mother had taken care to dress the boy for the cold. When the bodies were delivered to Halifax many people wanted to pay for the funeral of the "Unknown Child." The crew of the recovery ship wanted to do this so it is listed in the official reports as "Unknown child buried by crew of C. S. Mackay-Bennett, by special request." The funeral took place May 4 at Saint George's (Anglican) Church known locally because of its design as the "Round Church." Crowds attended and watched the small white coffin brought in for the service with the Reverend Kenneth Hind. People also lined the streets as the procession, including the seventy-five officers and crew of the *Mackay-Bennett*, moved off to the cemetery. Who was this unknown boy with blond hair? A review of the passenger list shows that only one child was lost in first class, a girl, Lorraine Allison. No young children were lost in second class. When the May 13th list for the disposition of bodies was prepared the unknown child was listed as "Baby? Paulson." A list prepared shortly after that recorded the boy as Leonard Paulsson. It was remembered by a survivor, August Wennerstrom, that the mother had handed this well-dressed boy to him as the ship was about to sink. The Swedish gentleman lost his grip on the boy as the ship went down. He also remembered that the mother had entertained her children with a mouth organ. Despite the identification offered and recorded, the stone was ordered and reads "Erected to the memory of an unknown child whose remains were recovered after the disaster to the '*Titanic*' April 15th 1912." The body number is not on the stone. The gravestone of the Unknown Child has come to represent the fifty-three young children who died when the *Titanic* sank; most of the bodies were never recovered.

Arthur Gordon McCrae,
Body #209.

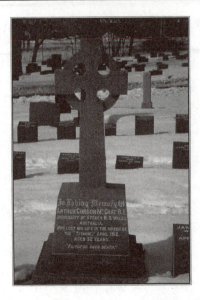

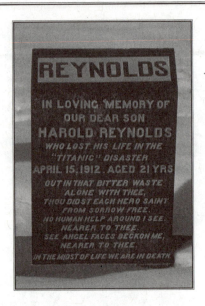

Row 2, from left to right:

#134. Unidentified male, possibly a steward, age about 25. Height 5 feet, 9 inches; weight: 150 pounds. Fair hair, brown moustache. Two prominent upper teeth. Jacket marked "A." No other aids to identification.

#209. Arthur Gordon McCrae, second-class passenger, age 32. The recovery crew originally estimated his age to be 45. Blue suit, white canvas shoes, flannel shirt. Diamond and emerald ring, gold links, two watches, key chain, keys, pencil case, foreign bills, letter case.

A wire was received from E. D. Upham, Denver, May 10 regarding disposition of the body. Arthur McCrae was travelling alone. He was an engineer from Australia who had worked in South Africa and Russia and was travelling to visit friends in Canada. His parents paid to replace the original small stone the White Star Line provided with a larger one in the shape of a Celtic cross. It is the largest stone of the 150 *Titanic* grave markers in Halifax. The body number is not on the stone. The inscription reads: "In loving memory of Arthur Gordon McCrae B. E. University of Sydney N.S. Wales who lost his life in the wreck of the *Titanic*, April 1912, aged 32 years. 'Faithful unto death.'"

#314. Jacob Alfred Wiklund, third-class passenger, age 18. He was from Finland and embarked from Southampton with his older brother, who was also lost. They were going to work on a farm in the Eastern Townships in Quebec.

#327. Harold Reynolds, third-class passenger, embarked from Southampton, age 21. He was travelling alone. A baker by trade, he was going to join a friend in Toronto. In his pocket was found the address of J. F. Cameron, 307 Yonge Street, Toronto. He was found clinging to a life preserver by the Canadian Department of Marine and Fisheries vessel *Montmagny*. His was one of four bodies picked up during the *Montmagny*'s search. His stone is larger than most others and has an inscription.

#330. James McGrady, first-class saloon steward, age 27. Was described as "bald head, dark hair; height 5 ft. 9 in.; weight 160 lbs. Body badly decomposed, about 50 years of age." Address: Platform Tavern, Southampton.

McGrady's body was picked up by the Bowring Brothers vessel, *Algerine*, and taken to St. John's then to Halifax on the *Florizel*. The twenty-three-year difference in the estimated age and his real age was probably due to the condition of the body. On June 12, 1912, he became the last *Titanic* victim to be buried in Halifax.

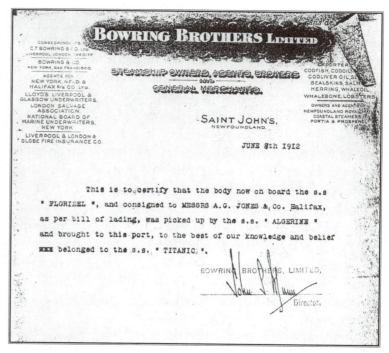

CORRESPONDENCE REGARDING THE LAST BODY BROUGHT TO HALIFAX; THE BODY WAS IDENTIFIED AS JAMES McGRADY, SALOON STEWARD. HE WAS THE LAST *TITANIC* VICTIM TO BE BURIED IN HALIFAX.

3RD ROW, FROM LEFT TO RIGHT:

#140. Achille Wallens, second-class passenger, age 28. Even though his last name is spelled the same on his ticket and all official reports the gravestone has it as "Waelens." Achille Wallens (his correct name) from Belgium is listed as having embarked Southampton as a third-class passenger. The ticket found on his body indicates he changed his class of accommodations. He may not have been satisfied with the people he had to share a cabin with. Changing cabins was not unusual on a ship, one simply went to the purser's office to pay to make the upgrade. (Hilda Slayter, a survivor, had changed her cabin because of the smell of fresh paint. She was moved from second class to first class as a courtesy to a refined young woman.)

#294. George Swane, second-class passenger, age 26. His estimated age was 18. Address found: 73 Little Cadogan Place, London SW. He was the chauffeur to Hudson Allison of Montreal. (See chapter 3.)

#11. John Shea, first-class saloon steward, age 39. Dark hair, light moustache. Address: 77 Portsmouth Road, Southampton.

#241. Unidentified male, probably a steward, estimated age 20. Black hair. Steward's uniform. Pocketbook, opera glasses, silver button hook. No marks on body or clothing.

This man was at first reported to be passenger Stephen W. Blackwell because of a calling card found on the body. In Halifax it was confirmed that it was not the body of Mr. Blackwell. While the list presented to the Public Archives of Nova Scotia in 1933 still has the wrong identification listed, the gravestone was not inscribed with a name. Mr. Blackwell was not a young steward but a forty-five-year-old first-class passenger from Trenton, New Jersey. He had been touring Europe in a motor car with his friend, Washington Roebling II, head of the Mercer Automobile Company. Roebling, the grandson of the man who built the Brooklyn Bridge, was also lost.

#163. F. Woodford, greaser, age 41. Carried two books, British Seafarer's Union No. 1802. Address found: 14 Clovelly Road, Southampton. His name was only inscribed in 1991.

#300. William Denton Cox, third-class steward, age 29. Fair hair and moustache. Address found: Denton Cox, 110 Shirley Road, Southampton.

William Denton Cox was one of the stewards that survivors remembered for his heroic efforts in guiding third-class passengers to the safety of the lifeboats. Despite his bravery, his gravestone is like most of the others and is inscribed with only his name, body number, and the date of death, April 15, 1912. His identity was known in 1912 but his gravestone was not inscribed until 1991 when a society interested in Titanic victims visited Halifax.

#83. William G. Dashwood, second-class saloon steward, age 19. Address: Sailor's Home, Southampton. Brown hair. Dark suit, steward's waistcoat with buttons, and white coat. Empty purse, road map, bank book, pawn tickets, army book, letter to Will Dashwood from mother: C. Dashwood, 31 Pallatt Road, E. Dulwich, England.

The coal strike had limited work opportunities and Will would have been happy to have secured a job on the Titanic. Many families depended on the wages earned to return to previous living standards, maybe even to regain items pawned in tough times.

#253. Frank Couch, able seaman, age 28. Tattoos: on left arm—eagle on branch with flower; on right arm—monument. Identified from effects.

This body was listed in the mortuary records twice. With the name W. Gough is the note that this person was not on the crew list. The note says to see the same body number with the name F. Couch. The name F. Couch of Port Issac, Cornwallis, is on the crew list. The gravestone was inscribed in 1991.

#290. Robert C. Bristow, third-class steward, age 31. Plain blue serge suit, steward's white

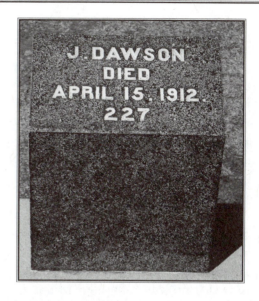

coat marked "Bristow," cholera belt, letter to R. C. Bristow, 49 West Ridge Road, Portswood, Southampton.

#161. George F. Bailey, second-class saloon steward, age 36. Rain coat over ship's uniform, second-class steward badge, No. 5. Address: Brooklands, Shepperton.

#227. Joseph Dawson, coal trimmer, age 23. Light brown hair and moustache. Dungaree coat and pants, grey shirt. Only item on body was dues book for N. S. & Fireman Union No. 35638, and the home address: 70 Briton Street, Southampton.

As with many of the workers on the *Titanic* not much is written of Joseph Dawson. He was Irish and living over a shop in Southampton. His job on the *Titanic* was to trim the piles of coal. He would take coal to the firemen or stokers. For all the men working in the engine department it was a dirty, hot, and smoky environment. Many of the bodies of the firemen found were not wearing much clothing, probably due to the fact they had come directly out of the engine rooms. The gravestone was inscribed "J. Dawson." For many

years his name was thought to be James instead of Joseph. With new research we have learned his correct first name.

The movie *Titanic*, released in 1997, brought notice to this coal trimmer buried in Halifax. Part of the movie production was based in Halifax. The lead male character has a similar name but a much different experience on the ship than Joseph Dawson, who came from the grimy tropical heat of the lower decks to the frigid temperatures of the Atlantic Ocean. In the buildup to the Academy Awards, the media focused on the graves in Halifax. The rumour started that there was a connection between the fictional character played by the actor Leonardo DiCaprio and the real Joseph Dawson. Quickly following the media were young teenage girls on spring break who wanted to place flowers and movie tickets on the J. Dawson grave, a practice that happily abated.

Now occasionally flowers are left but not always on the J. Dawson grave.

#251. William Carney, lift attendant, age 31. Address found: 11 Cairo Street, West Derby Road, Liverpool.

#242. Richard Hosgood, fireman, age 22. Black coat, grey singlet, and drawers. Address found: 19 Woodly Road, Southampton.

From the description of the bodies found it seems that many of the crew had no chance to dress. Richard Hosgood was one of the men that was hired at the last minute to replace crew who did not show up for work. His family would have said goodbye in hopes that he would get work that morning. He probably considered himself lucky to have the work.

#267. John Brown, fireman, age 25. Address found: 2 Russell Street, Southampton.

#205. Joseph Francis Akerman, assistant pantryman, age 25. Address: 25 Rochester Street, Southampton.

#221. Baptiste A. Allaria, assistant waiter in the À la Carte Restaurant, age 25. Address: 9 Orchard Place, Southampton.

#279. Unidentified male, possibly a steward, age about 45. Height: 5 feet, 9 inches; weight: 160 pounds. Sandy hair and moustache. Wore blue serge suit, white shirt, underclothes marked "BC." Tattooed on right arm with a monument (a cross in memory of my dear mother) and on left arm with "B. C." Clothing made by Wolf Bros., 50 East Street, Southampton.

With these clues to identity why could the name of this man not be found? There were a

LEFT: WILLIAM CARNEY, BODY #251. RIGHT: BAPTISTE ALLARIA, BODY #221.

number of firemen with these initials but only one person who might have passed as a steward. That was J. B. Crosbie, the Turkish bath attendant. Did he go by his middle name, which would account for the initials "B. C."? There is no record that this possibility was researched in 1912.

#228. Unidentified male, probably a fireman, age about 45. Height 6 feet, 1 inch; weight 195 pounds. Black hair; greyish moustache. Tattoos: cross and anchor on left arm; girl, "J. O. A.", cluster of roses, and scroll on right arm. Wore dungaree coat and trousers, grey shirt, drawers, body belt. No other aids to identification.

#139. Unidentified male, possibly an engineer, age about 30. Height 5 feet, 9 1/2 inches; weight: 180 pounds. Light brown hair; clean shaven. A gold tooth, 3rd from centre, on each side; scar on left small knuckle. Wore boiler suit and jacket. No other aids to identification.

#219. Unidentified male, estimated age 35. Dark and sallow. Brown overcoat, blue coat, fancy vest, striped shirt, black trousers, patent boots. Razor, comb, links, gold chain, sovereign purse, keys, chain, 10s. 8d., 40c.

There were some difficulties identifying this body. The disposition list has the name M. Rame, and a notation "was later identified from effects." It was also noted that this name was not on the crew list and that the man was probably a mail clerk. There were no sea post officers of that name in the mail room. Other lists have him as possibly a waiter from the restaurant. The waiter possibility was a guess based on the fancy vest and patent boots. The authorities decided to leave him as un-identified male crew and this is based on the other guesses. He could be a passenger.

#183. William McQuillan, fireman, age 26. Hardly any hair on head or face. Effects: shaving brush, soap, papers, National Fireman Union Book No. 932. Address found: 79 Sea View Street, Belfast, Ireland.

#273. Sidney Holloway, assistant clothes presser, age 20. Brown hair, smooth shaven. Ship's uniform, no vest or shirt, pyjama suit, false upper teeth. Address found: 60 Hartington Road, Southampton.

The recovery ship crew had this man listed as "probably a junior officer." Even a junior officer's uniform should have had some marking that set it apart from other crew. Was his uniform just a well kept one, or was the uniform one he had pressed and simply grabbed to put on over his pyjama suit? In Halifax, the undertakers worked with the White Star Line crew list and identified Sidney Holloway.

#138. Alfred J. Fellowes, assistant boots, age 30. This man, whose job it was to polish the shoes

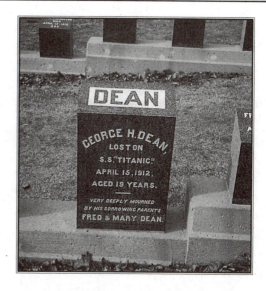

and boots of the passengers, was identified on the recovery ship *Mackay-Bennett* from his effects. Address: 51 Bridge Road, Southampton.

#252. George H. Dean, assistant second-class steward, age 19. Blue suit. Keys and second-class steward's badge No. 35. His family paid for a bigger stone. Body number is not on stone. Address: King Edward Avenue, London.

#222. Frank Goree, greaser, age 28. Address: 5 Belvedere Terrace, Southampton.

#276. Ernest E. Gradidge, fireman, age 32. Identified from effects. Address found: Redcliffe Road, Southampton.

#246. Robert Arthur Wareham, first-class bedroom steward, age 36. Identified from effects. Address: 46 Park Road, Southampton.

First-class passenger Edith Russell asked Robert Wareham if he should take her trunk keys to clear customs when the sinking ship was towed to a port. She remembered he told her to say good-bye to her things. In the British movie *A Night to Remember* this lady is portrayed as returning to her cabin and passing by her jewel case to pick up her toy mascot. In reality Edith recalled that her steward offered to fetch it for her. The toy pig played music when the tail was wound. This toy he retrieved was used by Edith to entertain children in her lifeboat while waiting for rescue. Edith always considered it her good luck charm. The luck did not extend to her steward, Robert Wareham.

#204. C. Ingram, coal trimmer, age 21. Union book 910. Address found: 18 Lower York Street, Southampton.

#211. George LeFebvre, first-class saloon steward, age 32. Address found: 17 Springfield Road, West Ham.

#235. Thomas Ferguson Baxter, linen keeper, age 48. Address: 81 Atherley Road, Southampton. The official disposition of bodies list prepared in 1912 and presented to the Public Archives of Nova Scotia in 1933 has T. F. Baxter listed as buried at Mount Olivet Catholic Cemetery, which is incorrect. There is nothing in the list of effects to identify him as Roman Catholic. The grave is at Fairview Lawn Cemetery.

#287. Robert Douglas Norman, second-class passenger, engineer, age 28. Fair hair, high forehead. Dark trousers, vest, no coat, green striped flannel shirt, no boots. Gold watch and chain, sovereign purse containing £5, £4.8s, and other coins, pocket knife, diary.

An engineer from Scotland, Robert was on his way to Vancouver, British Columbia. He

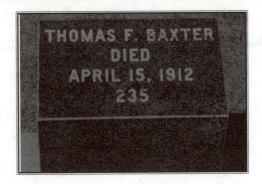

played the piano on April 14 for the Sunday evening hymn sing in the second-class dining saloon. He was last seen on deck with Doctor Alfred Pain of Hamilton, Ontario. The doctor was also lost but his body was not found.

4TH ROW, LEFT TO RIGHT:

#313. Luigi Gatti, manager of À la Carte (Ritz) Restaurant on the *Titanic*, age 36. He was seen on the boat deck in top hat with a grip (small bag) in hand, travel blanket over his arm, quietly waiting for rescue. Inside his coat he carried a small teddy bear his young son, Vittorio, had given him for good luck. Luigi Gatti had run fashionable restaurants in London and moved to Southampton to take over the concessions on the White Star's *Olympic* and *Titanic*. He had a house he called "Montalto" on Harborough Road in Southampton. The restaurant and café he ran had later hours than the first-class dining saloon and may have been a more appealing place to socialize. Passengers could receive a rebate from the purser's office on the meals that they did not take in the ship's dining saloon if they chose to pay to eat in the restaurant or café. Many of the wait staff Luigi hired were cousins of his or had worked in the London restaurants. Many of these men died in the sinking and some are buried in Halifax. In 1920, the "unsinkable" Margaret Brown of Denver, Colorado, made an unexpected stop in Halifax when the ship she was sailing on had to put in for repairs. She and her two nieces made 150 wreaths, one for each of the *Titanic* graves in the three cemeteries. "Luigi Gatti" may have been a name she recognized; he would have greeted his patrons on those too few happy days on the *Titanic*.

#32. Simon S. Sather, third-class passenger, embarked from Southampton, age 44. The only physical characteristic noted was "amputation of right foot."

#37. Malkolm Joachim Johnsson, third-class passenger, embarked from Southampton, age 33. Striped trousers, blue coat and vest, striped shirt, black boots. Gold watch and chain, gold tie pin, diamond set, purse, diamond solitaire ring, cheque for $1,200.00, two $20 pieces, $1.50 silver, $165.00 in notes, 6 pence, halfpenny, and odd coins.

The amount of money this man carried illustrates that being in third class did not mean all passengers were poor immigrants. Many of the passengers were travelling with money to buy or open a business. The people lost in the sinking often took with them all the wealth the family possessed.

#250. J. Hutchinson, assistant vegetable cook, age 29. Address: 91 Woodcroft Road, Liverpool.

HENRY P. HODGES, BODY #149.

#149. Henry Price Hodges, second-class passenger, age 50. He was a music store owner in Southampton and left a wife and eight children at home to mourn his loss.

#143. Jacob Alfred Johanssen, third-class passenger, age 34. Carried $264 in notes. From Finland, he was listed as Jakob Johnson when he embarked from Southampton.

#17. John Henry Chapman, second-class passenger, age 35. Effects included: lady's handbag, gold watch, chain and locket, gold watch, chain, and badge, £63 10s. in gold, letter, baggage receipt, baggage insurance, keys, tie clip, pipe, nail cleaner, marriage certificate. From St. Noets, Cornwall, England. His wife was also lost. It would seem from his effects that his wife gave him her handbag to carry.

#260. Albert Karvin Andersen, third-class passenger, embarked from Southampton, age 32. At first, Albert was unidentified as he carried three

ERNEST KING, BODY #321.

third-class tickets. The names on the tickets were: Albert Kaivin Anderson, Joham Martin Holten, and Henry Margive Olsen. The recovery crew added to their notes that the body was "probably Anderson by number of papers and pocketbook." The note on the report of disposition of bodies noted that Mr. Anderson "was later identified from effects." The three men were from Norway and all were lost in the sinking.

#304. Maurpre der Zakarian, third-class passenger, embarked from Cherbourg, age 26. Dark hair and slight moustache. Blue suit, striped shirt, brown pants, three shirts. Eighty francs in gold, $12.50 in gold in purse, empty purse. He was a Christian Armenian who, with other young men, had left Turkish-occupied Armenia to avoid persecution due to his religious beliefs. The "der" in his name signified that there was a priest in the family. Buried in Halifax at the request of his brother.

#321. Ernest Waldron King, assistant purser's clerk, age 28. Address: Currin Rectory, Clones, Ireland. His stone carries the inscription "Nothing in my hand I bring, simply to thy Cross I cling."

#323. Thomas A. Mullin, third-class saloon steward, age 30. Address: 12 Onslow Road, Southampton.

#201. Alphozo Meo Martino, third-class passenger, embarked from Southampton, age 48. Shown on embarkation list as Alphonso Meo, closer examination of effects indicated his name was Alphonse Meo Martino, from Bouremouth, England.

#308. Unidentified male, age about 50. Height: 5 feet, 8 inches; weight: 180 pounds. Dark hair, partly bald, sandy moustache. Handkerchief marked "A. H. F." No other aids to identification.

#315. Henry Wittman, first-class bedroom steward, age 34. Address: 12 Richville Road, Southampton.

LEFT: A. STANBROOK, BODY #315. RIGHT: ERNEST S. FREEMAN, BODY #239.

#316. Augustus Stanbrook, fireman, age 30. Address: 36 York Street, Southampton.

#319. Arthur Albert Howell, first-class saloon steward, age 31. Address: 12 Cliff Road, Itchen.

#165. Johan Henrik Kvillner, second-class passenger, age 31. Travelling from Sweden to New Jersey.

#239. Ernest Edward Samuel Freeman, chief deck steward, age 43. Dark hair, fair moustache.

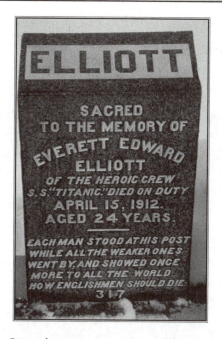

Blue suit, light overcoat, pyjamas. (At least twenty-three of the recovered bodies of men were wearing pyjamas under other clothing.) Address: 5 Hanley Road, Southampton.

Ernest Freeman is sometimes incorrectly listed as J. Bruce Ismay's private secretary. This may be because Ernest Freeman's stone was paid for by J. Bruce Ismay, president of White Star Line, who survived the sinking. At the base of the stone has been inscribed: "erected by J. Bruce Ismay, to commemorate a long and faithful service."

#261. Thomas Storey, third-class passenger, embarked from Southampton, age 51. Travelling alone from Liverpool, England. Southampton newspaper memorial placed by friends: Storey, Tom, late of SS *St. Paul*. No relatives but a good-hearted old pal. Liverpool papers copy.

#320. James Edward Cartwright, first-class saloon steward, age 32. Address: 77 Gossett Street, London.

#317. Everett Edward Elliott, coal trimmer, age 24. Address: 11 Wilmington Street, London. Body

THE FATE OF THE PALSSON FAMILY

The front pages of newspapers were devoted to the stories of the wealthy who were on the *Titanic*. Society photographs were published with descriptions of the jewellery that was lost. Short stories of the third-class passengers lost were sometimes found on the last pages of the paper. The Palsson family was one of those stories. Mr. Palsson's first name was "Nils" but he may have found it easier to use "Neil" in Chicago. The letter found in the purse of Alma has his name as Neil Paulsson, with the address as 94 Townsend Street, Chicago. The newspaper story gives his address as 754 Townsend Street. He may have moved since last writing his wife so that there would be room for her and the children. He probably bought household items to be ready for their arrival. The newspaper story read:

LOSES HIS FAMILY OF FIVE Nels Paulson Collapses in Grief at White Star Office. The tragedy of the *Titanic* reached more people in Chicago yesterday. When the conflicting stories of the last few days had been simmered down to facts it was discovered that at least seven more passengers who went down with the great boat either were bound for this city or had relatives here. In the local offices of the White Star line there was no display of wealth. Those who called to receive the news

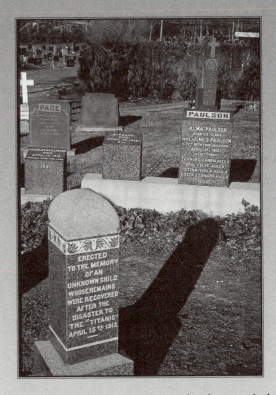

that their loved ones were dead visited the third class department of the company. Nels Paulson, 754 Townsend Street, whose wife and four children were on the *Titanic*, was informed that none of the members of his family had been rescued. Paulson looked pale and ill when he leaned hungry eyed over the desk and asked in broken English if his wife or children had been
accounted for. Chief Clerk Ivar Holmstrom scanned the list of third class passengers saved. He failed to find there any of the names enumerated by Paulson. "Perhaps they did not

sail," he suggested hopefully. Then he looked over the list of those who shipped third class on the *Titanic* at Queenstown. The process of elimination was now complete. "Your family was on the boat, but none of them are accounted for," said Clerk Holmstrom. The man on the other side of the counter was assisted to a seat. His face and hands were bathed in cold water before he became fully conscious. He was finally assisted to the street by Gust Johnson, a friend who arrived with him. Paulson's grief was the most acute of any who visited the offices of the White Star but his loss was the greatest. His whole family had been wiped out.

—*Chicago Daily Tribune*, April 20, 1912

number is not on stone; there is an inscription: "Each man stood at his post while all the weaker ones went by and showed once more to all the world how Englishmen should die." There had been many stories in the newspapers that crewmen had survived while women and children died in the sinking. Everett's family wanted the passing reader to know that he had died heroically.

#311. Italo Donati, assistant waiter, restaurant, age 19. Address: Tottenham Court Road, London. Like many of the restaurant waiters he came from London to work for Mr. Luigi Gatti (#313). A number of the restaurant staff were relatives of Mr. Gatti and they had worked in his London restaurants.

#226. Thomas Moore Teuton, second-class saloon steward, age 39. Light hair and moustache. Tattoos: on left arm—Japanese woman; on right arm—snake. He wore a steward's coat. Effects: army discharge book and papers, corkscrew, razor, keys, knife, brush, soap. The discharge book led the recovery crew to make the note, "probably old soldier." Address found: 98 N. E. Road, Scholing, Southampton.

#285. Gustav Joel Johansson, third-class passenger, embarked from Southampton, 33. Dark tweed suit, no shirt, grey drawers, black overcoat. From Sweden heading for North Dakota.

#305. Hans Christensen Givard, second-class passenger, age 30. Very fair hair and moustache. Dark brown striped suit, white shirt marked "D. M.," pocketbook with $55 in bills.

#187. Thomas James Everett, third-class passenger, embarked from Southampton, age 36. Black suit, red and white cholera belt, tobacco box, etc.

#284. Frederick C. Sawyer, third-class passenger, embarked from Southampton, age 23. Address found: Malshanger Cottage, Near Basingstoke, Hunts, England. Fred was travelling to Michigan.

#280. F. Reeves, fireman, age 31. Address found: 22 Cable Street, Northam Local, Southampton.

#231. Frederick Roberts, third butcher, age 36. Address found: Dawson Cottages, Reading Road, Farnborough Hants, England.

#272. J. White, glory hole mess steward, estimated age 32. Address: 41 Thackeray Road,

Southampton. The glory hole was the access area where the crew lived. Some officers referred to it as Scotland Road.

#192. David Matherson, able seaman, age 30. Blue serge suit, ship's jersey, and black boots. Tattoos included "D. Matherson" over cross. Address: 20 Richmond Street, Southampton.

#238. Alfred King, lift attendant, age 19. Steward's jacket marked "Alfred King." Address: 132 Mile Street, Gateshead-on-Tyne.

#218. Herbert Cave, first-class saloon steward, age 39. Fair hair and moustache. Black overcoat, steward's

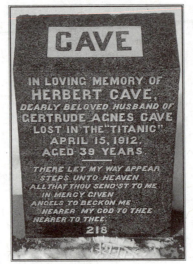
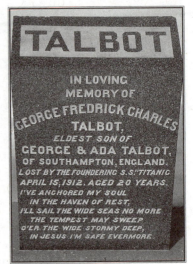

uniform and white coat, black boots, flannel shirt, cholera belt marked "H. C.", 5s. 6d., keys, corkscrew. First Class Steward Badge No. 27. Address: 17 Shirley Park Road,, London. Herbert Cave's body number is not on his gravestone but there is an inscription paid for by his wife.

Bodies number 3, 187, 218, 247, and 290 are all listed as wearing a cholera belt, a belt made of flannel to warm the intestines. It was an old-fashioned remedy to prevent catching disease or getting dysentery. They were usually worn when going to a hot climate, not when crossing the North Atlantic in winter. These people may have felt the hot conditions of a ship carrying immigrants was enough reason to wear these belts.

#191. Robert J. Davis, second saloon steward, age 26. Identified from effects. Address: 12 The Polygon Road, Southampton.

#34. Harry Wellesley Ashe, glory hole mess steward, age 32. Address found: 15 Wysdale Road, Aintree, Liverpool.

#282. Edward J. W. Rogers, assistant storekeeper, kitchen, age 32. Dark complexion, bandage on left leg. Address: 120 Oxford Avenue, Southampton.

#145. Henry Allen, fireman, age 32. Blue coat and vest, striped trousers, dungaree trousers, grey trousers. Name in discharge book. Address: 3 French Street, Southampton.

#150. George Frederick Charles Talbot, third-class steward, age 20. Address found: 4 Alpha Villas, Lemon Road, Shirley, Southampton. Body number not on stone. There is an inscription.

#10. Robert Henry Butt, first-class saloon steward, age 22. Fair hair. Ships uniform waistcoat, blue trousers, spring sided shoes. Address found: 6 Cawte Road, Freemantle, Southampton. There is a note on the *Mackay-Bennett* recovery list to see "Body #77." This referred to a burial at sea, body #77, W. Butt, fireman, estimated age 30. He was found with the same Cawte Road, Southampton, address. These men were brothers, however no note is made to that effect. Their last name was sent to New York through wireless messages from the recovery ship *Mackay-Bennett*. These messages caused a great stir in the press as it was thought the name referred to Major Archibald Butt, a first-class passenger and military aide to President Taft. The body of Major Butt was never found. (see Chapter 7)

#268. Frederick C. Marsh, fireman, estimated age 55, actually 39. Black hair and moustache, grey beard. British Seaman's Union No. 601. Address found: 24 Asenpart Street, Southampton.

#247. Arthur White, third-class assistant barber, age 37. Identified from effects. Address: 36 Purbrook Road, Portsmouth. His date of birth, "March, 11, 1875," is inscribed on the gravestone.

#195. Charles Shillabeer, coal trimmer, age 20. Union book 995. Address found: 21 Nelson Road, Southampton. His gravestone has the inscription: "Forever with the Lord." Left parents, brothers, and a sister.

#301. E. Poggi, waiter, restaurant, age 26. Black curly hair. Fawn rain coat, black suit, black patent shoes, vest, no shirt, drawers marked "P." Keys, corkscrew, comb, 17s. 2 1/2 d. Address: Bowling Green House, Southampton.

#206. Alma Cornelia Palsson (Paulson on stone), third-class passenger, housewife, age 29. Fair hair. Brown coat, green cardigan, dark skirt, brown skirt under, boots, no stockings. Wedding ring, brass keeper, mouth organ, purse and two coins, a letter, 65 kroner, letter from husband Neil Paulsson, 94 Townsend Street, Chicago. Third class ticket no. 349909 (five tickets).

LEFT: E. POGGI, BODY #301. RIGHT: ALMA CORNELIA PALSSON, BODY #206.

A survivor with a Halifax connection

Hilda Slayter was from Halifax, Nova Scotia, and the daughter of a local doctor. She lived in Europe for nine years, studying music in Italy. Her talent was not enough to establish a career and at age 27, she was returning to Canada to marry the son of an English aristocrat. She had filled her trunks with a trousseau gathered from fashionable shops and boarded the *Titanic* in second class. However her cabin smelled of fresh paint and she was relocated to a first class cabin. She survived the sinking and told her story to the newspapers on arriving in New York. Hilda was articulate and more readily available to newsmen as many first class passengers were rushed to private train cars, hotels, or home. While newspapers often misspelled her last name by leaving out the "y," Hilda did provide witness to the conduct of the orchestra and to John Jacob Astor. The *New York Herald* was one of the newspapers that carried her comments:

> Of all the heroes who went to their deaths when the *Titanic* dived to its ocean grave, none, in the opinion of Miss Hilda Slayter, a passenger in the last boat put off, deserved greater credit than the members of the vessel's orchestra. According to Miss Slayter, the orchestra played until the last. When the vessel took its final plunge the strains of a lively air mingled gruesomely with the cries of those who realized they were face to face with death. She added: "There were many touching scenes as the boat put off. I saw Colonel John Jacob Astor hand his wife into a boat tenderly and then ask an officer whether he might go. When permission was refused he stepped back and coolly took out his cigarette case. 'Goodbye,' he called gaily as he lighted a cigarette and leaned over the rail. 'I will join you later.'
>
> "Another man, a Frenchman, I think, approached one of the boats about to be lowered. He had with him two little beautiful boys. An officer waved him back sternly, but the man pleaded with him to take the boys for their mother waited in New York and the boys were taken aboard."

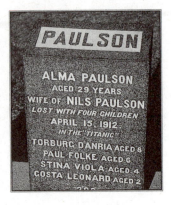

The gravestone of Alma Palsson. Her stone also records the names of her four children. The Swedish community in Chicago gave support to the father.

Listed as Alma Paulsson when she embarked from Southampton, this housewife had tickets for herself and her four children. Her husband had emigrated to Chicago in 1910 and was finally able to afford to send for his family. On the trip Alma used her mouth organ to entertain her children. She was remembered as having played music to calm her children while waiting for the rescue that never came. Her last name is on the stone as it was on the coroner's list. The stone reads "ALMA PAULSON aged 29 years, wife of NILS PAULSON lost with four children April 15, 1912 in the '*Titanic*' TORBURG DANRIA aged 8, PAUL FOLKE aged 6, STINA VIOLA aged 4, GOSTA LEONARD aged 2." At the bottom of the stone is the number 206, assigned to record her body. Her sons and her daughter were never found.

#186. Ernest Price, restaurant barman, estimated age 26 (some sources list him as 17). Address found: 93 Grove Road, Holloway, N. London.

#2. J. W. Marriott, first-class assistant pantryman, estimated age 24. Dark hair, mole under left nipple. Address found: 7 Chilworth Road, Shirley Warren, Southampton. With only his name on the stone, visitors often ask if he is of the Marriott Hotel family. There appears to be no family connection though a family tree might prove differently.

#297. Ralph Giles, second-class passenger, age 22. Address: West Kensington, London, England. Long medium brown hair, high forehead. Glasses, watch, gold ring, etc.

#64. John Reginald Rice, assistant purser's clerk, age 25. Dark hair. Officer's double-breasted uniform. Pocketbook, purse with £10s. 2d., cigarette case, scissors, silver watch with photo, silver matchbox and chain, pencil, keys, knife, stud, gold ring engraved "Elsie." Address found: "Leafield" 37 Kimberly Drive, Great Crosby, Liverpool. Inscribed on his stone are the words "Nearer my God to thee."

In the late 1990s, new cement foundations

In Lifeboat 13

Hilda Slayter was in lifeboat 13 and a man in the dark said he recognized her voice. He was Lawrence Beesley, a teacher from England. They were seated at the same table for dinner in the second class dining saloon.

Hilda thought it ironic to be seated in the same lifeboat. Laurence Beesley would be one of survivors to write a book on the sinking. He would note what a small world it was to sit in a lifeboat in the Atlantic Ocean and find through talking while waiting for rescue, that he and Hilda shared mutual friends in Ireland.

under the gravestones replaced the original 1912 footings. The lettering on the stones was also whitened. New directional signs were installed to assist visitors in finding the gravesite. This work was carried out using funds put in trust by the White Star Line in 1912, grants from three levels of government, and the generosity of groups and individuals interested in the care of the graves of the *Titanic* victims.

SAINT MARY'S (ROMAN CATHOLIC) CATHEDRAL, WHERE FUNERAL SERVICES WERE HELD FOR FOUR WOMEN. THE WHITE STAR OFFICIALS CALLED ON THE CLERGY AT SAINT MARY'S GLEBE TO THANK THEM FOR THE SOLEMN SERVICE.

CHAPTER 6

MOUNT OLIVET CEMETERY—19 VICTIMS

Holy Mary, mother of God, pray for us sinners now
and at the hour of our death. Amen.

—Part of the prayers of the rosary.

Established in 1896, Mount Olivet was the third Catholic Cemetery in Halifax. It is administered by the Catholic Cemeteries Commission. The land was originally part of the estate on which the Archbishop's Palace was situated in 1870. As the summer residence of Halifax archbishops, it also served as a retreat for clergy and as a picnic area for Catholic parishes and schools. As with most Halifax rural retreats, the property was subdivided for new housing developments and only the cemetery grounds still belong to the Roman Catholic Church.

THE HEROIC PRIESTS ON DUTY.

On Sunday, April 14, the captain led a service of devotion in the first-class dining room where the passengers and servants could attend. Later in the evening a minister would lead a hymn sing in the second-class dining room. In second class there were three Roman Catholic priests travelling on separate itineraries: Reverend Joseph Montvila from Lithuania going to Worcester, Massachusetts; Reverend Joseph M. Peruschitz, a Benedictine monk from Germany; and the Reverend Thomas R. D. Byles,

FATHER THOMAS BYLES. HIS BODY WAS NOT FOUND.

PRIESTS ON DUTY AS TITANIC SINKS

Gather Doomed Passengers About Them on Deck and Read Litany to All.

CALMLY AWAIT DEATH.

Survivors of the Titanic, especially those from the steerage, tell of the heroism of two Catholic priests who after assisting women and children into the last boat gathered about them the doomed passengers and calmly sought to comfort them in the face of approaching death.

The story of hope and faith evidenced in that hour by Father Byles of England and Father Peruschoetz, a German, entitles them to a high place in the roll of honor. The "America," a Catholic review of the week, repeats the story of eye witnesses.

The two priests had held Sunday services in the morning and evening for the Catholics of various nationalities, addressing them in German and English. The rosary and litanies had been recited by all.

Help in Preserving Order.

The first news of the disaster brought the priests to the scene, where they joined with the other men in assisting to preserve order and insure the safety of the women and children. When men of all nationalities gathered about them and sought comfort and hope the two priests raised their voices and calmly as if in the sanctuary repeated over and over again the rosary.

No man, according to the story of those present, was turned away. The priests ministered to Catholics and non-Catholics alike. As the sinking vessel listed more and more the crowd about the priests grew larger and all joined fervently in the prayers. Those in the boats pulling away from the vessel could see the men kneeling on the deck, but it is related that in the last moment, when

Chicago Tribune, April 28, 1912.

age 44, travelling from London, England, to the United States to officiate at the wedding of his brother. They held services in the morning and evening to meet the needs of the Roman Catholics, including the large number of Irish immigrants.

Along with masses held in second and third class, the rosary and litanies were recited by all.

Reported in the *Chicago Tribune* on April 20 was a story from the "America," a Catholic review of the week:

The first news of the disaster brought the priests to the scene, where they joined the other men in assisting to preserve order and ensure the safety of the women and children. When men of all nationalities gathered around them (Father Byles and Father Peruschitz) and sought comfort and hope the two priests raised their voices and calmly as if in the sanctuary repeated over and over again the rosary. No man according to the story of those present was turned away. The priest ministered to Catholics and non-Catholics alike. As the sinking vessel listed more and more the crowd around the priests grew larger and all joined fervently in the prayers. Those in the boats could see the men kneeling on the deck, but it is related that in the last moment when the lights went out, no shrieks were heard nor cries of terror from the group where the faithful pastors serenely and devoutly sought to comfort those about them.

A lovely story, but it would have been difficult for anyone in the lifeboats to see if people were kneeling around the priests. There is, however, confirmation of the actions of Father Byles in dispatches from New York on April 22. A group of third-class survivors from Ireland remembered that Father Byles's sermon at the Sunday mass "was on the necessity of being possessed of the life boat of religious consolation in the time of spiritual ship wreck."

"When the liner struck the iceberg, Father Byles came down in the steerage passageway with hand uplifted, commanding the people to be calm and giving them absolution and his blessing. He led us to where the boats were being lowered," said Miss Helen Mocklare, "the meanwhile saying prayers and helped the women and children into them. He whispered words of comfort and encouragement to all."

The three priests did not survive, and their bodies were not found. The newspapers noted that the requiem mass of the dead for Father Byles in New York was sung at the hour he would have presided over his brother's marriage. On Friday, May 3, a funeral mass for four women of the *Titanic* was held at Saint Mary's Cathedral in Halifax. The rector, Father John Foley, stated that Father Byles was on his way to his brother's marriage but "instead he stayed and married souls to God." The recovered dead of *Titanic* were buried as Roman Catholic, if crucifixes or medallions, sometimes called holy medals, were found on them. These medallions were often recorded as "charms." A number of recovered bodies carried "beads." These were rosary beads used for prayers to the Virgin Mary, mother of Jesus, another sign of Catholic faith.

There are nineteen *Titanic* victims buried at Mount Olivet. They are buried in two rows, and all the graves are marked with the same-sized stone. When the first bodies were brought to Halifax, a funeral mass for four women who at that point were unidentified was held. The requiem mass was sung by His Grace, Archbishop

cont. on p. 119

Titanic graves at Mount Olivet Cemetery.

THE MUSICIANS PLAYED AS THE WATER ROSE

The most remembered story from the *Titanic* legend is of the musicians who played on during the hours of the sinking. Their services were supplied through a contract with a music company (what today we would call a talent agency). The musicians were not employees of the White Star Line but had to sign on to obey the rules of the ship. They performed in two groups, one a band of five, sometimes referred to as the saloon orchestra, and the other a trio, referred to as the deck band. They were expected to play from the White Star booklet of music and to perform requests for the passengers. The musicians played during lunches, receptions, and dinners. They also provided the evening entertainment. At the end of the voyage they could expect a gratuity from some of the passengers. They were accommodated in the second-class passenger cabins.

The bandmaster was Wallace H. Hartley (see Chapter 3). He was remembered as a man with the highest sense of duty. "He often said that music was a bigger weapon for stopping disorder than anything on earth. He knew the value of the weapon he had and I think he proved his point," musician John

S. Carr was quoted as saying in New York papers on April 21, 1912. Bandmaster Hartley's body was returned to England for burial. John Law Hume, violinist, who was engaged to be married when he made the return trip,

Men assembling outside Snow's undertaking establishment, Argyle Street, Halifax, where bodies of some of the *Titanic* victims were held.

is buried at Fairview Lawn Cemetery. J. F. P. Clarke, bass viol player, who was making his first trip across the ocean, is buried at Mount Olivet Cemetery. The bodies of Percy C. Taylor, piano, a married man from Clapham, England; John W. Woodward, cello, Oxford, England; Roger M. Bricoux, cello, London, England; George A. Krins, viola, Brixton; and W. Theodore Bailey, pianist and an only son, Notting Hill, London, England; were never found.

There is some dispute as to what was the last music played. Part of this confusion arises from the fact survivors left the ship at different times. One of the women survivors told the waiting press in New York it was "Nearer My God to Thee" and many of the families on

shore wanted that last comfort, that a hymn had accompanied their loved ones in death. It was a hymn that was seized on by many of the clergy for sermons on the evils of material wealth and of being prepared for the end of life. Organizers of events for the *Titanic* Fund used it as part of the programme to satisfy the public demand to hear it again and again.

"Nearer my God to Thee" was a favourite of the late King Edward VII and the selection that Hartley had told others he wanted played at his funeral. The question is whether the musicians would all know the same version. Others hold the music played was a similar tune, "Autumn" or "Songe d'Automne," which were popular at the time. Two survivors who went down with the ship and swam

J. F. P. CLARKE. THE LOCAL AUTHORITIES DECIDED A PERSON'S IDENTITY BASED ON WHAT THEY FOUND ON THE BODY. MR. CLARKE HAD MANY ITEMS WITH HIS INITIALS ON THEM. CARD IN FILE AT NOVA SCOTIA ARCHIVES.

for the lifeboats—wireless operator Harold McBride and first-class passenger Colonel Archibald Gracie—offered different perspectives. McBride thought it was "Autumn." Colonel Gracie in the newspapers and his book *The Truth About the Titanic* stated, "the band began to play, and continued while the boats were being lowered…I did not recognize any of the tunes, but I know they were cheerful and not hymns. If as reported, 'Nearer My God to Thee' was one of the selections, I assuredly should have noticed it and regarded it as a tactless warning of immediate death to us all and one likely to create a panic that our special efforts were directed towards avoiding…"

Those that discount his account will point out that he also stated that the *Titanic* did not break in half, which is now proven to have happened. The *New York Times* reported that the majority of witnesses agreed that the last music they heard was "Autumn." Lawrence Beesley, who was widely quoted and wrote a book on surviving the sinking, also felt the musicians had not played the hymn. On seeing the movie *A Night to Remember*, he stated the hymn was a "fiction." He also noted that with the angle of the sinking ship it would have been impossible to play right up to the last moment. Certainly the piano would have gone down the deck as *Titanic* dipped further into the icy waters. Nonetheless it was certainly heroic for the band to play with the difficulty they faced wearing cumbersome life jackets and playing for over two hours in the cold air of the night.

Some weeks after the sinking, at least one of the musician's families received a letter from the supplier that hired the men to play on the ship asking for reimbursement for the uniform lost in the sinking. The musicians had signed contracts agreeing to pay for uniforms and alterations done to them. The supplier reasoned that with the large amounts being donated to the Musicians' Fund there was plenty to share. There is no record as to the actions of the families to the request but given the standards of the time there would be some who would have paid the debt.

cont. from p. 115

Edward McCarthy, and six priests at Saint Mary's Cathedral. There are other Catholics buried at Fairview Lawn Cemetery, and also Michel Navratil at the Jewish Cemetery. No request was made to remove any of them to the Catholic cemetery.

1ST ROW, START RIGHT, MOVING TO THE LEFT:

#298. H. Wenzel Linhart, third-class passenger, embarked from Southampton, age 32. Effects included pocketbook, purse, 220 kroner, and other bills and coins. A wire was received from Rud Linhart, May 6th, which gave instructions as to burial.

#302. Thomas Morgan, fireman, estimated age 26. Effects: pocketbook with crucifix, union book and discharge "A" book. Address found: Thomas Morgan, Spar Tavern, Spar Road, Southampton.

#244. Maurice Emil Debreucq, assistant waiter, restaurant, age 18. Fair hair. Address: 12 Meade Street, London.

#215. Baptiste Bernardi, assistant waiter, restaurant, age 22. Black coat, pants, singlet, no shirt, white apron, one button lost. Effects: purse, 7s. 2d., one link, comb, one horseshoe pin. Address: 113 High Street, Nottinghill Gate, London.

#5. Unidentified female, probably a third-class passenger, age about 40. Height: 5 feet, 9 inches; weight: 170 pounds. Dark brown hair. Blue waterproof, black jacket and skirt, pink and white striped jacket, blue and red petticoat and fur boa, black boots and ribbed stockings. Empty purse, crucifix, snuff box and medallion, one gold earring, four

rings—two silver, one turquoise, one garnet and pearl.

#202. J. Fred Clarke, John Frederick Preston (Fred) bass violinist, bandsman, age 34. Black hair. Grey overcoat, grey muffler, uniform with green facing, green socks. Crucifix. Diamond pin, gold watch, keys, knife, sovereign case No. 2, pocketbook, memo book, 8s. Gold ring marked "J. F. P. C." Address: 22 Tunstall Street, Smithdown Road, Liverpool. (See chapter 7.)

#288. Unidentified male, probably third-class passenger, probably a Greek, age about 50. Height: 5 feet, 1 12 inches; weight: 190 pounds. Black hair and moustache slightly grey. Hair very thin in front. Wore two gold rings, one a chain ring; white shirt with fancy front; light striped trousers; black waist coat; charms on gold chain around neck, left on. Belt with 140 francs in gold. Carried gun-metal watch. No other aids to identification.

#210. Unidentified female, age about 23. Height: 5 feet, 4 inches; weight: 130 pounds. Brown hair, false upper teeth. Wore long green overcoat, purple jacket, skirt, no corsets, brown shoes, black stockings. No guess was made as to the passenger class of this woman.

#13. Unidentified female, probably third-class passenger, age about 34. Height: 5 feet, 3 inches; weight: 150 pounds. Dark brown hair, false upper teeth (partial). Probably Italian, wore two green cotton blouses, green cotton skirt, striped petticoat, one shoe. No marks on clothing. Charm around neck. Nothing else to identify.

#12. Margaret Rice, third-class passenger, embarked from Queenstown, Ireland, age 39. Height: 5 feet, 5 inches; weight: 140 pounds. Black hair, turning grey. False upper teeth. Black velvet coat, jacket and skirt, blue cardigan, black apron, black boots and stockings. Shoes marked "Parsons Sons, Athlone." Medallion around neck, marked "B. V. M." On the recovery ship they recorded this medal as a "charm" around neck. Wore wedding ring, keeper, and another gold ring; locket and photo; one jet and one bead necklace. In purse, £3 in gold, £4 in Irish notes, gold brooch, plain gold wag earrings, £10 note, box pills.

Margaret Rice was originally listed as unidentified female; it was the box of pills that identified her. The address of the chemist was on the box, and the authorities in Halifax wrote to the chemist in Ireland and he knew her identity. She had left the United States after her husband had

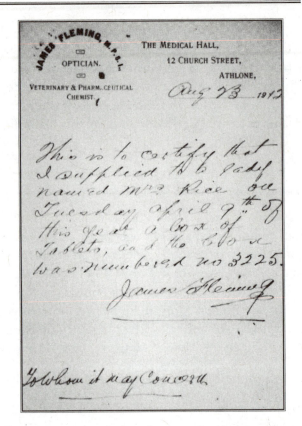

LETTER FROM CHEMIST IN IRELAND IDENTIFYING BOX OF PILLS AS BELONGING TO MARGARET RICE, A WIDOW TRAVELLING WITH HER FIVE SONS TO THE UNITED STATES; ALL WERE LOST.

died while working in a railway yard at Seattle, Washington. With his insurance money she went home to Ireland. She was travelling back to the United States, thinking there would be more opportunities for her five boys: Albert, age 10; George, age 9; Eric, age 7; Arthur, age 4; and Eugene, age 2. One can imagine this group of boys huddled

FROM THE NEWSPAPERS:

Boston Globe, April 18. "Good Luck of J. P. Morgan. He had intended to take passage on *Titanic* as had H. C. Frick before him. J. P. Morgan's star of good luck was still in the ascendant in the 75th year of his life, for the banker had thought earlier in the year to return to America on the ill-fated *Titanic*. Henry Clay Frick in February had engaged a suite on the *Titanic*, but Mrs. Frick sprained her ankle when the *Adriatic* stopped at Mareira and she went to hospital in Naples. Mr. Morgan took over Mr. Frick's bookings. Then Mr. Morgan decided to lengthen his stay abroad…"

around their mother saying their prayers. Her boys perished with her in the sinking. None of their bodies were found and their names are not recorded on their mother's stone. The initials "B. V. M." on the "charm" around her neck stood for "Blessed Virgin Mary."

SECOND ROW, RIGHT MOVING TO LEFT:

#328. Unidentified female, probably a third-class passenger, age about 14. Height: 4 feet, 6 inches; weight: 80 to 85 pounds. Golden brown hair, very dark skin, refined features. Wore lace trimmed red and black overdress, black underdress, green striped underskirt, black woolen shawl, and black slippers.

No further aids to identification. In 1991, a society interested in *Titanic* victims tentatively identified this girl as Hileni Zabour, age 16. This would make her the youngest victim buried in this plot.

#189. Servando Ovies, first-class passenger, age 28, dark. Black coat and vest, blue serge pants, grey shirt marked "J.R." The recovery crew listed this body as "probably a sailor" based on his clothes and maybe the roughness of his hands. The only description was "dark." There were no effects on the body so there were no clues to his identity. The body was buried in Fairview Lawn Cemetery. There was some doubt whether this was a sailor or first-class passenger, Servando Ovies y Rodrigues. His family was in Spain yet J. A. Rodriguez of

FROM THE NEWSPAPERS:

April 21. Cardinal Farley paid a visit to *Titanic* survivors at Saint Vincent's Hospital, New York. (A surgery wing would be named after Dr. Wm. O'Loughton, *Titanic*'s chief surgeon who was lost in the sinking.)

Prayer for all: At high mass at Saint James Cathedral in Montreal, the pastor recommended all the victims without distinction of race or creed to the prayers of the faithful.

"Emile Richard, one of the victims of the disaster, was a resident of Cognac, France, and was the son of P. H. Richard, the brandy distiller. The young man, who was in his twenty-third year, had just finished his term of service as an officer in the French army, and as he looked upon a military life with distaste, his father had promised him a six months' holiday in Canada and the United States. With this incentive he finished his term and then embarked on the voyage which ended in his death." The *Gazette*, Montreal, April 22, 1912. The body of this second-class passenger was not found.

Rodriguez & Co., Havana, Cuba was sure it was Servando. As Servando was Roman Catholic, his remains were exhumed from Fairview Lawn Cemetery and reburied at Mount Olivet on May 15, 1912. There was speculation that this claim was made to comfort a mother in Spain and to settle inheritance questions. Despite going to the trouble of moving the body to the Catholic cemetery, the stone marker is the same size as the others. A more elaborate memorial stone would have allowed for his complete name to be inscribed. Instead only "Servando Ovies" is inscribed with the date of death and the number 189.

#277. Henry Jaillet, pastry chef, restaurant, age 38. Very dark hair and moustache. Probably Italian. Checked trousers, blue coat and vest, dark overcoat, blue and white striped pyjamas, "H. J." on pyjamas, brown boots. A card with "H. Jallet (Chef)" found on body. Address: Jamison Street, London.

#306. Tozni Henderkovic, third-class passenger, embarked from Southampton listed as Ignaz Hendekovic, age 28. Fair hair, light moustache. Blue coat, blue stripe pants, no vest, white shirt with embroidered front, leather sandals, brown belt. One knife, purse with $12 in notes, small purse with 72 cents, two third-class tickets: one, No. 349245, for Matilda Petram, the other, No. 349243, for Toznai Hendekovic.

Henderkovic and his friend, Miss Matilda Petranec, were travelling from Croatia. Matilda also died in the sinking but her body was never found. His was the last body picked up by the first recovery ship, the *Mackay-Bennett*.

#188. Mansour Hanna, third-class passenger, embarked from Cherbourg, age 35. Black hair, very dark. Effects: pocket knife, amber beads, purse. On the passenger list as Mansour Hanna, the Halifax authorities listed him as Merne Hanna.

#79. William Ale (or Ala), third-class passenger, embarked from Southampton, listed as Wm. Ali, age 25. Dark hair and moustache. Black coat, velvet vest, checked trousers, green socks, black boots. Third-class ticket No. 310312 for William Ale, Argentina.

#312. Youssef Gerios, third-class passenger, embarked from Cherbourg, age 26. Black curly hair, brown moustache. Carried a rosary, scapulare, and crucifix. He was Turkish and was heading to the county of Luzerne, Wilkesboro, Pennsylvania.

#266. Pompeo Piazza, waiter, restaurant, age 30. Black trousers, dark coat, cotton shirt, patent leather shoes. Effects: knife. Address: 94 Newport Building, London, England.

#196. Petril Lemperopolis, listed as Peter Lemberopoulos, third-class passenger, embarked from Cherbourg, age 28. Green striped suit, heavy blue wool vest, no boots. Effects: gold watch, $15.45 Greek.

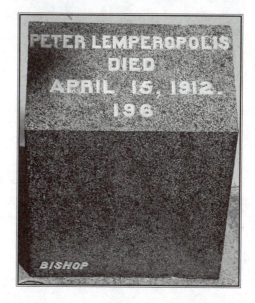

PETER LEMPEROPOLIS'S GRAVESTONE IS THE ONLY ONE OF 150 STONES TO HAVE THE NAME OF THE STONE CARVER (BISHOP) INSCRIBED ON IT.

Captain A. H. Rostron of the Carpathia and Loving Cup Given Him by Titanic Survivors.

MRS. MARGARET BROWN, LADY PRESIDENT OF THE COMMITTEE OF SURVIVORS, PRESENTING TO CAPTAIN ARTHUR ROSTRON, OF THE CUNARD LINER *CARPATHIA*, A LOVING CUP INSCRIBED WITH THE THANKS OF THE SURVIVORS OF THE *TITANIC*. COMMEMORATIVE MEDALS WERE PRESENTED TO EACH CREW MEMBER, JUNE 1912.

CHAPTER 7

"SINCE THE *TITANIC* WENT DOWN."—CARING FOR THE DEAD

"...in Halifax their graves will be kept forever green."

—Reverend MacKinnon, Presbyterian, Pine Hill College.

There was an immediate outpouring of help after the sinking of the *Titanic* as can be seen from the following newspaper accounts.

London, April 17. "It is with the deepest sympathy that I hear of the terrible disaster to the *Titanic* and of the awful loss of life. My heart is full of grief and sympathy for the bereaved families of those who have perished." Queen Mother Alexandra of Great Britain. The Queen Mother donated $1,000 to the Lord Mayor's *Titanic* Relief Fund. The King and Queen also made donations.

London, April 17. "Oscar Hammerstein has offered his opera house to the Lord Mayor of London for an entertainment to raise money for the *Titanic* Fund."

New York, April 18. "Eva Booth, Commander of the Salvation Army, and 50 of her officers met survivors on the pier to offer medical care and accommodation. Immigration officials allow ship to proceed to Cunard pier rather than put 3rd Class survivors through the ordeal of being processed through Ellis Island. Black robed Sisters of Charity took injured and destitute to Saint Vincent's Hospital."

New York, April 18. "A committee of thirteen of the most prominent women in the city...was formed to take care of the surviving steerage passengers. 'We do not know how many steerage passengers have been saved,' said Mrs. Henry, committee chair, 'but we feel that something should be done for their comfort on their arrival as there will probably be few of their friends to give them adequate care. We wish to give them what financial aid may be necessary to alleviate their sufferings as far as possible and assist the immigration authorities.'"

New York, April 19. "New York Stock Exchange men contribute $10,000 to fund for the destitute steerage passengers. Vincent Astor gives $10,000; Andrew Carnegie, $5,000; John D. Rockefeller, $2,500; George M. Cohen, $9,000. Pennsylvania Railway offers free train service for any survivor."

New York, April 22. "New York Giants and the Yankees played benefit game for destitute survivors. J. P. Sousa and other musicians offer to play benefit New York City concert. Enrico Caruso sings at benefit concert in New York.

"Queen of Norway donated money to the Lord Mayor of London *Titanic* relief fund. Government of the Dominion of Canada gives $10,000 to the *Titanic* Relief Fund. Princess Kawana Koa collected money in Hawaii for the Washington, D.C. *Titanic* memorials.

"Belden Avenue Baptist Church, Chicago, took up a collection for the needs of Nina Harper, the 6 year old daughter of the Reverend John Harper who was lost in the wreck of the *Titanic*. The Reverend Harper was to preach in Chicago churches. His charge in London, England also collected for the daughter's future education."

Many effects were felt in the lives of those who were connected to the *Titanic*. The captain and crew of the *Carpathia* were described as courageous heroes. The Cunard Line absorbed the costs of the rescue and the delayed voyage to Italy. The line also gave the crew an extra month's wages for their work in reaching the survivors. By June, Marconi and Company was unable to keep up with the demand of shipping companies wanting wireless operators. Mr. Marconi announced plans to open a new training school in London. His years of work were finally paying off.

Just as the rich and famous occupied the headlines in the days after the sinking, their stories continued to feature in the newspapers:

June 1912. Mrs. Madeleine Astor welcomed Captain Rostron and Doctor F. E. McGee of the *Carpathia* into her home to personally thank them for their kindness to her. Mrs. Astor and her stepson gave $2,000 to the crew of the recovery vessel, *Mackay-Bennett*.

On August 7, 1912, John Jacob VI was born. Mrs. Madeleine Astor was one of a number of *Titanic* widows who had children soon after the sinking. The provisions of the will of the late Mr. Astor made all the newspapers. The older son, Vincent, inherited the bulk of the estate with a share going to his sister. The baby boy was also provided for.

The London newspapers pointed out that Mrs. Madeleine Astor would have income from the investment of $3 million. If she remarried she would lose this sizable inheritance. Boston ladies were quoted in their city newspapers as saying this provision was very unfair to such a young widow.

A passenger that received a great deal of press notice after the sinking was the military aide to the president of the United States, Major Archibald W. Butt. The recovery of two *Titanic* crew members with the same last name caused a great deal of confusion at the White House. The president and staff had hoped that the major had survived but were also glad he went down with the ship, remembered for being an officer and a gentleman. His body was never found. Messages of sympathy came in from around the world. HRH Prince Arthur, the Duke of Connaught and Governor General of Canada sent, on April 18th, this message to President Taft at Washington: "I have delayed telegraphing to you in the hope that Major Butt might still be among the saved but fear there is now no hope. Accept the expression of my deepest sympathy on this gallant officer's tragic end and the loss to yourself of a devoted member of your staff... ARTHUR."

cont. on p. 130

HALIFAX MAN LOST ON TITANIC

Mr. Geo. Wright Latest Canadian Victim of Crash With Iceberg Reported.

One of the many people whose body was not found was first-class passenger George Wright, a Halifax millionaire. At the 1876 World's Fair in Philadelphia, George conceived of compiling a business directory. Soon, his business directories were considered a bible for the professional office. For information on respectable businesses around the world you could consult Wright's World Business Directory for information and addresses. After years of travel, he sold the business and retired to his home in Halifax. He was a land developer and built commercial and residential buildings. He enjoyed hunting, fishing, and bicycling. He owned horses and yachts. He also decried vulgarities and loose morals and his "name was almost synonymous with anti-profanity." He spent the winter holidaying around the Mediterranean. Travelling in Europe he was making all sorts of plans and was keeping in touch with his Halifax office. He made arrangements to take a cabin on the *Titanic* for

WRIGHT, AGE 62. HIS BODY WAS NOT FOUND. HEADLINE FROM *MONTREAL STAR*, APRIL 23, 1912.

his return to North America. He tried to convince friends, who were also from Halifax, to return with him but they declined. While in London, he went to his solicitor and made out his will. He signed it the day before he left for Southampton. On April 8th, a cable from the firm of Thompson and Adams, Saint Paul's Building, Barrington Street, Halifax, was sent to George Wright, Russell Hotel, London. The reply on April 9th, from the cable company, was that the message was undelivered as

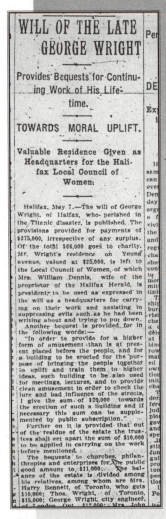

WILL OF THE LATE GEORGE WRIGHT

Provides Bequests for Continuing Work of His Lifetime.

TOWARDS MORAL UPLIFT.

Valuable Residence Given as Headquarters for the Halifax Local Council of Women.

Halifax, May 7.—The will of George Wright, of Halifax, who perished in the Titanic disaster, is published. The provisions provided for payments of $275,000, irrespective of any surplus. Of the total $66,000 goes to charity. Mr. Wright's residence on Young avenue, valued at $25,000, is left to the Local Council of Women, of which Mrs. William Dennis, wife of the proprietor of the Halifax Herald, is president, to be used as expressed in the will as a headquarters for carrying on their work and assisting in suppressing evils such as he had been writing about and trying to put down.

Another bequest is provided for in the following words:—

"In order to provide for a higher form of amusement than is at present placed before the people, and for a building to be erected for the purpose of bringing the people together to uplift and train them to higher ideas, such building to be also used for meetings, lectures, and to provide clean amusement in order to check the lure and bad influence of the streets, I give the sum of $20,000 towards the erection of such a building and if necessary this sum can be supplemented by public subscription."

Further on it is provided that out of the residue of the estate the trustees shall set apart the sum of $10,000 to be applied in carrying on the work before mentioned.

The bequests to churches, philanthropies and enterprises for the public good amount to $11,000; the balance of the estate is divided among his relatives, among whom are Mrs. Harry Bennett, of Toronto, who gets $10,000; Thos. Wright, of Toronto, $15,000; George Wright, city engineer, of London, Ont. $17,000; Mrs. John

GEORGE WRIGHT'S LAST WILL WAS PUBLISHED IN THE *MONTREAL GAZETTE* ON MAY 8, 1912.

Mr. Wright had left for Halifax. He had taken the train to Southampton and the next day boarded the *Titanic*. At the time of the sinking no one could remember the man from Halifax. George Wright was a quiet gentleman but large in size and distinguished looking. It is odd that no one that survived, not even those who were taking notice of others, including Hilda Slayter, formerly of Halifax, saw him. Friends said that George Wright was a man who retired early and was a sound sleeper. It is speculated that this prosperous gentleman from Halifax never left his cabin. He was travelling alone with no personal servant. It is possible that his steward did not knock on the door. After all there were many empty cabins in first class. As time passed maybe George Wright woke and discovered his door stuck. This was the case with a lady who had returned to her cabin and had to be rescued by a passing man. In that case the steward nearby complained about the damage to company property. Other stewards were going around locking cabin doors to protect valuables; could George Wright have been locked into his room and not been able to find his key? Others speculated that he may not have been on the ship, canceling his plans as others had done. Three weeks after the sinking it was agreed that George Wright was among the dead of the *Titanic* and on May 8, 1912, the terms of George Wright's will were disclosed in the newspapers. George Wright was sixty-two years old and had no wife or children so left much of his wealth to charities. The story in the *Montreal Gazette* read:

Halifax, May 7. The will of George Wright, of Halifax, who perished in the *Titanic* disaster is published. The provisions provided for payments of $275,000, irrespective of any surplus. Of the total $66,000 goes to charity. Mr. Wright's residence on Young Ave. valued at $25,000 is left to the Local Council of Women, of which Mrs. William Dennis, wife of the proprietor of the *Halifax Herald*, is president, to be used as expressed in the will as a headquarters for carrying on their work and assisting in suppressing evils such as he had been writing about and trying to put down. Another bequest is provided for in the following words: "In order to provide for a higher form of amusement than is at present placed before the people, and for a building to be erected for the purpose of bringing people together to uplift and train them to higher ideas, such building to be also used for meetings, lectures, and to provide clean amusement in order to check the lure and bad influence of the streets, I give the sum of $20,000 towards the erection of such a building and if necessary this sum can be supplemented by public subscription." Further on it is provided that out of the residue of the estate the trustees shall set apart the sum of $10,000 to be applied in carrying on the work before mentioned. The bequests to churches, philanthropies and enterprises for the public good amount to $11,000. The balance of the estate is divided among his relatives, among whom are Mrs. Harry Bennett, of Toronto, who gets $10,000; Thos. Wright, of Toronto, $15,000; George Wright, city engineer of London, Ont. $12,000; Mrs. John Fraser, Halifax, a sister, $35,000, and

THE HOUSE THAT GEORGE WRIGHT LEFT TO THE WOMEN'S COUNCIL OF HALIFAX.

Mrs. Daniel Johnstone, of Minneapolis, sister, $20,000. The executors are W. B. McCurdy and George Orman, Halifax, and George Wright, nephew, London. The will was executed in London the day before Mr. Wright sailed on the *Titanic*. He left the original with his London solicitors by whom a copy has been sent to the executors.

It took forty years before the money, for a building to "uplift" the citizens, was spent in the construction of a new YMCA. His house on Young Avenue in Halifax is still owned by the Local Council of Women.

A PHOTOGRAPH OF CHARLES HAYS HANGS NEXT TO THE ENTRANCE OF THE CHATEAU LAURIER SWIMMING POOL. THE OPENING OF THE CHATEAU LAURIER HOTEL IN 1912 DREW HUGE CROWDS BUT THE FESTIVITIES WERE KEPT TO A MINIMUM OUT OF RESPECT FOR THE LATE PRESIDENT, CHARLES HAYS.

cont. from p. 126

The political story did not end there. Major Archibald Butt had gone on a trip to Europe at the insistence of Frank Millet, who was also lost in the sinking. Richard B. Watrous, a friend, was quoted in the newspapers:

I was a witness of the manner in which Millet pleaded with Major Butt to go to Europe with him for a rest, and the manner in which Millet pleaded with the president to order Major Butt to go with him when he demurred. Millet noticed Major Butt was looking paler than usual and generally run down. He announced to us his determination that Major Butt should return with him to Rome for a little rest.

Major Archibald Butt, aide to President Taft, was the centre of controversy between Republican presidential candidates. Both President Taft and Colonel Theodore Roosevelt wanted their mutual friend, Major Butt, to work on their campaigns for the presidential nomination for the next election. These requests made Butt very uncomfortable as he did not want to take sides. This is why Frank Millet insisted on the trip away from Washington.

When Major Butt died, the political community of Washington paid their respects. President Taft described the lost aide: "He was like a member of my family and I feel his loss as if he had been a younger brother…He leaves the widest circle of friends whose memory of him is sweet in every particular." Colonel Theodore Roosevelt described him as "an officer and a gentleman. I and my family all loved him sincerely."

Shortly after the kind messages regarding his loss, Colonel Roosevelt used Major Butt's trip to Rome as ammunition against President Taft. Roosevelt hinted that the trip was a mission to seek the support of the Holy Father. This sort of mission would send a message to anti-Catholic factions within the party and the general public. Taft denied any secret mission and said only the normal diplomatic introductions were provided. It did not help the president's position that there was correspondence thanking Major Butt for arranging the precedence of American Cardinals over other clergy at official functions. When the sympathy message from His Holiness, Pope Pius, arrived, great compliments were paid to the major's loss. This added to the suspicion that President Taft was seeking foreign help to win the Roman Catholic vote. The exchange between these two presidential candidates was part of a larger debate that continued up until the election. Both men would run for president and lose.

MAJOR ARCHIBALD W. BUTT

THE *NEW YORK TIMES* REPORTED ON NOVEMBER 12, 1912, THAT MAJOR ARCHIBALD W. BUTT'S HOME SOLD IN WASHINGTON TO HOUSE REPRESENTATIVE MR. UNDERWOOD. THE BUSINESS OF SETTLING OF ESTATES AND INSURANCE CLAIMS OF *TITANIC* PASSENGERS WOULD TAKE YEARS.

THE FATE OF OTHER SURVIVORS:

Colonel Archibald Gracie, a survivor whose written account recorded the heroism of the sinking, died December 4, 1912. He had gone down with the ship and survived in the freezing water until

COLONEL ARCHIBALD GRACIE, SURVIVOR AND AUTHOR.

he could gain a place on an overturned lifeboat. Some would blame his death on the stress of what he had witnessed. His book *The Truth About the Titanic*, released in 1913, was a bestseller. It is still considered one of the most important chronicles of the sinking.

J. Bruce Ismay, president of the White Star Line, was vilified in the American press for surviving the sinking. The rumour was that it was he that insisted that Captain Smith maintain a dangerous speed going through the icefields.

The British press felt the Americans had no jurisdiction in holding an inquiry. Of Senator Smith, the chair of the inquiry, the *Daily Express* said, "There is no need to suppose because Senator Smith is an asinine American that the inquiry is purposeless." Others reported, "Senator Smith… remorselessly insists on specific replies to questions some of which are irrelevant and others painful."

There was mixed public reaction to Mr. Ismay's return to Britain. Testimony at the British inquiry brought out comments on the actions of Mr. Ismay that speak to the theory of women and children first. Stewardess Annie Robinson stated that Mr. Ismay pressed her to enter a lifeboat. She said "I am only a stewardess." His reply was "Never mind, you are a woman, take your place." Her hesitation in taking a seat also speaks to the class structure at the time. Sir Robert Finlay, addressing the British inquiry for the White Star Line, stated: "There was not the slightest ground for suggesting that any other life would have been saved if Mr. Ismay had stayed on the ship. Mr. Ismay violated no point of honour, and had he thrown away his life those who now attack him would have said that he did so to avoid inquiry!" Lord Mersey, head of the inquiry, said, "Mr. Ismay, after rendering assistance to many passengers, found Collapsible C being lowered (the last boat on the starboard side). No other people were there at the time. There was room for him and he jumped in. Had he not jumped in he would merely have added one more life, namely his own, to the number of those lost." Mr. Ismay retired as president of the White Star Line as had been planned before the sinking and lived quietly in the countryside.

Sir Cosmos Duff-Gordon, of England, would forever be associated with giving money to the crew of his near empty lifeboat, considered by some to have been a bribe to avoid returning to save others who might have swamped the boat. The lifeboat left with seven crew—Sir Cosmos, Lady Duff Gordon and her secretary, plus two

American gentlemen. There were twenty-eight empty seats in the boat. Sir Cosmos said he had responded to the comment of a crew member in his lifeboat that he had lost all his kit. Sir Duff Gordon offered each man £5 for his loss. He and Lady Duff Gordon posed on the *Carpathia* with the people they had shared a lifeboat with. This was considered in bad taste by some survivors. The British inquiry found no fault on the part of this couple but the press and unions made much of their story.

Major Arthur Peuchen of Toronto enjoyed a brief moment of fame for taking three oranges and leaving behind $200,000 in money and securities, but that did not last. He had volunteered to row an undermanned boat, climbing down a rope to prove his ability to be of use in a lifeboat. Even with a letter from an officer of the *Titanic* stating he was instructed to assist with rowing a lifeboat, Major Peuchen was never totally clear of the stigma of being a man who survived while women and children died in icy waters. (Obviously he knew there would be questions regarding his survival and that is why he requested the letter be written on the *Carpathia*.) Major Peuchen was often misquoted with regards to his opinion on Captain Smith and J. Bruce Ismay. He denied any negative comments attributed to him. Peuchen went to Washington from Toronto on the invitation of Senator Smith, the chairman of the American inquiry. The telegram from Senator Smith read: "Are you willing to come to Washington to testify on Monday before the Congressional Committee regarding the wreck of the steamer *Titanic*?" Major Peuchen

J. Bruce Ismay returning to Great Britain after the Senate hearings in the United States. His wife, who had gone on board to greet him, follows her husband down the gangway. She reacts to the positive greeting her husband receives from the people on the dock.

thought he had a duty to attend even though he was not legally required to be there. He appears in the background of photographs of the inquiry. When items were salvaged from the *Titanic*, in 1987, Major Peuchen's wallet was found. It contained tickets for the Toronto streetcar service.

THE WOMEN AT THE BRITISH INQUIRY WERE MORE
INTERESTED IN WHAT LADY DUFF GORDON WORE THAN
IN HER TESTIMONY.

Captain Lord, master of the *Californian* blamed for deaths because it was thought that he did not respond to the distress signals from the sinking ship, worked unsuccessfully until his death to clear his name. There is no firm answer as to the identity of the "mystery ship" several survivors reported seeing in the distance. Ships going to the rescue of the *Titanic* reported seeing small schooners on the way. These small vessels would not have had wireless so would not have known of the disaster. There is a story of a Norwegian sealing vessel, named the *Samson*, being in the area, which would fit the description given by surviving officers of the *Titanic*. If true, the crew of forty-five thought they might be in trouble for sealing on a Sunday or in open water. The first officer of the *Samson* at the time waited until 1963 to confess that his ship had been in the area and may have been the ship between the *Titanic* and the *Californian*. The *Samson* had no wireless and headed for Iceland. The story is one of those what-ifs of the *Titanic* saga. If the sealing ship had responded, how many of the *Titanic* lost could she have saved? In an interesting twist, the *Samson*—by then under the name *City of New York*—was wrecked off Yarmouth, Nova Scotia, in 1952.

Most of the lesser-known survivors disappeared into ordinary lives, always coloured by the sense of loss that accompanies sudden unexpected death.

The United States Senate Inquiry and the British Court of Inquiry would reach no specific conclusions regarding blame or innocence in the errors of the sinking. It is obvious in reading the minutes of these meetings that much testimony was not candid. This was to protect the reputation of the dead and that of the White Star Line. A number of improvements did come out of the tragedy. There was an International Convention for Safety of Life at Sea which set standards for safety, training, and radio watches. Drills for the lifeboats became standard on liners. Passengers and crew were assigned seats in specific lifeboats to cut out the confusion that had been experienced on the *Titanic*. Wireless operators became part of the safety program of ships with the requirement that there be twenty-four-hour coverage.

In 1913, the International Ice Patrol was established to track icebergs and give advisories to shipping. On April 15th every year the U.S. Coast Guard plane for Ice Patrol drops a wreath into the Atlantic Ocean where the *Titanic* sank.

The outbreak of war in 1914 led to the death of some of the men who survived the *Titanic* sinking, those who had gone to the rescue or had helped recover bodies. On December 6, 1917, a ship explosion in Halifax Harbour that killed two thousand residents of the city also destroyed the Mayflower Curling Rink. Lucy Maud Montgomery, author of the Anne of Green Gables books, would write in a letter to a friend in Scotland, of the war and the explosion in Halifax: "What horrors have been in the world since the *Titanic* went down!"

On July 17, 1918, four months before the end of World War I, the *Carpathia* was sunk off Fastnet, Ireland. Captain Rostron would survive the war and be knighted for his many fine deeds. He died peacefully and is buried in Southampton.

World War I and the Halifax Explosion killed some people who were involved with the *Titanic* tragedy. One example of was Captain James Murray. In the messages sent to the *Titanic* is one on Friday, April 12, three days before the sinking. It was from the Canadian Pacific liner *Empress of Britain* out of Halifax and bound for Liverpool. It read, "Officers and self send greetings and best of luck to the *Titanic*, her officers and commander. Murray. Empress of Britain." The reply was, "Many thanks for your kind message from all here. Smith."

A DESTROYED BUILDING—1917 HALIFAX EXPLOSION.

When Captain Murray reached Liverpool he reported ice three days out of Halifax, one hundred miles in extant. He reported the message he had wired to the *Titanic*.

Five years later on December 6, 1917, Commander Murray responded to the call of a ship on fire in Halifax Harbour. He was in naval service and gathered a crew to go to the assistance of the burning vessel. He, along with two thousand others, were killed when the burning munitions ship, *Mont Blanc*, exploded.

The Great Depression and World War II would overshadow *Titanic*, but the story continued to generate interest. After the release of the movie *A Night to Remember* in 1958, the medium of television interview shows preserved survivor memories. A number of *Titanic* historical groups

Copyright R. T. McCully

His Majesty's Transport *Olympic*, nicknamed "Old Reliable," was a frequent caller to Halifax during World War I. Refurbished after the war, she is shown here at Piers 20–21 in Halifax. She was sold for scrap in the 1930s. Some of her interior fittings are still in use, including panelling that has been installed on a cruise ship.

were established and survivors of the sinking were always honoured guests at these groups' special events. In Halifax the three cemeteries have always attracted visitors, including survivors of the sinking. Some visits drew at least local media attention, including that of the "unsinkable" Margaret Brown, who visited in 1920. Other visitors went unnoticed.

Robert Vaughan of Perth, Ontario, formerly of the rescue ship *Carpathia*, brought his wife to the city in 1965 to view the graves. He was a seventeen-year-old steward when the *Carpathia* picked up the survivors. He and the other crew were told to prepare for survivors quietly so as not to disturb the *Carpathia* passengers. Vaughan assisted Walter Lord with his book *A Night to Remember*.

Other visitors with a direct connection to the sinking have followed. In June 1972, Madeleine Mellenger Mann visited Halifax with her husband. They were vacationing from Toronto. They went to the offices of the *Halifax Herald* to gather information about the *Titanic* graves. They had the good fortune to meet Shirley Ellis, a writer with the *Herald* who was able to supply them with the required information. Miss Ellis also arranged for an interview with the newspaper. The interview revealed that Mrs. Mann was Madeline Mellinger, a thirteen-year-old survivor of the sinking. She was with her widowed mother in a second-class cabin, travelling to Vermont, where her mother was going to a new work position. The women were travelling under the protection of Mr. Charles C. Jones, a first-class passenger. He was able to secure a place for the two ladies in a lifeboat but he was lost in the sinking. His body was found and brought to Halifax (see Chapter 3). Mrs. Mann, age 73, asked Shirley Ellis to forward a copy of the newspaper interview. Miss Ellis received a thank-you letter from Mrs. Mann.

In 1985, the *Titanic* wreck site was discovered. It was found that the ship had broken up as it sank. This would prove the drawing of survivor John Thayer Jr. was accurate. His drawing published in newspapers around the world was supported by other eyewitnesses but was not believed. This is why in the intervening years there were many suggestions that the *Titanic* could be raised.

A plaque was later placed on the stern of the wreck "in memory those souls who perished in with the *Titanic*." The discovery of the wreck has led to many trips to the site, including those of a company that has made a profit bringing up artifacts and displaying them around the world.

In 1987 and 1991, several names of unidentified victims were discovered. In September of 1991, the gravestones of six of the "unidentified" were inscribed with their names: Frank Couch #253, William Denton Cox #300, F. Woodford #163, Alan Vincent Franklin #262, Jenny Lovisa Henriksson #3, and Vendla Maria Heininen #8. Present for the ceremony was Louise Kink Pope. As a four-year-old, she survived the sinking with her parents, passengers in third-class cabins. In 1996, Edith Haisman, age 99 (she passed away the next January), and Michel Navratil, age 88, visited the Halifax graves (see Chapter 4).

The 1997 movie *Titanic* created a new generation interested in the story of the sinking. Many people, even cruise ship passengers who visit Halifax, want to see the *Titanic* graves. While many of the buildings associated with the recovery of the bodies have been destroyed, there are still ships' horns and train whistles to be heard. The city has grown through the fields of 1912, and has surrounded the three cemeteries where the *Titanic* dead rest. There is a permanent *Titanic* display at the Maritime Museum of the Atlantic which incorporates many artifacts found by the recovery crews.

The people directly connected with the *Titanic* sinking have all passed away. The *Titanic* Relief Fund for widows and children of the crew of the White Star Line was wound up in 1998 (see chapter 10).

News items continue to remind us of the *Titanic*. For example, one April 26, 2000, story from St. John's, Newfoundland, by Michael MacDonald of the Canadian Press reported:

JOHN THAYER JR. SWAM TO SAFETY AND WAS VERY CLOSE TO THE *TITANIC* WHEN IT SANK. HIS SKETCH WAS FILLED IN BY L. P. SKIDMORE OF BROOKLYN, AN ART INSTRUCTOR AND *CARPATHIA* PASSENGER, ON THE TRIP TO NEW YORK.

The Daily Gleaner.

FREDERICTON, N. B., WEDNESDAY, APRIL 24, 1912.

Eye Witness Sketched Titanic in Last Moments

SKETCHES OF THE SUCCESSIVE STEPS IN THE FOUNDERING OF THE TITANIC, MADE BY JOHN B. THAYER, JR., FROM ONE OF THE TITANIC'S COLLAPSIBLE RAFTS. HIS SKETCHES WERE FILLED IN BY L. P. SKIDMORE, OF BROOKLYN, ON THE CARPATHIA, THE SAME DAY. MR. THAYER IS SON OF THE SECOND VICE PRESIDENT OF THE PENNSYLVANIA RAILROAD, WHO WAS ONE OF THE VICTIMS OF THE DISASTER.

THE *DAILY GLEANER*, FREDERICTON, NEW BRUNSWICK, APRIL 24, 1912.

"Water cannons mounted on supply ships are being used to blast icebergs drifting towards oil rigs on the Grand Banks." *Titanic* is such a powerful image that it has become part of popular culture. *Titanic* has been used as the setting for movies and plays. A television series from Great Britain, *Upstairs Downstairs*, wanted to remove the character of Lady Marjorie, so the writers booked her passage to New York on the *Titanic*. So exited Lady Marjorie! In politics a change of ministers in the cabinet of a tired government is described by opposition members as "like moving deck chairs on the *Titanic*."

Throughout the world, the name *Titanic* needs no translation. While in the history of time the sinking of the *Titanic* was but a brief moment, it is a moment that continues to play in our collective memory. After all, it was a night where the glamour and sparkle of human lives was replaced by the sparkle of stars, ice, and a new morning.

On May 17th, 2001, the graves of bodies #281 and #140 were opened to allow for DNA sampling by scientists from Lakehead University, Thunder Bay, Ontario.

CHAPTER 8

DEEPENING MY CONNECTION TO *TITANIC* VICTIMS

For long-time residents of Halifax, there is often a connection to the *Titanic* story. For others it may simply be that friends and relatives are buried in the Baron de Hirsch, Fairview Lawn, and Mount Olivet cemeteries where the *Titanic* victims are found. My very slender connection goes back to my paternal grandfather, John A. Beed. As a young boy he was hired to walk in front of funeral processions. He would wear a top hat with ribbons hanging from the back. As the "lead" mourner, a child was to evoke a picture of sadness and innocence in a procession that was attended mostly by adults. When he was in his twenties he worked as bookkeeper at Stroud and Eveleigh, "manufacturers and dealers in carriages of all kinds," at 143–147 Maynard Street, Halifax. Next door at 141 Maynard Street, the Nova Scotia Undertaking Company required extra help preparing the *Titanic* victims. My grandfather was hired to assist with the embalming work.

As a boy I looked for tadpoles in the little stream that flows on one side of the Mount Olivet Cemetery, where I have family members buried not far from the *Titanic* graves. Those graves would sometimes be mentioned in local newspapers on the anniversary of the sinking. The sinking of *Titanic* did not take "life" for me until I viewed the British movie *A Night to Remember* on our black and white television set. What a movie! What a story! In high school I read the poem "*Titanic*" by E. J. Pratt. Wow! The iceberg perspective! Unfortunately a little too long and old-fashioned a poem to share with classmates in a 1970s enriched English program.

My first summer job was at the local tourist bureau and included giving directions to the *Titanic* graves. Most motor coach groups would not have the time to stop there. Individuals who made the effort to go to Fairview Lawn Cemetery would find a large white sign with one word in black paint: *TITANIC*. Sixty years after my grandfather had helped prepare the *Titanic* dead, I started to conduct tours of Halifax, bringing some visitors to the *Titanic* gravesites. Most of the visitors on tour with me were satisfied with a stop outside the former house of victim George Wright. In 1978 I made a friend from Southampton, England, and we shared *Titanic* stories. Lesley and I are still friends. At the Southampton Maritime Museum, she was fascinated by the pay books of crew who had survived the sinking. Their books show that on April 15, 1912, they were discharged at sea. Their pay ended when the ship sank.

THE AUTHOR AT THE FAIRVIEW LAWN CEMETERY IN 1998 BEFORE IMPROVEMENTS TO THE *TITANIC* GRAVESITES WERE CARRIED OUT.

I have been fortunate in knowing many people who worked with the *Titanic* story in Halifax. The late Phyllis Blakeley, archivist, pointed me to the coroner's lists and photographs. The late Russ Louwds, a historian whose father worked for the agent of the White Star Line in Halifax, was always willing to share his knowledge. These people added to my understanding of the *Titanic* and the recovery efforts from Halifax.

One type of visitor that I often take to the gravesites are writers looking for a special angle that would appeal to their readers. One of those writers was kind enough to send me a copy of the Monday, April 19, 1982, edition of *The Age*, a Melbourne newspaper from Australia. In the travel section is a photo of children from the Halifax School for the Blind tracing the letters on the *Titanic* stones. The interest for Melbourne readers, wrote Nancy Dexter, is that "Among the few elaborate [*Titanic*] stones was that inscribed by Arthur Gordon MacCrae, B. E. University of Sydney, New South Wales, age 32."

Occasionally I would meet other visitors in the cemetery but the interest was very low-key. The number of visitors changed with the release of the 1997 movie *Titanic*. I did not go to see the movie but heard from others that no mention is made of Halifax and its connection to the real tragedy. Halifax received attention from the media in the lead-up to the Academy Awards ceremony and the many other award shows where the movie was acclaimed. The graves were part of the background of stories from the real sinking. I finally saw the movie in a hotel room in Boston some years later.

With the wider interest in the graves of *Titanic* victims there were concerns regarding access to the sites. When visiting Fairview Lawn Cemetery with a media group I was startled to observe a tour vehicle had been driven onto the grass. I watched as two costumed characters jumped out to lead a group. This prompted media coverage of my concerns about appropriate conduct of tour leaders and the need for alternative parking arrangements for motor coaches. A committee of municipal and provincial officials worked with the cemetery directors to arrange appropriate signage and site improvements that would meet the expectations of the growing number of visitors. At the same time the arrangements took into account the fact that the three cemeteries are visited by grieving families. Respectful behavior during visits is paramount. The committee members are to be congratulated for their efforts.

The gravestones have been refurbished so you can see the inscriptions. In most cases of the *Titanic* victims there is not much to read. As with other professional tour guides, I have always more to tell than time allows. This book has been my solution to that problem. I also hope that people will use the information I have assembled to correct some of the information they give out. The false stories I hear in the cemetery give me a headache. George Bernard Shaw said the disaster caused an "explosion of outrageous romantic lying." There is some truth to that even today.

Before and during the writing of this book I have found answers to questions of what happened on the night of the sinking. As a child I wondered why people did not swim to an iceberg. I now know more about cold water and icebergs. Another thing that always bothered me was why did the men of third class not take charge of protecting their families? With all the wood on the *Titanic* why did those strong workers not use the two hours and forty minutes before the ship sank to do something? Could they not have put children into the huge crates that held cargo and supplies? Would the large travelling trunks of the

well-dressed ladies have floated as rowboats until the rescue ships arrived? It was only in March of 2000 that I finally had my answer. The two hours and forty minutes was simply not enough time for people to think of alternatives to what was happening. Many of the people did not have the experience or knowledge to judge that rescue would not arrive in time so they took no action.

I came to this understanding as I visited a ship at Pier 20 in Halifax. Growing up in a harbour town, I have had the opportunity to visit many different ships, even the occasional cruise ship. On this particular rainy day I was taking advantage of an open house on the United States Coast Guard cutter *Healy*. The ship was on its maiden voyage to the Arctic. Imagine, visiting an icebreaker while writing a book on the *Titanic*! That rainy afternoon the groups visiting were small. As we went up the gangway we were passed by heavily scented young men going ashore, so typical of the arrival of sailors in our harbour town for 250 years. Our guide was Jeff, an engineer. We viewed the bridge, lifeboats, research rooms, equipment, and the engines. Jeff led and we followed. Groups of technical people, designers, and builders worked around us as they tested the systems of this new vessel that had only been commissioned in November of 1999.

As our group only consisted of six, Jeff was most obliging in taking us to see the mess, a cabin to be shared by three scientists, the library, and the dining and recreation rooms. We even had a closer look at the dual electric propulsion system. While the other guests were asking about details of the ship, my mind was making *Titanic* comparisons. The ship was less than half the length of *Titanic* and had seven decks to *Titanic*'s ten; it would carry 140 people compared to over 3,000. Up and down stairs we went, trusting a complete stranger to guide us safely. When we passed through a control room we heard buzzers making warning noises and saw red lights flashing. Jeff assured us that the alarm signals were malfunctioning as systems were being tested and there was nothing to worry about. Around corners and along corridors, travelling seven decks we reached an exercise room deep in the ship. At that point, I wondered if I could find my way back to the gangway deck on my own. I realized how dependent I was on our guide. Jeff cheerfully took us back to the exit onto the dock. After one hour and forty-five minutes our tour of the *Healy* was over and I was exhausted and cold.

I now understood how the *Titanic*'s third-class passengers, especially those who could not speak English, were unable to take control of their destiny that last night. They would trust that the crew of the big ship would take charge and know what to do. The parents might act brave for their children's sake. They might gather up a few possessions to take on the hoped-for rescue ship. However, in the time needed to dress and reach the upper decks, there was no opportunity for anyone to organize a plan other than what was being offered. The passengers and crew of *Titanic* were already cold and exhausted before the ship even sank. While a few people did throw deck chairs into the water, there was no chance to think of ripping the ship apart

for wood. There was simply not enough time. I am indebted to our cheerful guide on the *Healy* for unknowingly helping me to understand this. It has added to my Halifax tours.

In May of 2001, three graves of *Titanic* victims were opened at Fairview Lawn Cemetery. The application for this process had taken over a year to complete. It had begun when a family of a *Titanic* passenger asked permission to inscribe the woman's name on a stone at the grave of body #281, an unidentified female. This request was passed from the Halifax Regional Municipality to a committee of three citizens knowledgeable on the *Titanic* and the burial sites.

The information given the committee did not match the description of body #281 from the 1912 coroner's report. Alan Ruffman, a member of the committee, suggested DNA testing and sought out Dr. Ryan Parr with the department of anthropology at Lakehead University in Thunder Bay, Ontario. While exploring the possibilities of DNA sampling, two other families were approached regarding bodies #240 and #4. Mr. Ruffman and others presented their case to the provincial medical officer, Dr. Robert Strang, who agreed to sign the order for exhumations.

This planned exhumation was only a rumour among Haligonians. For some of us it was hard to believe that permission would be granted. The first news report gave the impression that the regional municipality, owners of the cemetery, had given permission for the work. On making an inquiry, I was informed that this was not the case. The municipality was only following the order of the

medical officer. A press release was subsequently issued on May 16, 2001, explaining that the municipality would ensure that all relevant protocols would be followed for the handling of remains, that no artifacts would be removed, and that the situation would be handled in a dignified and respectful manner.

My position was that after eighty-nine years there were no immediate family waiting for news of identification. There were also no estate questions to be resolved. My view opposing the exhumations attracted media inquiries from all over North America, which was somewhat disconcerting. While I did not like the idea of people peering into the graves, I also did not want to become part of a circus. However, when it was put forward that identification would allow for proper religious services I reminded listeners on radio that services were conducted at the time of burials in May 1912. While there was no Catholic priest at the service,

I had to agree with a priest who had once said a prayer is never lost.

I felt that the exhumations were being carried out more to prove the science than to prove the identities for families. This feeling was reinforced when I heard one of those involved say it was tantalizing to be able to open the graves looking for DNA. The families had been promised that there was no financial cost to agreeing to allow their names to be used in the application process. A company donated the equipment used in the DNA work. The scientists were using funds from the province of Ontario heritage fund. The families were guaranteed privacy but had to promise to allow the results to be published in scientific papers and to be presented at conferences.

Words like closure were used to try to justify what I considered to be scientific curiosity. We knew the people died in the sinking of the *Titanic*. We also know that it was upsetting for people in

ANOTHER VIEW AT FAIRVIEW LAWN
CEMETERY OF THE TENT COVERING
THE GRAVES OF BODIES #281 AND
#240, WHICH WERE OPENED FOR
DNA TESTING IN 2001. NO HUMAN
REMAINS WERE FOUND.

Halifax who have cared for the dead to have this work carried out.

On Thursday, May 17, digging started at the graves of the unidentified female, body #281, and the unidentified male, #240, which were side by side. After an excavator had cleared the first few feet of soil a tent was place over the graves to keep the media from taking pictures of the open graves. Local media drove me to the cemetery to conduct an interview outside the gate. I was soon surrounded by media from across the nation. Part of the reason for this interest was that the people doing the research tried to control where and when the media would have access to the scientists. A neighbour came along and offered a drive that I quickly accepted. I did return later to assure myself that everything was being handled with dignity. At that point I was discouraged to see what I thought were too many people looking down the open graves. However, I was later to learn that on the first day of work they had only reached the top of the coffins, which seemed to be in good condition. The sides of the tent were down so the workers could close the graves with boards for the night. The scientists were conducting interviews in the cemetery—something they had promised not to do. The police security was leaving and the way was open to take photographs.

On Friday, May 18, the tops of the coffins of the two adults were lifted only to reveal that time had taken its toll on the remains. As the coffins had been buried in a large trench on the slope of a hill, the trench had acted like a conduit for all the water runoff. This, together with the type of soil present and the other forces of nature, had eliminated any remains suitable for DNA testing. My question is why they did not make a better study of these factors before putting us through this process. The scientists made contact with the family interested in the unknown child to tell them of the controversy surrounding the exhumations and some members were hesitant with going ahead. The closest possible relative, however, agreed to allow the exhumation to proceed.

Later that same day scientists opened the grave of the unknown child, who was identified as Gosta Leonard Palsson in 1912 (see chapter 5). While his name was never inscribed on the stone, the

identity was accepted by the coroner in 1912. There are those who have wondered if it was another boy of the same age who was lost in the sinking. My feeling is that the grave of the unknown child has come to represent all fifty-three young children lost in the sinking. When they opened the grave they did find some remains and took samples but because of the age of the child it was not certain whether it would reveal anything. Also found was a red funeral decoration inscribed "Our Dear Babe," an item that was often put into the casket of young children. That same afternoon the grave was closed. That evening Alan Ruffman and I were invited to appear on a television news programme where the host, Steve Murphy, asked us our points of view. I had not changed my mind and still opposed that sort of testing. I feel that living in a Maritime city like Halifax, we will always have

identities that will never be known in our coastal graveyards. Mr. Ruffman came out on the side of science but agreed that there was probably nothing more to be learned at the *Titanic* gravesites. Mr. Murphy thanked us for our "civilized discussion." The *Titanic* victims deserved nothing less from the media and they got it. Later that night the scientists cancelled their news conference as the media had moved on.

I received telephone messages from friends and supporters of my view for the next week. I answered letters from complete strangers who wanted to add their voice to everything that had gone on that week. A few days later, while conducting a tour to the cemetery, I noticed the new grass sods where the digging had occurred. I was satisfied that things were back to normal once again.

The headstone of *Titanic* survivor Hilda Slayter Lacon, Camp hill Cemetery, Halifax.

CHAPTER 9

TRAVELS WITH *TITANIC*

Even if another port had been chosen for receiving *Titanic*'s dead, Halifax would have still had a connection to the disaster. Haligonian George Wright died in the disaster and left his house to the Women's Council of Halifax. His memorial stone remains in the family plot in Christ Church Cemetery in Dartmouth. Halifax would also have had the story of resident Hilda Slayter, who survived the sinking.

However, as the port that was home to the "death ship" *Mackay-Bennett*, Halifax is as important to the story of *Titanic* as the port of Belfast, where she was built, and the ports she steamed from with passengers and crew.

Since my interest in *Titanic* was first sparked I have travelled to numerous places to conduct research for this book. I have stayed at the Charing Cross Hotel, London, where Michel Navratil stayed with his two boys before leaving for Southampton. I have stayed at the Russell Hotel in London where George Wright stayed before taking the train for Southampton. I have attended numerous events and conventions related to *Titanic*. One convention was in Ottawa, appropriately at the Chateau Laurier. Victim Charles Hays had intended to preside at the opening of the Laurier on his return from Europe. From that hotel our group travelled into the countryside to

THE COUNTRY HOME WHERE HUDSON ALLISON INTENDED TO STABLE THE TWENTY-FIVE HORSES THAT ARRIVED FROM ENGLAND AFTER THE SINKING.

GRAVESIDE MONUMENT TO THE ALLISON FAMILY.

WREATH FLOATING ALONG THE *TITANIC* DOCK AT SOUTHAMPTON.

SIGN AT THE CHURCHYARD IN BARKING, LONDON, WHERE A MEMORIAL INSCRIPTION TO TWO COUSINS LOST IN THE SINKING IS FOUND.

see a church that had a memorial window for the Allison family. Outside Chester, Ontario, we saw the county home that was built for them. Lastly, we visited the family plot to see the inscriptions for the three lost in the sinking.

On numerous visits to Southampton there has always been something new to find. The city has sixteen public memorials as well as stones in local graveyards. At the British Titanic Society meetings there are always new stories to learn, often brought by local people whose relatives were on-board the ship. The laying of the wreath in the water at the dock from which *Titanic* departed is always a moving experience.

At the 2009 convention I was successful in having purchased a taxi tour of London's *Titanic*-related sites. It was led by well-known *Titanic* exhibitor and London cabbie Alex Toouli, who offered the tour as a way to raise funds for senior

home care for *Titanic* survivor Millvina Dean. On the tour we started in the area of Barking, where we entered the graveyard of the ancient parish church of East Ham St. Mary Magdalene.

As the gate was locked it was suggested we hop the stone wall. This is where the line between *Titanic* fanatic and enthusiast might be drawn. With the help of Alex and fellow passenger Patrick Murphy of Halifax, over the wall I went in search of two *Titanic* inscriptions. Finding them was in no way diminished by the means of access. To stand at the headstone marked "RJ & PS Rogers" one finds "also Edward James William son of the above age 31 years, also Edward Henry Bagley their nephew age 33, who lost their lives on the Titanic April 15, 1912. Out of the deep I call to thee O Lord."

But these two men are not buried in that cemetery. Edward James William Rogers, assistant

The former London home of Lord Pirrie. It was here over dinner that Pirrie, chair of the Harland and Wolff shipyards in Belfast, and J. Bruce Ismay, president of the White Star Line, discussed building the Olympic class ships.

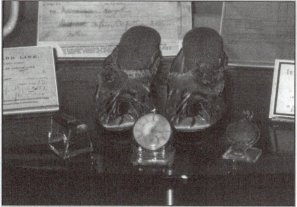

In front of the evening slippers of survivor Edith Russell is the watch found on the body of victim Robert Douglas Norman.

storekeeper, was married with three children and lived in Southampton; his wife could not afford to bring his body home. He is buried in Fairview Lawn Cemetery, Halifax, body #282. Edward Henry Bagley was a first-class saloon steward and was never identified as being found. Scaling over the wall we returned to our London cab parked on a side street, where in great embarrassment we noted that there was an open gate to the churchyard.

We drove for hours to see other monuments and buildings associated with *Titanic*, including Downshire House, the former London home of Lord Pirrie, where a dinner was held in July 1907 to discuss the building of the Olympic class of ships. The building is now used as an embassy.

The National Maritime Museum (with its *Titanic* memorial garden and exhibit) at Greenwich has displayed the evening slippers of survivor Edith Russell, who is famously remembered for taking her music box shaped like a pig (with a wind-up tail) into the lifeboat. In front of the slippers is the watch found on second-class passenger Robert Douglas Norman. Mr. Norman was body #287 and is buried in the Fairview Lawn Cemetery in Halifax.

Sometimes I do not have to go far from home to find connections to the *Titanic*. At a small museum in Lower Selma, Nova Scotia, there is an embalming table that was taken to Halifax and said to have been used for the body of John Jacob Astor.

In 2007 to commemorate the ninety-fifth anniversary of the sinking, *Titanic* societies from around the world met in Halifax for the first time as a group. Among the events was a memorial

Embalming table in museum in Lower Selma, Nova Scotia.

Deck chair that was presented by the crew of the *Minia* to the Rev. Henry W. Cunningham.

service—held at the time the ship would have struck the iceberg—in the ballroom of a hotel overlooking the harbour. The Halifax Regional Municipality also planned a service at the Fairview Lawn Cemetery for the time of the sinking of the ship. This 2:20 a.m. time would have been a very cold event for people dressed in evening clothes from the hotel. However hardy Halifax residents gathered in the cemetery on the newly paved pathway with temporary lighting installed and other conveniences.

The Maritime Museum of the Atlantic in Halifax houses the largest collection of wooden objects from *Titanic* in the world. The items were picked up at the time of the recovery of the bodies. It was a tradition of the sea to pass the time making items from recovered wood. So in the display cases of the museum there are many examples, including a cribbage board, a rolling pin, and frames made from *Titanic* wood. There is a cutting board from *Titanic*'s kitchen; it was brought home to a wife who needed a new one but she refused to cut into it. There are large pieces of wood from the decorative panels of the ship. Visitors can stand in front of a stairway photograph and reach out towards an actual piece of the carved stair wood. The exhibit features a boat deck scene where visitors can sit on a replica deck chair. Nearby is a deck chair from *Titanic* that was presented by the crew of the *Minia* to the Reverend Henry W. Cunningham for his work performing memorial services and burials at sea.

Families donated some of the pieces, while others were sold to the museum. In 2000 the museum bought a cabinet from a first-class cabin for eighty thousand dollars. It was kept by crew member Theodore Smith of the recovery vessel CS *Minia*, whose family used it and knew it as "the

<small>CABINET FROM THE *TITANIC*.</small>

Titanic medicine cabinet." It was confirmed to be from *Titanic* as it was marked on the back for what cabin it should go in (B-Deck) and was stamped with the name "J. Cobain," a Belfast carpenter. Among the other items on display are a mortuary bag with the number 41 and a tag listing that it carried the effects of E. J. Stone, a first-class steward buried in the Fairview Lawn Cemetery.

In July 2009 I joined a tour from Halifax to Ireland. The highlight was a specially arranged tour for me with local *Titanic* enthusiast and professional tour guide Nollaig Neill. We visited the private offices of the Belfast Harbour Commissioners. In a small anteroom was the dining furniture commissioned by the White Star Line for the private quarters of the captain of the SS *Titanic*. It was not ready for the maiden voyage and was sent to Southampton to be placed onboard when the ship returned. It remained in storage for many years and was returned to Belfast.

<small>THE DINING TABLE AND CHAIRS COMMISSIONED FOR THE SS *TITANIC* SET AS IF WAITING FOR THE ENTRANCE OF THE CAPTAIN.</small>

At Belfast City Hall we stopped to take a photo of the *Titanic* memorial but I could not see it as there was a ferris wheel placed over it. The wheel was removed the following year. Along with the docks and buildings of the Harland and Wolff yard, Nollaig also took me on board the *Nomadic*, former tender of the White Star Line.

SS *NOMADIC*: PASSENGER FERRY TO THE SS *TITANIC*

With the largest passenger ships crossing the North Atlantic, the White Star Line was ahead of its competitors. The ships also put the company

EVEN IN NEED OF RESTORATION, INTERIOR CONSTRUCTION SHOWS *NOMADIC* WAS BUILT TO PLEASE FIRST-CLASS PASSENGERS.

NOMADIC AT DOCK WAITING RESTORATION FUNDING, SHOWING NAME AND HOMEPORT OF CHERBOURG, FRANCE.

ahead of the available docks in ports of call. This was remedied in Southampton and New York by the building of larger docking facilities. At Cherbourg and Queenstown (Cobh), servicing the liners meant smaller vessels delivered passengers, luggage, and mail to the anchored ships. One of these passenger ships, SS *Nomadic*, still exists and after many years she has returned to the port of its building: Belfast.

SS *Nomadic* was to carry first- and second-class passengers from the shore at Cherbourg. A sister vessel, the *Traffic*, was to carry third-class passengers and mail cargo. Launched April 25, 1911, *Nomadic* steamed to France and served the passengers of SS *Olympic* until the one voyage out to the SS *Titanic* April 10, 1912. Twenty-two passengers were taken off the *Titanic* and 274 passengers were delivered by the two ferries. The most

famous of the passengers to board at Cherbourg were John Jacob Astor and his wife, Madeline, and Mrs. Margaret Brown of Denver, Colorado.

The ferries continued to be used until the Second World War interrupted passenger service. The *Nomadic* was described in a promotional film as "almost a large steamer herself." *Nomadic* ultimately became a floating restaurant in the River Seine, Paris, in the 1970s. There she rose and fell in the swell of passing tourist boats and suffered from conversion and neglect. She came up for auction in 2006 and many thought she would be scrapped. Finally she was bought and brought back to Belfast.

I first saw *Nomadic* in Belfast on a private tour to its mooring site in July 2009. Touring inside and out was a tremendous experience along with meeting people filled with optimism about the

Monument in Cobh, Ireland, includes an illustration of the ship and of a woman surrounded by her boys. The woman depicted is Margaret Rice, who is buried in Halifax's Mount Olivet Roman Catholic Cemetery.

Service held at Fairview Lawn Cemetery by the International Ice Patrol Service of the United States Coast Guard for dedication of wreaths to be dropped at the site of the sinking of *Titanic*.

restoration of the ship. I again visited the *Nomadic* in July 2011 when it was in drydock in the process of being restored. When fully restored it is expected that thousands of people will visit this floating link to *Titanic*.

Belfast will become the largest centre for display of items related to the *Titanic*.

***

As my tour headed for the south of the island I was continually looking for *Titanic* mentions. I left the group at Killarney and took a bus and a train to Cobh (formerly Queenstown), Ireland—the last departure point for *Titanic* before heading to open sea. I stayed at the Commodore Hotel (where the survivors of the *Lusitania* stayed) and explored the town. Cobh has displays on the *Titanic* in the heritage centre at the railway station, and in the centre of town is a monument to *Titanic*. The town has also created a "Titanic Trail." This walk along the streets of the town includes pubs and hotels where passengers stayed, White Star Line dockside offices and waiting rooms, and other sites related to the only visit *Titanic* made to the port. Local guides can be hired to provide a colourful description of life in 1912.

On April 14, 2010, while in the Fairview Lawn Cemetery for an evening memorial service, I was invited by Commander Scott Rogerson of the International Ice Patrol Service of the United States Coast Guard to join them at a ceremony in the cemetery the next day, April 15, to dedicate three wreaths that would later be dropped by airplane in the Atlantic Ocean at the site of the sinking.

On October 11, 2010, I received an email from Virginia Hopwood, a descendant of a *Titanic* victim:

Dear Mr. Beed

I am a descendant of a *Titanic* victim. I understand that you wrote a book called "Titanic Victims In Halifax Graveyards" and I thought you might find the enclosed information of interest.

Yours sincerely

Virginia Hopwood

England

I am writing to tell you a *Titanic* story, in which I thought you might be interested.

As you can see from the enclosed letter, which is a copy of the original sent by the White Star Line to my great-grandmother, my family believed that my great-grandfather Frederick Woodford had been drowned on the *Titanic*, recovered by the Cable Steamer *Mackay-Bennett* and buried at sea.

As a descendant of a *Titanic* victim, I have naturally been drawn to museums and exhibitions relating to the great ship. In 2002, my husband and I decided to visit Canada and one of the places we stayed was Halifax, which we knew had a *Titanic* connection, being the place where the recovered victims were brought. However, as my great-grandfather was buried at sea, this fact was not of apparent interest.

We visited the Maritime Museum of the Atlantic and discovered that the victims, who had been brought to Halifax, had been buried in a special section of the city's cemetery. In the hope of finding a general memorial to all the victims of the *Titanic*—a sort of war memorial—we walked all the way to the cemetery. It is a long way on foot and many times we thought of giving up our wild goose chase as we wandered through the suburbs of Halifax. Eventually we got to the cemetery and began to read the information boards about the *Titanic* section. As we read down to the final paragraph, the boards talked about the re-dedication of four of the previously blank gravestones, which had been identified, and, to our surprise, we made the momentous discovery that my great-grandfather was one of them. He had not been buried at sea after his recovery by the *Mackay-Bennett* at all, but was lying only a few yards away from where we stood, and I was the first of his descendants to visit his grave, almost exactly ninety years to the day that he was buried there

We returned in something of a state of shock to the Maritime Museum where one of the Curator's assistants kindly gave us an article relating to the role of the Titanic International Society in the identification and re-dedication of the bare stone which had marked my great-grandfather's grave for almost eighty years.

Sadly, my grandmother died in 1985

never knowing that her father had been buried in Halifax. This was particularly poignant as she had once told me how sad it was that she had no grave to visit—her mother and siblings were all dead by 1916, leaving her an orphan—and their graves were removed by Southampton Council. Little did she know that her father's unnamed grave existed. Fortunately my father and his brother are still alive, and I duly phoned my father from Halifax with news of our discovery. He was shocked by our revelations and told his brother, who was equally amazed by this new information.

Looking at the guidebook we used in Canada, I see that the entry for the Maritime Museum of the Atlantic, reads, "After the 1912 catastrophe, many of the bodies that were recovered were brought to Halifax, and 150 are buried in the town." Little did we know when we planned our trip to Halifax that we would discover that one of the 150 would be my great-grandfather.

Yours sincerely
Virginia Hopwood

***

Later I heard a story of two *Titanic* survivors who lived into old age in California. In the summer of 2011 while giving a tour in Halifax, I met Jackie Waldon and her son Russell Hall from Grants Pass, Oregon. Hearing my *Titanic* stories they wanted to share theirs. Jackie Waldron was a literary agent for author Rustie Brown, who wrote a book on premonitions (*The Titanic, the Psychic and the Sea*) and had

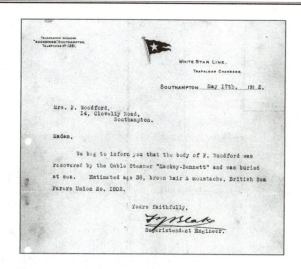

COPY OF LETTER SENT TO THE FAMILY OF F. WOODFORD STATING HE HAD BEEN BURIED AT SEA.

interviewed survivors Edwina Troutt and Ruth Becker. Jackie had a calling card with a photo and the printed words "Edwina MacKenzie, *Titanic* Survivor" and an illustration of the ship. In handwriting on the front is "Born in 1884, Edwina C. MacKenzie saved in life boat 13." On the back was written "With all my love to you Always, Edwina C. MacKenzie nee Troutt." It appears the card was given to Rustie Brown in 1980. What an interesting calling card for a woman who was by then ninety-six years old. The last name MacKenzie came from her third husband; she had outlived all three. In 1983 Jackie was invited to a party in Hermosa, California, to celebrate Edwina's ninety-ninth birthday. There, Jackie took a photograph of happy seniors Ruth Becker and Edwina Troutt. Edwina would die the next year after her one-hundredth birthday. Ruth Becker lived in Santa Barbara, California, until she died in 1990 at the age of ninety.

The shoes of the "Unknown Child."

CHAPTER 10

CONTINUING CONTROVERSIES AND THE END OF AN ERA

Most touching of the exhibit pieces at the Maritime Museum of the Atlantic in Halifax are the shoes of a third-class passenger, known as the "Unknown Child," next to the gloves of a first-class passenger, railway president Charles Hays. While travelling in different classes of accommodation they were united in death.

For over eighty years the Unknown Child was thought to be Swedish boy Gosta Leonard Palsson, who was travelling with his mother and three siblings. In 2002 after digging for remains at the Fairview Lawn Cemetery in Halifax, it was decided that the boy was thirteen-month-old Eino Vijami Panula from Finland. A documentary company even brought in descendents of the family to visit the grave. In 2003 the museum came into the possession of a pair of shoes that had belonged to the Unknown Child but they seemed too large for the child identified. (The shoes had been kept by a Halifax police officer who was part of a group that was to see to the disposal of the clothing of the victims. Most items were burned but the shoes remained in his possession.) The shoes seemed too big for a thirteen-month-old and the research and testing of the scientists was reviewed. Other agencies became involved. Finally, in 2011 it was announced that the grave of the Unknown Child is

SIDNEY LESLIE GOODWIN, THE "UNKNOWN CHILD."

that of nineteen-month-old English boy Sidney Leslie Goodwin. His parents had boarded the *Titanic* with their six children and the entire family was lost in the sinking.

With the one hundredth anniversary of the sinking there is much discussion of all aspects

THE GRAVESTONE IN FAIRVIEW LAWN CEMETERY FOR BODY #308.

Alfred Vanderbilt, George's nephew, was a wealthy world traveller. In 1915 during the First World War he did take passage on the *Lusitania*. That ship was famously torpedoed off Ireland and Alfred Vanderbilt was one of the hundreds of passengers and crew lost in the sinking. The two stories of the ships and the Vanderbilt name became linked through newspaper accounts. It made a good story of a passenger surviving one sinking and going down on another. There were certainly similar stories of other passengers and crew having that kind of life and death experience. It is just not true about Alfred Vanderbilt.

• • •

of the *Titanic* and with more research more corrections are made to previous stories. One of these concerns Alfred Vanderbilt versus George Vanderbilt II and the unlucky valet.

It is often mistakenly printed that Alfred Vanderbilt was booked on the *Titanic* but never sailed. This would have made Alfred Vanderbilt one of those who truly missed the ship. But this was not the case. It was actually a relative, George Vanderbilt II, and his wife Edith, who decided to not travel on the *Titanic*. Their valet/driver Edwin (Fred) Wheeler did travel on the *Titanic* with the couple's luggage. There is a photograph of twenty-four-year-old Edwin (Fred) Wheeler walking along the deck in second class with two other passengers before *Titanic* arrived at Queenstown, Ireland. Fred did not survive the sinking. George Vanderbilt II died only two years later in 1914 after an operation.

There are many theories as to why the *Titanic* hit an iceberg and sank. In 2010 I spent a half hour on a radio program discussing the *Titanic* in light of the news story that the Lady Louise Patten, the granddaughter of Charles Lightoller, had the theory that the *Titanic* was steered in the wrong direction when the iceberg was spotted. Unfortunately Lady Patten does not have any real evidence from her grandfather. But this theory has now joined the continuing debate regarding how the crew handled the ship.

Another theory often discussed is what caused the ship to sink. It was long thought to be a gaping hole although some suggested it was caused by small gashes. Others have suggested the plates were weak. Lately it has been thought the rivets did not hold. The Maritime Museum of the Atlantic in Halifax has a caption near a photograph

THE DRAWING BUILDING OF THE HARLAND AND WOLFF YARD WAS OPEN TO THE PUBLIC FOR THE BELFAST TITANIC FESTIVAL.

became common during the Second World War."

If the ship's construction does not interest you it may be the people onboard that do. There has been a long-running debate on the number of people who died in the sinking. Long accepted was 1,517, but now 1,497 is considered the more accurate number by experts around the world who are compiling an authoritative list of those on board. This revision to the list of those who travelled on the ship will likely also mean there were more survivors that the official number of 705.

Many such discussions now take place online among *Titanic* historians and enthusiasts. A contributor has put forward the theory that body #308 must be Anton Ferrari, since the only identifying item on the body was a handkerchief with the initials AHF. With the body's original description as that of an assistant engineer, other possible owners of the handkerchief, especially "A. Foster" would be eliminated. Enthusiasts attending the Belfast Titanic Convention seem to agree with this new proposed identity. However, the identity is not universally accepted and is unlikely to ever be known for certain. There will be no attempt to inscribe a name on the stone at the Fairview Lawn Cemetery. The debate on identities will continue.

BELFAST CLAIMS THE *TITANIC* STORY

"Built in Belfast" is the slogan on many items for sale in that city. Belfast was built partly on the success of its shipbuilders, with Harland and Wolff the largest of those operations. With the sinking

of rivets stating "Titanic was an outstanding example of the art of riveted steel shipbuilding. Her steel plates were fastened by three million thick, steel pins called rivets. Riveting reigned supreme in shipbuilding for over a century, relegating wooden shipyards to oblivion and lasting until welding

Belfast is building a £100 million Titanic Centre to mark the area's shipbuilding history. The building is designed to look like the bows of ships pointed to the four corners of the earth. It is being constructed on the site where the *Titanic* and her sister ships were built and launched.

Sign at the Harland and Wolff drydock where *Titanic* was given final touches after launch.

of *Titanic* there was sorrow but the shipbuilding continued. Hundreds of ships were built and a number sank but only *Titanic* left a black mark on the city's history. Belfast now wants to reclaim the glory of the shipbuilding days, including the building of *Titanic*, which employed many.

On May 31, 2011, Belfast, Northern Ireland, celebrated the one-hundredth anniversary of the successful launch of the SS *Titanic* from the Harland and Wolff yard. Many events were held leading up to this important day in shipbuilding history. Rockets were fired to recreate what was done on the day in 1911 to signal to the thousands that crowded the shoreline that she was coming down the ways. One hundred years later

the crowd was much smaller, but there was an assembly of small craft in the water, and on shore groups of school children cheered the event. The City of Belfast has designated the area where the *Titanic* was built at the Harland and Wolff yards as the Titanic Quarter.

One of the speakers during the Titanic Festival events in Belfast was award-winning Irish newspaper journalist Senan Molony. He has written about the Irish on the *Titanic*, including victim Joseph Dawson, buried in the Fairview Lawn Cemetery. Molony has also written about the unidentified ship's stewards whose bodies were buried at sea and in Halifax. He argues one of those buried in the Baron De Hirsch Hebrew Cemetery listed as unidentified may be T. Ryan. The body had no papers for identity purposes, but the man was wearing drawers marked "H. Lyons." There was no such name on the stewards' list; however,

Senan Molony at the Lord Mayor's Dinner and Dance at Belfast City Hall, May 2011, to celebrate the one hundredth anniversary of the successful launch of *Titanic*.

if the written marks were misread this could explain the discrepancy.

Molony's talk at Belfast City Hall concerned whether the crew on the *Californian* that was blamed for not assisting the *Titanic* ever saw *Titanic* or instead saw flares over another ship. (Several *Titanic* survivors reported seeing a ship's lights in the distance and the identity of this "mystery ship" has long been assumed to be the *Californian*.) Over the years Senan and I have corresponded and I have tried to track down more information on a ship that has a Nova Scotia connection. The *Kevindale* was bound for Louisbourg, Nova Scotia. After the *Titanic*'s sinking, another captain was quoted in New York newspapers as stating the *Kevindale* was steaming through the area of the sinking around the time of the disaster. Molony is hoping to one day prove that the

captain of the *Californian* was not in a position to render assistance, and that his vessel was not, in fact, the "mystery ship." He feels that there were one or two ships that may have been closer.

Ninety-nine years after the *Titanic*'s sinking, his talk in Belfast generated heated discussion. On one side were those who feel that the *Californian*'s Captain Lord should have his reputation restored, and on the other side were those who continue to believe the captain should have done more to come to *Titanic*'s aid.

***

With the passing of *Titanic* survivors, diaries and letters now allow us to see how these survivors got on in life after the sinking. In June 1972, sixty years after the sinking, Shirley Ellis of Halifax received a letter from survivor Madeleine (Mellinger) Mann thanking her for newspaper clippings of an interview done while Madeleine was in Halifax to visit the *Titanic* graves.

In the *Mail Star* article by reporter Al Herron on June 16, 1972, he relates that Madeleine "slept while *Titanic* hit [the] iceberg." He wrote at the time, "The nice little old lady looked rather frail, she walked with a slight limp, but there was neither hesitation nor faltering in either her memory or her speech."

Mrs. Mann wrote to Shirley:

Dear Shirley
Thank you so much for your kindness in sending me the extra copies of the paper. I had to laugh at the bit about the "frail little lady with the limp", tho' guess I am a

"Little old lady" at 73 but never thought of myself that way. I had a bad illness in 1929 which caused the stiffness on my left side, it was caused by a "quinsey" (sore throat) and in those days we didn't have the "wonder drugs" & it broke and the poison went to all my joints in the left side. I have lived with it and am used to it, unless I get careless and move too quickly. I got quite a lot of mail when I got home, or I should have written sooner. We went on to <u>Fredericton</u> & had a nice visit with a friend I met in England when on a visit few years ago. She is a well known lady there in NB a poetess & painter of lovely <u>flower</u> <u>pictures</u> & has won many awards there & in Europe. Perhaps you have heard of her—Miss Marguerite McNair. We had lovely weather all the way until we got home, then got real cold wind & rain storms. I have had so much to do in my flower garden & it looks lovely. I love flowers too, being <u>English</u> first of all, but became a Canadian Citizen 3 yrs ago, after living here since 1913, it was <u>real</u> <u>kind</u> of them and me having 4 wonderful sons, two of them were in the 2nd world war too. Where in England did your mother come from? I was born in Essex but went to school in <u>Wimbledon</u> where the famous Tennis Courts are. I don't suppose we will meet again but it was nice of you to be so thoughtful.

Sincerely
Madeleine (Mellinger) Mann

<u>P.S.</u>
Excuse the scribble & errors but I am real tired after so much gardening & my hand is stiff so will be off to bed, but did not want another day to go by before writing you. I have lots to answer yet.
M. V. M

Mrs. Mann gave the initial V. for Violet, her middle name. Madeleine Mann died in Toronto on May 27, 1976.

Shirley Ellis, who arranged the interview in 1972, recounted the story of meeting this *Titanic* survivor in a newspaper article, "Night to remember," on January 28, 1998, which she wrote after seeing the movie *Titanic*. Shirley Ellis kept Madeleine Mann's thank you letter for thirty-nine years until her own death in May 2011.

MILLVINA DEAN—*TITANIC* SURVIVOR

Born February 2, 1912, Millvina (Elizabeth Gladys) Dean was only nine weeks old when she was put into Lifeboat 10 in the early morning hours of April 15, 1912, with her mother Georgetta (Light) Dean and one-year-old brother Bertram. She was the youngest survivor of the ill-fated *Titanic*.

Her father was Bertram Frank Dean, and he had purchased tickets for third-class accommodation for the April 10 sailing with the aim to start a new life for his family in Wichita, Kansas. He intended to open a tobacconist shop. He went down with the ship and his body was not identified by the Halifax boats.

After the tragedy Millvina's mother decided to return to England with her children. On the White Star liner *Adriatic* Millvina was a star attraction, according to the *Daily Mirror*: "she was the pet of the liner during the voyage and so keen was the rivalry between the women to nurse the lovable mite of humanity that one of the ship's officers decreed that 1st and 2nd Class passengers might hold her in turn for no more than 10 minutes." She and her brother would have received money from various *Titanic* funds to help with their upbringing.

Millvina lived a quiet life, if you can call working through the bombing of England quiet. She worked for the government and then an engineering firm, never married, and stayed in the Southampton area in retirement. Her mother died in 1975 and her brother died in 1992. Her place in the survivor category became more noted as other survivors with memories of the night passed away. She eventually became the Honourary President of the British Titanic Society.

In the fall of 2008 she made headlines around the world by sending to auction the suitcase given her mother in 1912 for the return trip to England, along with other mementoes of that time. The sale was to raise funds so that she could continue to live in the nursing home where she had moved in 2007 after breaking her hip. A very shrewd woman, she realized the publicity would help raise the prices. She stated she hoped the sale would raise £3,000. The items wound up selling for over

MILLVINA DEAN WEARING THE AUTHOR'S COAT WHILE WAITING FOR THE ALL-CLEAR FROM THE FIRE DEPARTMENT, APRIL 2003.

£30,000 pounds ($61,000 Canadian). A variety of people began to work on setting up a fund to support Millvina so that she could continue to live in her private nursing home. Miss Millvina Dean passed away May 31, 2009. As the last survivor of the *Titanic*, she was once again the centre of attention.

I first met Millvina Dean over lunch at the British Titanic Society Convention at Southampton in 2002. Just days prior to the convention, I had walked in the streets of London with the crowds to the viewing of the casket and crown of the late Queen Mother Elizabeth at Westminster Hall. I told Millvina about being in the Hall when members of the Royal Family were present and she nodded with keen interest to hear all the details. Then after lunch Millvina was surrounded by many other people looking to have time with a *Titanic* survivor.

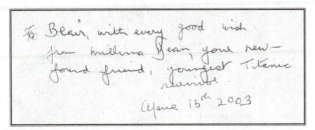

To Blair, with every good wish from millvina Dean your new-found friend, youngest Titanic survivor. April 13th 2003

Inscription from Millvina Dean to the author.

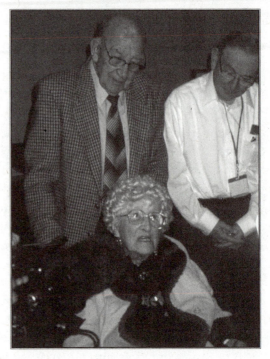

Millvina Dean dressed for the April cold giving an interview at Southampton in 2009, a month before she passed away. Behind her is longtime companion Bruno Nordmanis on the left and David Hill of the British Titanic Society on the right.

In 2003 I returned to the Titanic Convention as one of the lecturers and had the opportunity to speak to Millvina a number of times and discovered her sense of humour. She commented on how many people telephoned and wrote her to find out about her *Titanic* connection and that she would never hear from them again. She enjoyed the conventions as she met many people who had become her friends from around the world. On the night of the gala dinner there was a small problem in the hotel kitchen and the building was evacuated into the parking lot. I took a chair from the banquet hall as Millvina needed to sit while waiting for the all-clear. I offered my jacket as she was only wearing a thin dress and jacket and the night air was cool.

As we waited hotel staff called the names of the registered guests to make sure we were accounted for. There in various sorts of attire from evening gowns to dressing gowns people from around the world gathered in the dark under a parking lot light. As they called the names I was reminded that after the sinking of the *Titanic* many of the survivors called out the names of their loved ones, most of whom were lost to the ocean. The moment when the hotel staff called "Millvina Dean" seemed most poignant. With the arrival of the fire service and blankets my jacket was no longer required and Millvina took great delight in the attention of the firefighters. Shortly after their arrival we were able to return to our conversations in the hotel lounge. After Sunday lunch Millvina inscribed a note to me in a book: "To

Blair with every good wish from Millvina Dean, your newfound friend, youngest *Titanic* survivor, April 13, 2003."

I continued to read her notes in the British Titanic Society Bulletin—short, cheery words to tell us what was going on in her life. I last spoke to Millvina at the April 2009 British Titanic Society Convention in Southampton. She was able to briefly visit the hotel in the afternoon. She greeted me as her "Canadian friend."

Millvina was unable to attend the gala dinner that night where plans were made to launch a fund for her care starting with a dinner auction. The next month Miss Millvina Dean passed away. Her headstone reads "the youngest and last *Titanic* survivor."

At the sinking of the *Titanic* hundreds of children were suddenly without a parent. Many of the crew who went down with the ship were from Southampton and were the only income earner of the family. Funds were immediately set up for subscribers to donate not only to the families who survived the sinking but also for the crew members' families. These children were often referred to as the "orphans" of the *Titanic*. A system of payments was established for the widows and children based on the job the husband had on the ship. The payments were made as long as the widow was of good character and did not drink or have a man living with her. The children received support until age sixteen for boys and eighteen for girls as long as they were in school or training.

Body #178 was buried at sea from the cable ship *Mackay-Bennett*. The body was identified as

SIDNEY SEDUNARY (DECEMBER 4, 1912–FEBRUARY 6, 2010) PHOTOGRAPHED IN 2002 AT THE FAIRVIEW LAWN CEMETERY, AT THE MONUMENT TO THE UNKNOWN CHILD. HIS FATHER'S BODY WAS FOUND BUT WAS BURIED AT SEA SEVEN AND A HALF MONTHS BEFORE SIDNEY WAS BORN.

Sidney Francis Sedunary, a third-class steward. The personal belongings were sent to his wife, who was expecting a child. The child, a boy named Sidney after his father, was born seven and a half months after the sinking.

I met Sid at the 2002 British Titanic Society convention in Southampton, and learned his story as one of the orphans. He was what people would describe as a quiet, kindly man. With a sense of humour, he described the woman involved with the fund payments as wearing a long black coat and skirt and black hat riding a bicycle. His description seemed to match the wicked witch from the movie *Wizard of Oz*. As the youngest person receiving the payments, Sid obviously was the last of the boys to benefit from the local *Titanic* fund. He donated a watch that was found on his father and other items to the Southampton Maritime Museum.

I was able to see him again during a visit the society made to Halifax in 2002. One of the most fascinating parts of his story was when Sid showed the last letter written by his father to his mother. There was also the letter of reply from his mother, which was found with the effects on his father's body. This was a moment of living history and the two letters were probably worth thousands of dollars to collectors. But Sid's intention was never to sell them. While at the Fairview Lawn Cemetery I asked if Sid would mind if I took his photograph next to the grave of the Unknown Child where the British Titanic Society had placed a wreath, and he graciously agreed. Even though he was almost ninety at the time, I was left with the feeling that here was a child mourning the loss of a father he never knew. While at the April 2009 British Titanic Convention in Southampton I overheard a woman say she was there to pay the membership dues of Sid Sedunary as he was unable to make the event. Sid Sedunary died February 6, 2010, at the age of ninety-seven.

***

The *Titanic* survivors have passed away, yet their story will continue to be retold to a new generation. New groups have formed such as the Addergoole Titanic Society, County Mayo, to remember eleven from the parish who died on the *Titanic*. one of those was Mary Mangan, who was buried at sea by the recovery crew of the *Mackay-Bennett*. The village of Comber, County Down, has schoolchildren who use the Memorial Hall, dedicated to Thomas Andrews, Harland and Wolff managing director and the nephew of Lord Pirrie, to create thoughtful projects on the subject of *Titanic*.

I am asked if it is strange to walk a tour into a cemetery. In the case of Halifax cemeteries, I am very comfortable, as I am walking past the graves of many people I have known or to whom I have a family connection. The tradition in graveyards is to erect a monument to the dead and often a tribute is inscribed as families want their loved one remembered. By reading the tribute on the stone, the visitor is paying respect to the loss of the family. The *Titanic* gravesites in Halifax also represent the many victims who were never found. Not everyone will see the situation as I do. Not all tour groups want to go to graveyards. Each tour group I take to the *Titanic* graves has someone who does not wish to walk among the graves. Even school groups have those students who are reluctant to visit. Others, however, are fascinated by visiting a place so deeply connected to a story they have grown up hearing about. The visits are done with great respect. The words of the Reverend Clarence

MacKinnon, principal, Pine Hill Presbyterian College, said at the memorial service for *Titanic* victims in Halifax, May 3, 1912—"their story shall be told to our children and our children's children"—are being fulfilled. The *Titanic* dead will never be forgotten.

TITANIC LEAVING IRELAND ON ITS MAIDEN VOYAGE.

MACKAY-BENNETT BODY DISPOSAL LIST

THE LIST SHOWING HOW BODIES WERE DISPOSED OF FROM THE RECOVERY VESSEL *MACKAY-BENNETT*. BODY #150, GEORGE TALBOT, WAS ACTUALLY BROUGHT TO HALIFAX. BODY #151 WAS BURIED AT SEA. THERE WERE NO BURIALS AT SEA FOR THE LAST 106 BODIES AS PUBLIC PRESSURE DEMANDED ALL BODIES BE BROUGHT ASHORE.

No.	Code	No.	Code	No.	Code	No.	Code	No.	Code
1	U. M.	63	U. B.	124	M.	185	U. B.	246	M.
2	M.	64	M.	125	U. B.	186	M.	247	U. M.
3	U. M.	65	U. B.	126	M.	187	M.	248	U. M.
4	U. M.	66	· B.	127	U. B.	188	M.	249	M.
5	U. M.	67	B.	128	U. M.	189	U. M.	250	U. M.
6	U. M.	68	B.	129	U. M.	190	B.	251	M.
7	M.	69	B.	130	M.	191	U. M.	252	M.
8	U. M.	70	B.	131	M.	192	U. M.	253	U. M.
9	M.	71	U. B.	132	U. B.	193	U. M.	254	U. M.
10	M.	72	B	133	M.	194	U. B.	255	M.
11	M.	73	U. B.	134	U. M.	195	M.	256	M.
12	U. M.	74	U. B.	135	M.	196	M.	257	U. M.
13	U. M.	75	B.	136	U. M.	197	M.	258	M.
14	B.	76	U. B.	137	U. M.	198	U. M.	259	M.
15	M.	77	B.	138	M.	199	U. B.	260	M.
16	M.	78	U. M.	139	U. M.	200	B.	261	M.
17	M.	79	M.	140	M.	201	M.	262	U. M.
18	M.	80	M.	141	U. M.	202	M.	263	M.
19	M.	81	B.	142	M.	203	U. M.	264	M.
20	U. B.	82	B.	143	M.	204	M.	265	U. M.
21	U. B.	83	M.	144	U. M.	205	M.	266	M.
22	M.	84	U. B.	145	M.	206	M.	267	M.
23	U. B.	85	B.	146	B.	207	M.	268	M.
24	U. B.	86	U. B.	147	M.	208	M.	269	M.
25	B.	87	U. B.	148	M.	209	M.	270	M.
26	U. B.	88	U. B.	149	M.	210	U. M.	271	M.
27	B.	89	B.	150	B.	211	M.	272	U. M.
28	U. B.	90	M.	151	M.	212	U. M.	273	M.
29	U. M.	91	U. B.	152	B.	213	U. M.	274	U. M.
30	U. B.	92	U. M.	153	B.	214	U. M.	275	M.
31	U. B.	93	U. B.	154	U. B.	215	M.	276	M.
32	M.	94	U. M.	155	B.	216	U. M.	277	M.
33	U. B.	95	U. B.	156	B.	217	U. M.	278	U. M.
34	M.	96	M.	157	B.	218	M.	279	U. M.
35	M.	97	M.	158	B.	219	U. M.	280	M.
36	U. B.	98	B.	159	B.	220	U. M.	281	U. M.
37	M.	99	U. B.	160	U. B.	221	M	282	M.
38	M.	100	B.	161	M.	222	U. M.	283	M.
39	U. B.	101	U. B.	162	U. B.	223	U. M.	284	M.
40	U. B.	102	U. B.	163	M.	224	M.	285	M.
41	B.	103	B.	164	U. B.	225	M.	286	M.
42	U. B.	104	B.	165	M.	226	M.	287	M.
43	M.	105	U. B.	166	M.	227	M.	288	U. M.
44	U. B.	106	U. B.	167	B.	228	U. M.	289	U. M.
45	B.	107	B.	168	B.	229	U. M.	290	M.
46	B.	108	B.	169	M.	230	M.	291	U. M.
47	B.	109	M.	170	U. B.	231	M.	292	M.
48	U. B.	110	M.	171	B.	232	M.	293	M.
49	B.	111	U. B.	172	M.	233	U. M.	294	M.
50	B.	112	U. B.	173	B.	234	M.	295	M.
51	B.	113	U. B.	174	M.	235	M.	296	U. M.
52	B.	114	U. B.	175	M.	236	M.	297	M.
53	B.	115	B.	176	B.	237	U. M.	298	M.
54	U. B.	116	U. B.	177	B.	238	M.	299	M.
55	U. B.	117	U. B.	178	U. B.	239	M.	300	M.
56	U. B.	118	U. B.	179	U. M.	240	U. M.	301	M.
57	U. B.	119	M.	180	U. B.	241	U. M.	302	M.
58	B.	120	B.	181	B.	242	M.	303	U. M.
59	B.	121	B.	182	U. B.	243	U. M.	304	M.
60	U. B.	122	M.	183	M.	244	M.	305	M.
61	B.	123	B.	184	B.	245	M.	306	M.
62	M.								

Key to accompanying List, showing how Bodies have been disposed of:

B	=	IDENTIFIED BODIES BURIED AT SEA.
UB	=	UNIDENTIFIED BODIES BURIED AT SEA.
M	=	IDENTIFIED BODIES TAKEN TO MORGUE.
UM	=	UNIDENTIFIED BODIES TAKEN TO MORGUE.

BARON DE HIRSCH CEMETERY

Row 2

Row 1

FAIRVIEW LAWN CEMETERY

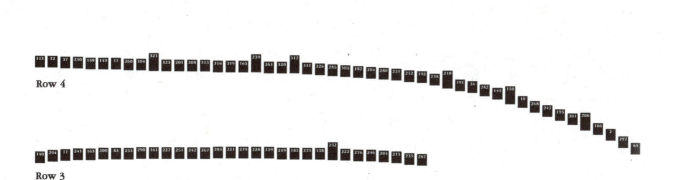

Row 4

Row 3

Row 2

Row 1

MOUNT OLIVET CEMETERY

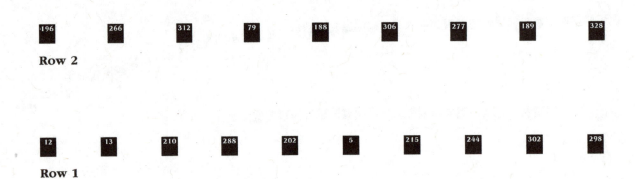

196 266 312 79 188 306 277 189 328

Row 2

12 13 210 288 202 5 215 244 302 298

Row 1

SELECTED BIBLIOGRAPHY

Brown, Rustie. *The* Titanic, *the psychic and the sea.* Lomita, CA: Blue Heron Press, 1981.

Bolger, Francis W. P. and Elizabeth R. Epperly, eds. *My dear Mr. M: letters to G. B. MacMillian from L. M. Mongomery.* Toronto: Oxford University Press, 1992.

Eaton, John P., and Charles A. Haas. Titanic: *triumph and tragedy.* London: W. W. Norton, 1986.

Eaton, John P., and Charles Haas. Titanic: *destination disaster: the legends and reality.* New York: W. W. Norton, 1996.

Everett, Marshall, ed. *Story of the wreck of the* Titanic: *the ocean's greatest disaster.* Memorial edition. New York: L. H. Walter, 1912.

Foster, John Wilson, ed. *The* Titanic *reader.* Toronto: Penguin, 1999.

Garrison, Webb. *A treasury of* Titanic *tales.* Nashville: Rutledge Hill Press, 1998.

Geller, Judith B. Titanic: *women and children first.* New York: W. W. Norton, 1998.

Hustak, Alan. Titanic, *the Canadian story.* Montreal: Véhicule Press, 1998.

Hyslop, Donald, Alastair Forsyth, and Sheila Jemima. Titanic *voices: memories from the fateful voyage.* Gloucestershire, England: Sutton, 1997.

Landau, Elaine. *Heroine of the* Titanic: *the real unsinkable Molly Brown.* New York: Clarion Books, 2001.

Lord, Walter. *A Night to Remember.* New York: Bantam, 1956.

MacLeod, Mary K. *Whisper in the air: Marconi, the Canada years, 1902-1946.* Hantsport, NS: Lancelot Press, 1992.

Maxtone-Graham, John, ed. Titanic *survivor: the newly discovered memoirs by Violet Jessop who survived both the* Titanic *and* Britannic *disasters.* Dobbs Ferry, NY: Sheridan House, 1997.

McCluskie, Tom, Michael Sharpe, and Leo Marriott. Titanic *and her sisters:* Olympic *and* Britannic. Canada: Prospero Books, 1999.

Molony, Senan. *The Irish Aboard* Titanic. Dublin: Wolfhound Press, 2000.

Pellegrino, Charles. *Her name* Titanic: *the untold story of the sinking and finding of the unsinkable ship.* New York: Avon Books, 1990.

Pratt, E. J. *The collected poems of E. J. Pratt.* Toronto: Macmillan, 1958.

Ruffman, Alan. Titanic *remembered: the unsinkable ship and Halifax.* Halifax: Formac, 1999.

Tanaka, Shelley. *On board the* Titanic. Toronto: Scholastic/Madison Press, 1997.

Tibballs, Geoff. *The* Titanic: *the extraordinary story of the 'unsinkable' ship*. Vancouver: Raincoast, 1997.

Tyler, Sidney F. *A Rainbow of Time and Space: Orphans of the* Titanic. Tuscon, AZ: Aztex Corporation, 1981.

Wade, Wyn Craig. *The* Titanic: *End of a Dream*. McClelland and Stewart Ltd, 1979.

Watson, A. *Roster of valor:* Titanic, *Halifax legacy*. Riverside, CT: 7C's Press, 1984.

Winocour, Jack, ed. *The story of the* Titanic: *as told by its survivors: Lawrence Beesley, Archibald Gracie, Commander Lightoller, Harold Bride*. New York: Dover, 1960.

DOCUMENTS, BOOKLETS AND MAGAZINES, NEWSPAPERS:

VanBeck, Todd W. "Call to duty: the funeral director's response to the *Titanic* disaster—1912." Boston: presentation for the National Funeral Directors' Convention, October 1998.

Groffand, John M., and Jane E. Allen. *The* Titanic *and her era*. Philadelphia: Philadelphia Maritime Museum, 1982.

Ticehurst, Brian. Titanic: *Southampton's memorials*. Settle, North Yorkshire, England: Waterfront, 1998.

Ticehurst, Brian J. Titanic: *Southampton and district information sheet*. Southampton: B & J Publications, 1995.

Ticehurst, Brian J. Titanic's *memorials, worldwide*. Southampton: B & J Printers, 2000.

Titanic Commutator, various issues. Indian Ocean Massachusetts: *Titanic* Historical Society. Inc., 1970–2000.

New York Herald, European Edition, Paris, April 1912. *Times*, London, April 1912. *Boston Globe*, Boston, April–May 1912. *Chicago American*, Chicago, April 1912. *Chicago Daily Tribune*, Chicago, April–May 1912. *New York Times*, New York, April 1912. *Globe*, Toronto, April–May 1912. *Hamilton Spectator*, Hamilton, Ontario, April–May 1912. *Gazette*, Montreal, April–May 1912. *Montreal Daily Star*, Montreal, April–May 1912. *Daily Gleaner*, Fredericton, New Brunswick, April–May 1912. *Evening Mail*, Halifax, Nova Scotia, April 1912. *Mail Star*, Halifax, Nova Scotia. various issues 1975–2000. Archives of Ontario, Toronto: F 229-162-0-5 Container 1 T. Eaton Co. Records, Accidents and Disasters, RMS *Titanic* menu.

NOVA SCOTIA PUBLIC ARCHIVES AND RECORDS MANAGEMENT, HALIFAX, NOVA SCOTIA:

VF V380#9 A tract, The sinking of SS *Titanic* by Wm. H. Ferguson, from Words in season, Lakewood, Ohio 1912.

VF V182#10 Memorial Service pamphlet.

VK 1255 T6 R35 *Titanic*, Record of Bodies and effects.

VK 1255 T6 R35 C.3 Record of Bodies, buried at sea and bodies delivered at the morgue in Halifax, N.S.

D/S VK T53 D63 C.4 Disposition of Bodies ex *Titanic*, recovered up to May 13, 1912. List of bodies identified and disposition of same, list of bodies unidentified and disposition of same.

IMAGE CREDITS

Key: L – left, R – right, T – top, B – bottom

Eaton Collection, Archives of Ontario: 55, 56, 57

Father Francis M. Browne, S. J., Collection Provincial of the Irish Province of Society of Jesus: 2

Library and Archives Canada: 130R

Maritime Command Museum: x, xivT, 42, 136

McCord Museum, Montreal: 47

Nova Scotia Archives: xi, xii, 24B, 27, 40, 45, 49, 51L, 54, 69, 72, 74, 97, 118, 120, 127, 135

All other images from the author's collection

OTHER BOOKS BY THE AUTHOR

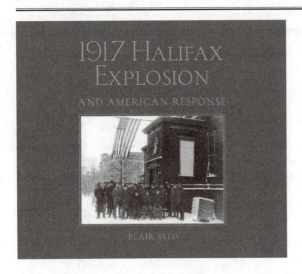

OTHER BOOKS ABOUT *TITANIC*

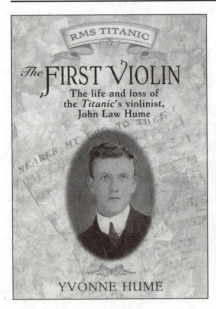

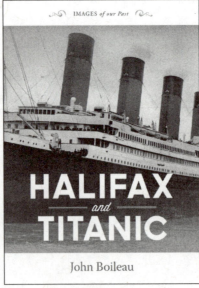

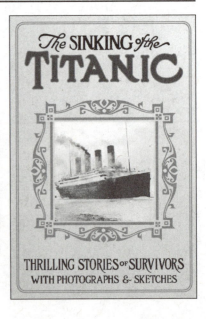